Taste of Home
30-MINUTE
COOKBOOK

TASTE OF HOME BOOKS • RDA ENTHUSIAST BRANDS, LLC • MILWAUKEE, WI

T0036032

Visit us at **tasteofhome.com** for other Taste of Home
books and products.

International Standard Book Number:
978-1-62145-782-4

Executive Editor: Mark Hagen
Senior Art Director: Raeann Thompson
Art Director: Courtney Lovetere
Deputy Editor, Copy Desk: Dulcie Shoener
Copy Editor: Sara Strauss
Contributing Designer: Jennifer Ruetz

Cover
Photographer: Dan Roberts
Set Stylist: Melissa Franco
Food Stylist: Shannon Norris

Pictured on front cover: One-Skillet Lasagna, p. 84; Great Garlic Bread, p. 218
Pictured on spine: Quick & Healthy Turkey Veggie Soup, p. 67
Pictured on back cover: Raspberry White Chocolate Pancakes, p. 37; Five
Cheese Baked Fonduta, p. 23; Turkey Breast Tenderloins with Raspberry Sauce,
p.105; Simple Turtle Cheesecake, p. 238; Garden Salad with Chickpeas, p. 216

INSTANT POT is a trademark of Double Insight Inc.
This publication has not been authorized, sponsored
or otherwise approved by Double Insight Inc.

Printed in China
1 3 5 7 9 10 8 6 4 2

Southwest Chicken
Dinner, p. 107

DINNER JUST GOT EASIER!

There's always time to settle in for home-cooked comfort, even when life's a whirlwind. Sound too good to be true? Simply check out the lip-smacking specialties inside **30-Minute Cookbook** complied by the *Taste of Home* Test Kitchen.

Inside, you'll find **317 full-flavored recipes** that come together in just half an hour...or less! This is the one kitchen tool you'll turn to most when a tasty meal is top priority but time isn't on your side.

Not only are these quick-to-fix favorites table-ready in a pinch, but they call for **everyday ingredients,** satisfy everyone at the table and come from today's home cooks. These busy chefs know what it's like to make dinner in short order and have generously shared all of their 30-minute dishes here.

From easy entrees and speedy sides to no-fuss appetizers and last-minute sweets, you'll always find the ideal **half-hour recipe,** no matter how busy your schedule might be.

You'll also enjoy...

- A chapter of **quick breakfast options,** featuring grab-and-go staples and brunch-buffet delights.

- Dozens of **meatless main dishes** guaranteed to appease even your biggest beef eater.

- **No-bake desserts** that keep the kitchen cool when sweet cravings come calling.

Best of all, a special **5-ingredient icon** 🔟 highlights recipes that require only a handful of items (not including salt, pepper, oils and optional ingredients such as garnishes). What could be easier or quicker?

It's a snap to build exciting menus, whip up midnight snacks and wow the crowd with an impressive dessert. Let **30-Minute Cookbook** show you how!

TABLE OF CONTENTS

MORE WAYS TO CONNECT WITH US: 📘🐦📷📌

SNACKS & APPETIZERS

Need an appetizer in a flash? Skip the standard bag of chips, tub of dip or can of nuts, and go with one of these quick-to-fix party pleasers.

⑤ EASY PUPPY CHOW

This version of everyone's favorite sweet-salty snack mix uses a whole box of cereal, so there's less messy measuring. And there's enough to feed a hungry crowd.
—*Taste of Home* Test Kitchen

TAKES: 15 MIN. • **MAKES:** 13 CUPS

- 1 box (12 oz.) Corn Chex
- 2 cups semisweet chocolate chips
- ¾ cup creamy peanut butter
- ⅓ cup butter, cubed
- 3 cups confectioners' sugar

1. Pour cereal into a very large bowl. In a large microwave-safe bowl, combine chocolate chips, peanut butter and butter.
2. Microwave on high 30 seconds. Stir gently. Continue microwaving on high, stirring every 30 seconds, until melted and blended. Pour over cereal; gently stir to coat.
3. In batches, place confectioners' sugar in a gallon-sized bag, add cereal mixture and shake until well coated. Spread cereal on a baking sheet. Let stand until set. Store in airtight containers.

½ cup: 229 cal., 10g fat (5g sat. fat), 6mg chol., 146mg sod., 35g carb. (23g sugars, 2g fiber), 3g pro.

GARLIC MOZZARELLA BREAD BITES

These little balls of deliciousness are ridiculously easy to make and insanely tasty! They are the perfect low-carb, keto-friendly, gluten-free appetizer, snack or side dish. To make them extra cheesy, sprinkle the tops with more mozzarella cheese after taking them out of the oven the second time, and then return them to the oven until the cheese is melted. Serve with your favorite low-carb dipping sauce.
—Anna Bowden, Littleton, CO

TAKES: 30 MIN. • **MAKES:** 1 DOZEN

- 1½ cups shredded part-skim mozzarella cheese
- 3 oz. cream cheese, softened
- 1 large egg, room temperature
- 1 cup almond flour
- ½ tsp. onion powder
- ½ tsp. garlic powder
- ½ tsp. salt
- ½ tsp. pepper

TOPPING

- 2 Tbsp. unsalted butter, melted
- 1½ tsp. minced garlic
  Prepared pesto, optional

1. Preheat oven to 400°. In a microwave-safe bowl, combine mozzarella cheese and cream cheese; microwave, covered, on high until melted, 30-60 seconds. Stir until smooth. Stir in egg. In another bowl, mix almond flour and seasonings; stir into cheese mixture until combined (mixture will be thick).
2. With wet hands, shape into 12 balls. Place 1 in. apart on a parchment-lined baking sheet. Bake 12 minutes. Combine butter and garlic; brush over rolls. Bake until light brown, 2-4 minutes longer. Let cool 5 minutes before serving. If desired, serve with prepared pesto.

1 appetizer: 144 cal., 12g fat (5g sat. fat), 37mg chol., 224mg sod., 4g carb. (1g sugars, 1g fiber), 6g pro.

SPICY POPCORN

When I allow myself to indulge in a snack, I make this spicy popcorn. One batch doesn't last long at our house. You can add more or less red pepper flakes to suit your family's tastes.
—Kay Young, Flushing, MI

TAKES: 5 MIN. • **MAKES:** 10 SERVINGS

- 10 cups popped popcorn
- ¼ cup butter, melted
- 1 tsp. paprika
- ½ tsp. ground cumin
- ¼ to ½ tsp. crushed red pepper flakes
- ⅓ cup grated Parmesan cheese

Place popcorn in a large bowl. In a small bowl, combine the butter, paprika, cumin and red pepper flakes. Pour over popcorn; toss to coat. Sprinkle with Parmesan cheese and toss again.

1 cup: 204 cal., 16g fat (7g sat. fat), 27mg chol., 337mg sod., 13g carb. (0 sugars, 2g fiber), 3g pro.

GRILLED LOADED POTATO ROUNDS

My go-to recipe for outdoor potlucks is an awesome potato side. I prep everything beforehand, then assemble and grill at the party. Serve with sour cream, cheese, bacon and chives.
—Fay Moreland, Wichita Falls, TX

TAKES: 30 MIN.
MAKES: 16 APPETIZERS

- 4 large potatoes, baked and cooled
- ¼ cup butter, melted
- ¼ tsp. salt
- ¼ tsp. pepper
- 1 cup sour cream
- 1½ cups shredded cheddar cheese
- 8 bacon strips, cooked and crumbled
- 3 Tbsp. minced chives

1. Trim ends of potatoes. Slice potatoes into 1-in.-thick rounds. Brush with butter; sprinkle with salt and pepper. Place potatoes on grill rack, buttered side down. Grill, covered, over medium heat, or broil 4 in. from heat until browned, 5-7 minutes. Brush with remaining butter; turn. Grill or broil until browned, 5-7 minutes longer.
2. Top with sour cream, cheese, bacon and chives.

1 potato round: 188 cal., 11g fat (6g sat. fat), 26mg chol., 212mg sod., 17g carb. (1g sugars, 2g fiber), 6g pro.

CONFETTI SNACK MIX

I've made this quick party mix for many years, and I usually double the recipe. It makes a delightful gift, and everyone always asks how I make it.
—Jane Bray, Temple Terrace, FL

TAKES: 10 MIN. • **MAKES:** 7 CUPS

- 4 cups Golden Grahams
- 1 cup dry-roasted peanuts
- 1 cup dried banana chips
- 1 cup raisins
- 1 cup milk chocolate M&M's

In a large bowl, combine all ingredients. Store in an airtight container.

¼ cup: 125 cal., 6g fat (3g sat. fat), 1mg chol., 98mg sod., 18g carb. (12g sugars, 1g fiber), 2g pro.

HERB-ROASTED OLIVES & TOMATOES

Eat these roasted veggies with a crunchy baguette or a couple of cheeses. You can also double or triple the amounts and have leftovers to toss with spaghetti the next day.
—Anndrea Bailey, Huntington Beach, CA

TAKES: 25 MIN. • **MAKES:** 4 CUPS

- 2 cups cherry tomatoes
- 1 cup garlic-stuffed olives
- 1 cup Greek olives
- 1 cup pitted ripe olives
- 8 garlic cloves, peeled
- 3 Tbsp. olive oil
- 1 Tbsp. herbes de Provence
- ¼ tsp. pepper

Preheat oven to 425°. Combine the first 5 ingredients on a greased 15x10x1-in. baking pan. Add the oil and seasonings; toss to coat. Roast until the tomatoes are softened, roughly 15-20 minutes, stirring occasionally.

Note: Look for herbes de Provence in the spice aisle.

¼ cup: 71 cal., 7g fat (1g sat. fat), 0 chol., 380mg sod., 3g carb. (1g sugars, 1g fiber), 0 pro.

ASPARAGUS WITH FRESH BASIL SAUCE

Add zip to your appetizer platter with an easy asparagus dip that can also double as a flavorful sandwich spread.
—Janie Colle, Hutchinson, KS

TAKES: 15 MIN. • **MAKES:** 12 SERVINGS

- ¾ cup reduced-fat mayonnaise
- 2 Tbsp. prepared pesto
- 1 Tbsp. grated Parmesan cheese
- 1 Tbsp. minced fresh basil
- 1 tsp. lemon juice
- 1 garlic clove, minced
- 1½ lbs. fresh asparagus, trimmed

1. In a small bowl, mix the first 6 ingredients until blended; refrigerate until serving.

2. In a Dutch oven, bring 12 cups water to a boil. Add asparagus in batches; cook, uncovered, until crisp-tender, 2-3 minutes. Remove and immediately drop into ice water. Drain and pat dry. Serve with sauce.

1 serving: 72 cal., 6g fat (1g sat. fat), 6mg chol., 149mg sod., 3g carb. (1g sugars, 1g fiber), 1g pro. **Diabetic exchanges:** 1½ fat.

⑤ⱼ CHOCOLATY CHIPS

My two little guys can't get enough of this sweet and salty snack that uses just three ingredients and is ready to eat in 15 minutes. The boys like to drizzle on the melted chocolate. Sometimes we replace the potato chips with apple slices.
—Jami Geittmann, Greendale, WI

TAKES: 15 MIN.
MAKES: 6 SERVINGS

- 3 cups regular or kettle-cooked potato chips
- ½ cup semisweet chocolate chips
- 1 tsp. shortening

1. Arrange potato chips in a single layer on a waxed paper-lined baking sheet.

2. In a microwave, melt chocolate chips and shortening; stir until smooth. Drizzle mixture over chips. Refrigerate 5 minutes or until set.

½ cup: 140 cal., 9g fat (4g sat. fat), 0 chol., 75mg sod., 16g carb. (8g sugars, 1g fiber), 1g pro.

TEST KITCHEN TIP

You can use either regular or kettle-cooked chips for this snack. Kettle-cooked chips, however, tend to keep their crisp texture slightly better than regular chips.

FRESH CORN & AVOCADO DIP

I alter my sister's recipe by adding finely chopped jalapeno for a little heat. This is a different way of serving corn as a dip that can be made ahead of time and refrigerated until serving.
—Pat Roberts, Thornton, ON

TAKES: 20 MIN. • **MAKES:** 4 CUPS

- 2 cups fresh or frozen corn, thawed
- 1 medium ripe avocado, peeled and diced
- 1 small peach, peeled and chopped
- 1 small sweet red pepper, chopped
- 1 small red onion, chopped
- 2 Tbsp. olive oil
- 2 Tbsp. white wine vinegar
- 1 Tbsp. lime juice
- 1½ tsp. ground cumin
- 1 tsp. minced fresh oregano
- 1 garlic clove, crushed
  Salt and pepper to taste
- 1 minced and seeded jalapeno pepper, optional
  Baked tortilla chips

Combine first 11 ingredients; add salt and pepper and, if desired, jalapeno. Serve with tortilla chips.
¼ cup: 52 cal., 3g fat (0 sat. fat), 0 chol., 4mg sod., 6g carb. (2g sugars, 1g fiber), 1g pro. **Diabetic exchanges:** ½ starch, ½ fat.

CREAMY CHICKEN ENCHILADA PIZZA

This is a twist on a family favorite. We wanted the taste of my chicken enchilada recipe, but we wanted it even faster. This kicked-up pizza was our fun creation.
—Crystal Jo Bruns, Iliff, CO

TAKES: 30 MIN. • **MAKES:** 6 SERVINGS

- 1 tube (11 oz.) refrigerated thin pizza crust
- 1 pkg. (8 oz.) cream cheese, softened, cubed
- 1 cup shredded Mexican cheese blend, divided
- 2 tsp. ground cumin
- 1½ tsp. garlic powder
- ½ tsp. salt
- 2 cups ready-to-use fajita chicken strips, cubed
- ½ cup salsa
- ¼ cup green enchilada sauce

Optional toppings: Shredded lettuce, chopped tomatoes and sliced ripe olives

1. Preheat oven to 400°. Unroll and press dough onto bottom and ½ in. up sides of a greased 15x10x1-in. baking pan. Bake 5 minutes.
2. Meanwhile, in a small saucepan, combine cream cheese, ½ cup cheese, cumin, garlic powder and salt over medium heat; cook and stir for 5 minutes or until blended. Remove from heat. Add chicken; toss to coat.
3. Spread over crust. Drizzle with salsa and enchilada sauce; sprinkle with remaining cheese. Bake until the crust is golden and cheese is melted, 8-12 minutes longer. Serve with toppings of your choice.
1 piece: 428 cal., 25g fat (12g sat. fat), 83mg chol., 1061mg sod., 30g carb. (5g sugars, 1g fiber), 20g pro.

TEST KITCHEN TIP

The super creamy topping on this pizza will prevent the bottom of the crust from crisping as much as a traditional pizza.

2 chipotle peppers in
  adobo sauce, finely minced
1 Tbsp. grated lime zest
¼ cup lime juice
¼ tsp. kosher salt
¼ tsp. pepper
1 can (14 oz.) water-packed
  artichoke hearts, drained and
  coarsely chopped
1 pkg. (10 oz.) frozen chopped
  spinach, thawed and
  squeezed dry
3 green onions, chopped
1 large garlic clove,
  finely chopped
  Optional: Baked pita chips,
  tortilla chips, sliced
  French bread baguette
  or assorted crackers

1. Preheat oven to 400°. Combine mozzarella cheese, cream cheese, mayonnaise and ¼ cup grated Parmesan cheese. Stir in next 9 ingredients. Spoon into a deep-dish pie plate; sprinkle with remaining Parmesan.

2. Bake until golden brown and bubbly, 20-25 minutes. Serve as desired with pita or tortilla chips, baguette slices or crackers.

¼ cup: 164 cal., 14g fat (6g sat. fat), 28mg chol., 318mg sod., 4g carb. (1g sugars, 1g fiber), 6g pro.

HOT CHIPOTLE SPINACH & ARTICHOKE DIP WITH LIME

I make spinach and artichoke dip for party guests all the time, but I wanted to give it a Mexican twist. I amped up this app with smoky chipotle chiles and tangy lime for an unexpected kick.
—Joseph Sciascia, San Mateo, CA

TAKES: 30 MIN. • **MAKES:** 4 CUPS

2 cups shredded
  mozzarella cheese
1 pkg. (8 oz.) cream cheese,
  softened
½ cup mayonnaise
½ cup grated Parmesan cheese,
  divided

TEST KITCHEN TIP

Try this dip as a delicious sandwich spread or as a schmear on bagels. Got a crowd coming? Extend this dip even further by adding shredded rotisserie chicken.

HOT DOG SLIDERS WITH MANGO-PINEAPPLE SALSA

For parties, we shrink down lots of foods, including these quick hot dogs, to slider size. Pile on the easy but irresistible fruit salsa for a burst of fresh flavor.
—Carole Resnick, Cleveland, OH

TAKES: 30 MIN.
MAKES: 2 DOZEN (2 CUPS SALSA)

- 3 **Tbsp. lime juice**
- 2 **Tbsp. honey**
- ¼ **tsp. salt**
- 1 **cup cubed fresh pineapple (½ in.)**
- 1 **cup cubed peeled mango (½ in.)**
- ¼ **cup finely chopped red onion**
- 2 **Tbsp. finely chopped sweet red pepper**
- 12 **hot dogs**
- 12 **hot dog buns, split**

1. In a small bowl, whisk lime juice, honey and salt until blended. Add pineapple, mango, onion and pepper; toss to coat.
2. Grill hot dogs, covered, over medium heat or broil 4 in. from the heat until heated through, 7-9 minutes, turning occasionally.
3. Place hot dogs in buns; cut each crosswise in half. Serve with the fruit salsa.

1 slider with 1 Tbsp. salsa: 146 cal., 8g fat (3g sat. fat), 13mg chol., 361mg sod., 15g carb. (5g sugars, 1g fiber), 5g pro.

WAFFLED PIZZA BITES

The whole family will love this playful twist on waffles. Mozzarella and Parmesan cheeses are sandwiched between two layers of dough and cooked up in the waffle iron. It's like a pizza grilled cheese waffle!
—Deirdre Cox, Kansas City, MO

TAKES: 20 MIN. • **MAKES:** 8 APPETIZERS

- 1¼ **cups shredded part-skim mozzarella cheese**
- ¼ **cup shredded Parmesan cheese**
- ½ **tsp. dried basil**
- ½ **tsp. dried oregano**
- 2 **tubes (8 oz. each) refrigerated crescent rolls**

- 32 **slices pepperoni (about 2 oz.)**
- 1 **jar (14 oz.) pizza sauce, warmed**
  Optional toppings: Sliced pepperoni, shredded mozzarella cheese and basil

1. In a small bowl, combine cheeses, basil and oregano. Separate each roll of crescent dough into two 7x6-in. rectangles; seal perforations.
2. Place 1 rectangle on a preheated and greased 8-in. square waffle iron (dough will not cover entire surface). Layer with half the cheese mixture and half the pepperoni to within ½ in. of edges; top with another rectangle. Bake until golden brown, 4-5 minutes. Repeat.

3. Remove to a cutting board and cool slightly. Cut each rectangle into 4 triangles; serve warm with pizza sauce and, if desired, toppings.

1 serving: 329 cal., 19g fat (4g sat. fat), 21mg chol., 909mg sod., 29g carb. (9g sugars, 1g fiber), 12g pro.

GOAT CHEESE MUSHROOMS

Stuffed mushrooms are superstars in the hot appetizer category. I use baby portobello mushrooms and load them with creamy goat cheese and sweet red peppers.
—Mike Bass, Alvin, TX

TAKES: 30 MIN. • **MAKES:** 2 DOZEN

- 24 **baby portobello mushrooms (about 1 lb.), stems removed**
- ½ **cup crumbled goat cheese**
- ½ **cup chopped drained roasted sweet red peppers**
  Pepper to taste
- 4 **tsp. olive oil**
  Chopped fresh parsley

1. Preheat oven to 375°. Place mushroom caps in a greased 15x10x1-in. baking pan. Fill each with 1 tsp. cheese; top each with 1 tsp. red pepper. Sprinkle with pepper; drizzle with oil.
2. Bake 15-18 minutes or until mushrooms are tender. Sprinkle with parsley.

1 stuffed mushroom: 19 cal., 1g fat (0 sat. fat), 3mg chol., 31mg sod., 1g carb. (1g sugars, 0 fiber), 1g pro.

FESTIVE SLIDERS

My mini turkey sandwiches with cranberry sauce, horseradish and ginger keep well in the refrigerator. I like to have a batch on hand for holiday get-togethers.
—Pamela Miller, Big Rapids, MI

TAKES: 30 MIN. • **MAKES:** 2 DOZEN

- 1 **pkg. (8 oz.) cream cheese, softened**
- ½ **cup mayonnaise**
- ¼ **cup Creole mustard**
- 2 **Tbsp. minced fresh gingerroot**
- 1 **Tbsp. grated orange zest**
- 1½ **tsp. prepared horseradish**
- 1 **cup whole-berry cranberry sauce**
- 4 **green onions, sliced**
- 2 **pkg. (12 oz. each) Hawaiian sweet rolls or 24 dinner rolls, split**
- 1½ **lbs. thinly sliced cooked turkey**

1. Beat the cream cheese and mayonnaise until smooth. Beat in mustard, ginger, orange zest and horseradish. In another bowl, mix cranberry sauce and green onions.
2. Spread cream cheese mixture onto roll bottoms. Top with turkey, cranberry mixture and roll tops.

1 slider: 231 cal., 10g fat (4g sat. fat), 54mg chol., 221mg sod., 22g carb. (10g sugars, 1g fiber), 13g pro.

SPICED HONEY PRETZELS

If your tastes run to sweet and spicy, you'll love these zesty pretzels with a twist. Their coating is so yummy, you won't need a fattening dip to enjoy them! They're so delightful for munching that your family will request you make them often.
—Mary Lou Moon, Beaverton, OR

TAKES: 15 MIN. • **MAKES:** 8 SERVINGS

- 4 **cups thin pretzel sticks**
- 3 **Tbsp. honey**
- 2 **tsp. butter, melted**
- 1 **tsp. onion powder**
- 1 **tsp. chili powder**

1. Line a 15x10x1-in. baking pan with foil; coat foil with cooking spray. Place the pretzels in a large bowl.
2. In a small bowl, combine the honey, butter, onion powder and chili powder. Pour over pretzels; toss to coat evenly. Spread into prepared pan.
3. Bake at 350° for 8 minutes, stirring once. Cool on a wire rack, stirring gently several times to separate.

½ cup: 98 cal., 1g fat (1g sat. fat), 3mg chol., 487mg sod., 20g carb. (0 sugars, 1g fiber), 2g pro. **Diabetic exchanges:** 1½ starch.

5i
BROCCOLI & CHIVE STUFFED MINI PEPPERS
Crunchy peppers perfectly balance the creamy filling in these party appetizers. Fresh chives help them stand out.
—Jean McKenzie, Vancouver, WA

TAKES: 30 MIN. • **MAKES:** 2 DOZEN

- 12 miniature sweet peppers
- 1 pkg. (8 oz.) cream cheese, softened
- ⅓ cup minced fresh chives
- ⅛ tsp. salt
- ⅛ tsp. pepper
- ⅔ cup finely chopped fresh broccoli
- ⅔ cup shredded cheddar cheese

1. Preheat oven to 400°. Cut peppers lengthwise in half; remove seeds. In a bowl, mix cream cheese, chives, salt and pepper; stir in broccoli. Spoon into pepper halves.
2. Place on a foil-lined baking sheet; bake until heated through, 9-11 minutes. Sprinkle with cheddar cheese. Bake until cheese is melted, 3-4 minutes longer. Cool slightly before serving.

1 stuffed pepper half: 48 cal., 4g fat (2g sat. fat), 14mg chol., 68mg sod., 1g carb. (1g sugars, 0 fiber), 1g pro.

PARMESAN-RANCH SNACK MIX
This is a quick, easy and delicious snack, especially for kids. No one I've made it for can have just one handful—they always come back for more, and more! So if you're thinking about cutting the recipe in half to make less, I wouldn't recommend it.
—Tammy Landry, Saucier, MS

TAKES: 15 MIN. • **MAKES:** 3 QT.

- 9 cups Corn, Rice or Wheat Chex
- 2 cups miniature pretzels
- 2 cups Goldfish cheddar crackers
- ½ cup butter, melted
- ½ cup grated Parmesan cheese
- 1 envelope ranch salad dressing mix

1. In a large bowl, combine cereal, pretzels and crackers. Drizzle with butter. Sprinkle with cheese and salad dressing mix; toss to coat.

2. Microwave in batches on high 3 minutes, stirring every minute. Spread onto a baking sheet to cool. Store in an airtight container.
Note: This recipe was tested in a 1,100-watt microwave.
¾ cup: 365 cal., 9g fat (5g sat. fat), 18mg chol., 826mg sod., 67g carb. (7g sugars, 6g fiber), 7g pro.

SHRIMP & FETA CUCUMBER ROUNDS
I love the contrasting tastes and textures of these rounds. Each bite balances the refreshing burst and crunch of cucumber with the rich flavor and smoothness of the filling.
—Donna Pochoday-Stelmach, Morristown, NJ

TAKES: 30 MIN.
MAKES: ABOUT 3 DOZEN

- 1 pkg. (8 oz.) cream cheese, softened
- 1¼ cups (5 oz.) crumbled feta cheese
- 2 tsp. snipped fresh dill
- ¼ tsp. salt
- ¼ tsp. chili powder
- ⅛ tsp. pepper
- ⅔ cup peeled and deveined cooked shrimp (61-70 per pound), chopped
- ¼ cup finely chopped roasted sweet red pepper
- 2 large English cucumbers, cut into ½-in. slices
  Optional: Fresh dill sprigs or additional chopped roasted sweet red peppers

In a large bowl, beat the first 6 ingredients until blended. Stir in shrimp and red pepper. Place about 2 tsp. shrimp mixture on each cucumber slice. Refrigerate until serving. If desired, top with dill or additional chopped red pepper before serving.
1 appetizer: 41 cal., 3g fat (2g sat. fat), 14mg chol., 90mg sod., 1g carb. (1g sugars, 0 fiber), 2g pro.

51 FRUIT & CEREAL SNACK MIX

I mix dried cranberries, cherries, raisins and apple chips with cinnamon cereal for a kid-friendly snack. It's wonderful all year, but we enjoy it at holiday parties in particular.
—John Lancaster, Union Grove, WI

TAKES: 10 MIN. • **MAKES:** 2½ QT.

- 8 cups Cinnamon Toast Crunch cereal
- ¾ cup dried cranberries
- ¾ cup raisins
- ½ cup dried cherries
- 1 pkg. (2½ oz.) dried apple chips, broken into large pieces

Place all ingredients in a large bowl; toss to combine. Store in airtight containers.

¾ cup: 223 cal., 5g fat (0 sat. fat), 0 chol., 162mg sod., 47g carb. (28g sugars, 3g fiber), 2g pro.

HOT SHRIMP DIP

I came across a recipe for crawfish dip, and it sounded amazing, but we don't have a lot of crawfish available in my area. However, I'm a big fan of shrimp, so I used that instead. This dish has become a family favorite. You can increase the heat with your favorite hot sauce or add a bit of acidity with a squeeze of lemon.
—Jill Burwell, Renton, WA

TAKES: 25 MIN. • **MAKES:** 4 CUPS

- ½ cup butter, cubed
- 8 green onions, thinly sliced
- 1 small green pepper, finely chopped
- 1 lb. peeled and deveined cooked shrimp (61-70 per lb.)
- 1 jar (4 oz.) diced pimientos, drained
- 2 garlic cloves, minced
- 2 tsp. Creole seasoning

- 1 pkg. (8 oz.) cream cheese, cubed
  Chopped fresh parsley
  French bread baguette slices or assorted crackers

1. In a Dutch oven, melt butter over medium heat. Add green onions and green pepper; cook and stir until tender, 3-4 minutes. Add shrimp, pimientos, garlic and Creole seasoning. Cook and stir until heated through.
2. Stir in cream cheese until melted; sprinkle with parsley. Serve with baguette slices or crackers.

¼ cup: 136 cal., 11g fat (7g sat. fat), 73mg chol., 217mg sod., 2g carb. (1g sugars, 0 fiber), 7g pro.

TEST KITCHEN TIP

Leftover dip? Spoon it onto a flour the tortilla and top with leafy greens for a fast no-fuss wrap, or heat the dip up and toss with cooked pasta.

🄍 SUGAR & SPICE POPCORN

Our family can't get enough of this light, cinnamon-sweet popcorn. The baked kernels are wonderfully crunchy and coated just right. Try mixing some to have on hand as an anytime nibble.
—Naomi Yoder, Leeseburg, IN

TAKES: 20 MIN. • **MAKES:** 4 QT.

- 4   qt. air-popped popcorn
- 3   Tbsp. butter
- ¼   cup sugar
- 1   Tbsp. water
- 1   tsp. ground cinnamon
- ¼   tsp. salt

1. Place popcorn in a large roasting pan coated with cooking spray. In a small saucepan, melt butter over low heat. Add the sugar, water, cinnamon and salt; cook and stir over low heat until the sugar is dissolved.
2. Pour over the popcorn; toss to coat. Bake, uncovered, at 300° for 10-15 minutes. Serve immediately.
1 cup: 62 cal., 2g fat (1g sat. fat), 6mg chol., 59mg sod., 9g carb. (0 sugars, 1g fiber), 1g pro. **Diabetic exchanges:** ½ starch.

🄍 PEANUT BUTTER S'MORES SANDWICH

Your favorite s'more flavors come together in this tasty peanut butter sandwich—no campfire required.
—James Schend, Pleasant Prairie, WI

TAKES: 10 MIN. • **MAKES:** 1 SERVING

- 1   Tbsp. creamy peanut butter
- 1   slice crusty white bread
- 1   Tbsp. milk chocolate chips
- 2   Tbsp. miniature marshmallows

Spread peanut butter over bread. Place on a baking sheet; top with chocolate chips and marshmallows. Broil 4-5 in. from heat until lightly browned, 30-60 seconds.
1 open-faced sandwich: 249 cal., 12g fat (4g sat. fat), 2mg chol., 224mg sod., 29g carb. (12g sugars, 2g fiber), 7g pro.

SMOKED SALMON BITES WITH SHALLOT SAUCE

A tangy Dijon-mayo sauce adds zip to layers of crisp arugula, smoked salmon and shaved Asiago cheese. I make these a couple of times a year.
—Jamie Brown-Miller, Napa, CA

TAKES: 30 MIN.
MAKES: 25 APPETIZERS

- 1   sheet frozen puff pastry, thawed

SAUCE
- 2   shallots
- 2   Tbsp. Dijon mustard
- 1   Tbsp. mayonnaise
- 1   Tbsp. red wine vinegar
- ¼   cup olive oil

FINISHING
- 1   cup fresh arugula or baby spinach, coarsely chopped
- 4½ oz. smoked salmon or lox, thinly sliced
- ½   cup shaved Asiago cheese

1. Preheat oven to 400°. Unfold puff pastry; cut into 25 squares. Transfer to greased baking sheets. Bake the squares 11-13 minutes or until golden brown.
2. Meanwhile, grate 1 shallot and finely chop the other. In a small bowl, combine shallots, mustard, mayonnaise and vinegar. While whisking, gradually add oil in a steady stream. Spoon a small amount of sauce onto each pastry; layer with arugula and salmon. Drizzle with remaining sauce and sprinkle with cheese.
1 appetizer: 89 cal., 6g fat (1g sat. fat), 3mg chol., 105mg sod., 6g carb. (0 sugars, 1g fiber), 2g pro.

- 1 loaf (1 lb.) frozen pizza dough, thawed
- 20 slices pepperoni
- 8 oz. part-skim mozzarella cheese, cut into 20 cubes
- ¼ cup butter
- 2 small garlic cloves, minced
  Dash salt
  Marinara sauce, warmed
  Optional: Crushed red pepper flakes and grated Parmesan cheese

1. Preheat oven to 400°. Shape dough into 1½-in. balls; flatten into ⅛-in. thick circles. Place 1 pepperoni slice and 1 cheese cube in center of each circle; wrap dough around the pepperoni and cheese. Pinch edges to seal; shape into a ball. Repeat with remaining dough, cheese and pepperoni. Place seam side down on greased baking sheets; bake until light golden brown, 10-15 minutes. Cool slightly.
2. Meanwhile, in a small saucepan, melt butter over low heat. Add garlic and salt, taking care not to brown butter or garlic; brush over puffs. Serve with marinara sauce; if desired, sprinkle with red pepper flakes and Parmesan.
Freeze option: Cover and freeze unbaked pizza puffs on waxed paper-lined baking sheets until firm. Transfer to a freezer container; seal and return to freezer. To use, preheat oven to 325°; bake pizza puffs on greased baking sheets as directed, increasing time as necessary to heat through.
1 pizza puff: 120 cal., 6g fat (3g sat. fat), 15mg chol., 189mg sod., 11g carb. (1g sugars, 0 fiber), 5g pro.

PIZZA PUFFS

What's more fun than a pizza puff? Skip the kind sold in the frozen-foods aisle and try this homemade version. You can substitute any meat or vegetable for the pepperoni and any cheese for the mozzarella.
—Vivi Taylor, Middleburg, FL

TAKES: 30 MIN. • **MAKES:** 20 SERVINGS

🄵 BARBECUE & BEER MEATBALLS

This simple meatball recipe relies on time-saving ingredients like frozen meatballs and barbecue sauce. It's the perfect last-minute appetizer!
—*Taste of Home Test Kitchen*

TAKES: 30 MIN. • **MAKES:** 20 SERVINGS

- 1 pkg. (22 oz.) frozen fully cooked Angus beef meatballs
- 1 cup barbecue sauce
- ⅓ cup beer
   Thinly sliced jalapeno pepper, optional

1. Prepare meatballs according to package directions.
2. Meanwhile, in a small saucepan, combine barbecue sauce and beer; heat through. Add meatballs; stir to coat. If desired, top with jalapenos to serve.
1 meatball: 106 cal., 6g fat (3g sat. fat), 17mg chol., 338mg sod., 7g carb. (5g sugars, 0 fiber), 4g pro.

HERBED CHEESE STICKS

We love the breadsticks we get hot from the oven at our local pizza parlor. Now I can serve that same wonderful goodness at home.
—*Heather Bates, Athens, ME*

TAKES: 30 MIN.
MAKES: 16 CHEESE STICKS

- 1 pkg. (6½ oz.) pizza crust mix
- 1½ tsp. garlic powder
- 1 Tbsp. olive oil
- 1 cup shredded part-skim mozzarella cheese
- ¼ cup shredded Parmesan cheese
- 1 tsp. Italian seasoning
   Pizza sauce

1. Preheat oven to 450°. Mix pizza dough according to the package directions, adding garlic powder to dry mix. Cover; let rest 5 minutes.

2. Knead dough 4-5 times or until easy to handle. On a greased baking sheet, press dough into an 8-in. square. Brush top with oil; sprinkle with cheeses and Italian seasoning.
3. Bake 6-8 minutes or until cheese is lightly browned. Cut square in half; cut each half crosswise into 8 strips. Serve with pizza sauce.
1 cheese stick: 72 cal., 3g fat (1g sat. fat), 5mg chol., 117mg sod., 8g carb. (1g sugars, 0 fiber), 3g pro.

🄵 CHUTNEY-TOPPED CREAM CHEESE SPREAD

I've had the pleasure of introducing many of my friends and family to chutney, that sweet and savory fruit sauce. Prepare this spread even faster by simply using chive-flavored whipped cream cheese.
—*Michelle Torkelson, Ham Lake, MN*

TAKES: 10 MIN. • **MAKES:** 1¾ CUPS

- 1 pkg. (8 oz.) cream cheese, softened
- 3 green onions, chopped
- ¾ cup chutney
- ¼ cup chopped salted peanuts
   Assorted crackers

1. In a small bowl, beat cream cheese until smooth; stir in green onions. Spread into a shallow serving dish.
2. Top with chutney; sprinkle with peanuts. Serve with crackers.
2 Tbsp.: 146 cal., 8g fat (4g sat. fat), 19mg chol., 242mg sod., 16g carb. (10g sugars, 0 fiber), 2g pro.

GRILLED GARDEN VEGGIE FLATBREADS

Grilled flatbread is a tasty way to put fresh garden vegetables to use. It's so versatile: Simply change the vegetables and cheese to suit your family's taste. It also works well cooked indoors, on a grill pan with a lid.
—Carly Curtin, Ellicott City, MD

TAKES: 20 MIN. • **MAKES:** 8 SERVINGS

 2 whole grain naan flatbreads
 2 tsp. olive oil
 1 medium yellow or red tomato, thinly sliced
 ¼ cup thinly sliced onion
 ½ cup shredded part-skim mozzarella cheese
 2 Tbsp. shredded Parmesan cheese
 1 Tbsp. minced fresh basil
 ½ tsp. garlic powder
 1 tsp. balsamic vinegar
 ½ tsp. coarse sea salt

1. Grill the flatbreads, covered, over indirect medium heat 2-3 minutes or until bottoms are lightly browned.
2. Remove from grill. Brush grilled sides with oil; top with tomato and onion to within ½ in. of edges. In a small bowl, toss cheeses with basil and garlic powder; sprinkle over vegetables. Drizzle with vinegar; sprinkle with salt. Return to grill; cook, covered, 2-3 minutes longer or until cheese is melted. Cut flatbreads into wedges.
1 wedge: 132 cal., 5g fat (2g sat. fat), 8mg chol., 390mg sod., 16g carb. (2g sugars, 2g fiber), 5g pro.
Diabetic exchanges: 1 starch, 1 fat.

FIVE CHEESE BAKED FONDUTA

If melted cheese isn't one of the most mouthwatering foods of all time, I don't know what is! Substitute your favorite cheese for any you don't like.
—Cheri Gilmore, Festus, MO

TAKES: 30 MIN. • **MAKES:** 3 CUPS

 3 Tbsp. melted butter, divided
 1 pkg. (8 oz.) cream cheese, softened
 2 cups shredded part-skim mozzarella cheese
 1 cup shredded fontina cheese
 1 cup shredded cheddar cheese
 ½ cup grated Parmesan cheese
 4 garlic cloves, thinly sliced
 1 tsp. dried rosemary, crushed
 1 tsp. dried thyme
 ½ tsp. pepper

Optional: Toasted French bread baguette slices, baked pita chips or assorted fresh vegetables

Preheat oven to 450°. Brush an 8-in. cast iron or other ovenproof skillet with 1 Tbsp. butter; set aside. In a large bowl, beat the cream cheese and the mozzarella, fontina, cheddar and Parmesan cheeses with garlic, rosemary, thyme, pepper and remaining 2 Tbsp. butter until combined. Spread into prepared skillet. Bake until bubbly and golden brown, 15-20 minutes. Serve with baguette slices, pita chips or vegetables.
¼ cup: 237 cal., 20g fat (12g sat. fat), 61mg chol., 402mg sod., 4g carb. (1g sugars, 0 fiber), 11g pro.

DID YOU KNOW?

Fonduta is not the same as fondue. Unlike fondue, Italian fonduta isn't thickened with flour or cornstarch.

BREAKFAST
IN A HURRY

Busy mornings got you hustling? Don't skip breakfast.
Stave off hunger until the noon bell rings with eye-opening,
quick and easy dishes.

WHAT'S IN THE FRIDGE FRITTATA

Great for a last-minute breakfast, brunch or lunch, this special frittata has a combination of crab and Swiss cheese that my guests rave about. I also like to use sausage and cheddar cheese with asparagus.
—Deborah Posey, Virginia Beach, VA

TAKES: 25 MIN. • **MAKES:** 4 SERVINGS

- 6 **large eggs**
- ⅓ **cup chopped onion**
- ⅓ **cup chopped sweet red pepper**
- ⅓ **cup chopped fresh mushrooms**
- 1 **Tbsp. olive oil**
- 1 **can (6 oz.) lump crabmeat, drained**
- ¼ **cup shredded Swiss cheese**
- 1 **Tbsp. minced fresh parsley, optional**

1. In a small bowl, whisk eggs; set aside. In an 8-in. ovenproof skillet, saute the onion, pepper and mushrooms in oil until tender. Reduce heat; sprinkle with crab. Top with eggs. Cover and cook until nearly set, 5-7 minutes.
2. Uncover skillet; sprinkle with cheese and, if desired, parsley. Broil 3-4 in. from the heat until the eggs are completely set, 2-3 minutes. Let stand for 5 minutes. Cut into 4 wedges.

1 wedge: 215 cal., 13g fat (4g sat. fat), 361mg chol., 265mg sod., 3g carb. (2g sugars, 1g fiber), 21g pro. **Diabetic exchanges:** 3 lean meat, 1½ fat.

YANKEE RANCHEROS

After my in-laws began affectionately referring to me as a Yankee, I decided I needed to learn to make a few Mexican dishes. These rancheros are super easy and make my Tex-Mex-loving family happy—even if they do come from a northerner.
—Darla Andrews, Boerne, TX

TAKES: 25 MIN. • **MAKES:** 4 SERVINGS

- 5 **cups frozen shredded hash brown potatoes (about 15 oz.)**
- 1 **cup refried beans**
- ¼ **cup salsa**
- 2 **naan flatbreads, halved**
- 4 **large eggs**
- ½ **cup shredded cheddar cheese or Mexican cheese blend**
  Additional salsa, optional

1. Cook potatoes according to package directions for stovetop.
2. Meanwhile, in a microwave-safe bowl, mix beans and salsa. Microwave, covered, on high until heated through, 1-2 minutes, stirring once. In a large skillet, heat naan over medium-high heat until lightly browned, 2-3 minutes per side; remove from pan. Keep warm.
3. Coat same skillet with cooking spray; place over medium-high heat. Break eggs, 1 at a time, into pan; reduce heat to low. Cook until whites are set and yolks begin to thicken, turning once if desired.
4. To serve, spread bean mixture over naan. Top with potatoes, eggs and cheese. If desired, serve with additional salsa.

1 serving: 430 cal., 23g fat (6g sat. fat), 202mg chol., 703mg sod., 40g carb. (4g sugars, 4g fiber), 16g pro.

TEST KITCHEN TIP

Bring the forks and knives to these flatbreads; they're a hearty meal-in-one! Chop some fresh cilantro, if you're a fan, for a perfect garnish.

ZUCCHINI & GOUDA SKILLET FRITTATA

This is a version of a skillet dish that my mother-in-law, Millie, created to use up all that extra summertime zucchini. The Gouda melts beautifully, but you can make it with Swiss or sharp cheddar, too.
—Susan Marshall, Colorado Springs, CO

TAKES: 30 MIN. • **MAKES:** 6 SERVINGS

- 6 large eggs
- 2 Tbsp. 2% milk
- 1 tsp. chopped fresh oregano
- ½ tsp. salt
- ⅛ tsp. pepper
- 2 Tbsp. butter
- 2 medium zucchini (7 to 8 oz. each), thinly sliced
- 1 medium onion, chopped
- 2 Tbsp. olive oil
- 1 medium tomato, diced
- 1 cup shredded Gouda cheese
- 2 Tbsp. minced fresh basil

1. Combine the first 5 ingredients; set aside. In a large nonstick skillet, melt butter over medium heat. Add the zucchini and onion. Cook until tender, 6-8 minutes; remove.
2. In same skillet, heat oil over medium heat. Add the egg mixture. Cook until set, gently lifting edges of cooked egg to allow liquid to run underneath. Top with zucchini mixture, diced tomato and cheese. Cover and cook until cheese is melted, 2-3 minutes. Sprinkle basil on top.
1 wedge: 238 cal., 19g fat (8g sat. fat), 218mg chol., 462mg sod., 6g carb. (4g sugars, 1g fiber), 12g pro.

WHOLE GRAIN BANANA PANCAKES

My kids love homemade banana bread, so why not make it in pancake form? These freeze well for a special breakfast any day.
—Ally Billhorn, Wilton, IA

TAKES: 30 MIN. • **MAKES:** 8 SERVINGS

- 1 cup whole wheat flour
- 1 cup all-purpose flour
- 4 tsp. baking powder
- 1 tsp. ground cinnamon
- ½ tsp. salt
- 2 large eggs
- 2 cups fat-free milk
- ⅔ cup mashed ripe banana (about 1 medium)
- 1 Tbsp. olive oil
- 1 Tbsp. maple syrup
- ½ tsp. vanilla extract
  Sliced bananas and additional syrup, optional

1. Whisk together the first 5 ingredients. In another bowl, whisk together the eggs, milk, mashed banana, oil, 1 Tbsp. syrup and vanilla. Add to flour mixture; stir just until moistened.
2. Preheat a griddle coated with cooking spray over medium heat. Pour batter by ¼ cupfuls onto griddle; cook until bubbles on top begin to pop and bottoms are golden brown. Turn; cook until second side is golden brown. If desired, serve with sliced bananas and additional syrup.

Freeze option: Freeze cooled pancakes between layers of waxed paper in a freezer container. To use, place pancakes on an ungreased baking sheet, cover with foil and reheat in a preheated 375° oven until heated through, 10-15 minutes. Or, place a stack of 2 pancakes on a microwave-safe plate and microwave on high until heated through, 45-60 seconds.
2 pancakes: 186 cal., 4g fat (1g sat. fat), 48mg chol., 392mg sod., 32g carb. (7g sugars, 3g fiber), 7g pro.
Diabetic exchanges: 2 starch, ½ fat.

CHORIZO & GRITS BREAKFAST BOWLS

Growing up, I bonded with my dad over chorizo and eggs. My fresh approach combines them with grits and black beans. Add a spoonful of pico de gallo.
—Jenn Tidwell, Fair Oaks, CA

TAKES: 30 MIN. • **MAKES:** 6 SERVINGS

- 2 tsp. olive oil
- 1 pkg. (12 oz.) fully cooked chorizo chicken sausages or flavor of choice, sliced
- 1 large zucchini, chopped
- 3 cups water
- ¾ cup quick-cooking grits
- 1 can (15 oz.) black beans, rinsed and drained
- ½ cup shredded cheddar cheese
- 6 large eggs
  Optional: Pico de gallo and chopped fresh cilantro

1. In a large skillet, heat oil over medium heat. Add sausage; cook and stir until lightly browned, 2-3 minutes. Add zucchini; cook and stir until tender, 4-5 minutes longer. Remove from pan; keep warm.
2. Meanwhile, in a large saucepan, bring water to a boil. Slowly stir in grits. Reduce heat to medium-low; cook, covered, until thickened, stirring occasionally, about 5 minutes. Stir in beans and cheese until blended. Remove from heat.
3. Wipe skillet clean; coat with cooking spray and place over medium heat. In batches, break 1 egg at a time into pan. Immediately reduce heat to low; cook until whites are completely set and yolks begin to thicken but are not hard, about 5 minutes.

4. To serve, divide grits mixture among 6 bowls. Top with chorizo mixture, eggs and, if desired, pico de gallo and cilantro.
1 serving: 344 cal., 14g fat (5g sat. fat), 239mg chol., 636mg sod., 30g carb. (4g sugars, 4g fiber), 24g pro.
Diabetic exchanges: 3 medium-fat meat, 2 starch.

HEALTH TIP

Black beans are part of the legume family and a rich source of iron, which helps transport oxygen to the muscles.

5i

EGG BASKETS BENEDICT

A little puff pastry turns Canadian bacon and eggs into a tasty update on eggs Benedict. We use a packaged hollandaise or even cheese sauce for the finish.
—Sally Jackson, Fort Worth, TX

TAKES: 30 MIN.
MAKES: 1 DOZEN (1 CUP SAUCE)

- 1 sheet frozen puff pastry, thawed
- 12 large eggs
- 6 slices Canadian bacon, finely chopped
- 1 envelope hollandaise sauce mix

1. Preheat oven to 400°. On a lightly floured surface, unfold puff pastry. Roll into a 16x12-in. rectangle; cut into twelve 4-in. squares. Place in greased muffin cups, pressing gently onto bottoms and up sides, allowing corners to point up.
2. Break and slip an egg into center of each pastry cup; sprinkle with Canadian bacon. Bake until pastry is golden brown, the egg whites are completely set, and the yolks begin to thicken but are not hard, 10-12 minutes. Meanwhile, prepare hollandaise sauce according to package directions.
3. Remove the pastry cups to wire racks. Serve warm with the hollandaise sauce.

1 pastry cup with about 1 Tbsp. sauce: 237 cal., 15g fat (6g sat. fat), 201mg chol., 355mg sod., 14g carb. (1g sugars, 2g fiber), 10g pro.

THE BEST FRENCH TOAST

There's no question that this is the best French toast recipe. The caramelized exterior meets a soft, custardlike center that practically melts in your mouth. Not only that, but it's quick and easy, too!
—Audrey Rompon, Milwaukee, WI

TAKES: 15 MIN. • **MAKES:** 4 SERVINGS

- 1½ cups half-and-half cream
- 3 large egg yolks
- 3 Tbsp. brown sugar
- 2 tsp. vanilla extract
- ¾ tsp. ground cinnamon
- ½ tsp. salt
- ¼ tsp. ground nutmeg

- 8 slices day-old brioche bread (1 in. thick)
  Optional toppings: Butter, maple syrup, fresh berries, whipped cream and confectioners' sugar

1. In a shallow dish, whisk together the first 7 ingredients. Preheat a greased griddle over medium heat.
2. Dip bread into egg mixture, letting it soak 5 seconds on each side. Cook on griddle until golden brown on both sides. Serve with toppings as desired.

2 pieces: 546 cal., 24g fat (15g sat. fat), 263mg chol., 786mg sod., 64g carb. (25g sugars, 2g fiber), 13g pro.

TEST KITCHEN TIP

Using day-old bread from a bakery helps the French toast to be more stable. If using commercially produced brioche, be sure to allow the bread to become slightly stale for best results.

¼ cup finely chopped fresh
  pineapple
6 large eggs, beaten
6 Tbsp. marinara sauce
2 Tbsp. shredded part-skim
  mozzarella cheese
2 Tbsp. grated Parmigiano-
  Reggiano cheese
2 Tbsp. minced fresh parsley

1. Preheat broiler. In a 10-in.
ovenproof skillet, cook sausage,
mushrooms, onion and pepper over
medium heat until sausage is no
longer pink and vegetables are
tender, 6-8 minutes, breaking
sausage into crumbles; drain.
2. Return sausage mixture to skillet;
stir in pineapple. Pour in beaten
eggs. Cook, covered, until nearly
set, 4-6 minutes. Spread marinara
over top; sprinkle with cheeses.
3. Broil 3-4 in. from heat until eggs
are completely set and cheese is
melted, 2-3 minutes. Let stand
5 minutes. Sprinkle with parsley;
cut into wedges.
1 wedge: 226 cal., 15g fat (5g sat. fat),
299mg chol., 459mg sod., 7g carb. (4g
sugars, 1g fiber), 16g pro.

SAUSAGE & MUSHROOM
PIZZA FRITTATA

*I love this frittata because the combo of
fresh flavors makes it special. It's the
perfect sunny South Florida breakfast.*
—Wolfgang Hanau, West Palm Beach, FL

TAKES: 30 MIN. • **MAKES:** 4 SERVINGS

4 oz. bulk Italian sausage
2 cups sliced fresh mushrooms
2 Tbsp. finely chopped red onion
2 Tbsp. finely chopped green
  pepper

DID YOU KNOW?

Packaged shredded
cheeses may be tossed
with potato flakes to keep
the shreds separate. By
shredding cheese yourself,
you'll get more flavor and
a better consistency when
the cheese melts.

BREAKFAST BRUSCHETTA

My family loves bruschetta, so why not have it for breakfast? This gives us a healthy start to the morning, and takes very little effort to set on the table. You get wonderful flavor, and with egg added, it makes a meal.

—Kallee Krong-McCreery, Escondido, CA

TAKES: 25 MIN. • **MAKES:** 4 SERVINGS

- 3 plum tomatoes, seeded and chopped
- ⅓ cup crumbled feta cheese
- ¼ cup sliced ripe olives
- 3 Tbsp. minced fresh basil or ¾ tsp. dried basil
- 3 Tbsp. olive oil
- 2 Tbsp. finely chopped red onion
- 4 English muffins, split and toasted
- 6 large eggs
- ⅛ tsp. salt
- ⅛ tsp. pepper
  Additional minced fresh basil

1. Preheat oven to 375°. Mix the first 6 ingredients. Place English muffin halves on a baking sheet; top with tomato mixture. Bake until heated through, 10-12 minutes.
2. Meanwhile, whisk together eggs, salt and pepper. Heat a small nonstick skillet coated with cooking spray over medium heat. Pour in eggs; cook and stir until eggs are thickened and no liquid egg remains. Top each English muffin half with scrambled eggs; sprinkle with basil. Serve immediately.

2 English muffin halves with topping: 381 cal., 21g fat (5g sat. fat), 284mg chol., 583mg sod., 31g carb., (4g sugars, 3g fiber), 17g pro.

DENVER SCRAMBLE TOSTADA

My tostadas feature the ingredients of a classic Denver omelet: ham, cheddar and green pepper. I also make a zesty Mexican version with chorizo and pepper jack and a Reuben with corned beef and Swiss.

—Joi Sinclair, Atchison, KS

TAKES: 15 MIN. • **MAKES:** 6 SERVINGS

- 1 Tbsp. butter
- ½ cup finely chopped green pepper
- ⅓ cup finely chopped onion
- ¼ tsp. pepper
- ⅛ tsp. salt
- 12 large eggs, beaten
- 1 cup cubed fully cooked ham
- ¾ cup shredded cheddar cheese
- 6 tostada shells, warmed
  Additional shredded cheddar cheese

In a large nonstick skillet, melt butter over medium heat. Add green pepper, onion, pepper and salt; cook and stir 2-3 minutes or until vegetables are crisp-tender. Add eggs, ham and cheese; cook and stir until eggs are thickened and no liquid egg remains. Serve over tostada shells; sprinkle with additional cheese.

1 tostada: 302 cal., 19g fat (8g sat. fat), 405mg chol., 626mg sod., 9g carb. (1g sugars, 1g fiber), 22g pro.

PUMPKIN CREAM OF WHEAT

This autumn-inspired breakfast tastes like pumpkin pie but without the guilt! Simply double the recipe if you feel like sharing.

—Amy Bashtovoi, Sidney, NE

TAKES: 10 MIN. • **MAKES:** 1 SERVING

- ½ cup 2% milk
- ¼ cup half-and-half cream
- 3 Tbsp. Cream of Wheat
- ¼ cup canned pumpkin
- 2 tsp. sugar
- ⅛ tsp. ground cinnamon
  Additional 2% milk

In a small microwave-safe bowl, combine the milk, cream and Cream of Wheat. Microwave, uncovered, on high for 1 minute; stir until blended. Cover and cook for 1-2 minutes or until thickened, stirring every 30 seconds. Stir in the pumpkin, sugar and cinnamon. Serve with additional milk.

1 cup: 314 cal., 9g fat (6g sat. fat), 39mg chol., 96mg sod., 46g carb. (18g sugars, 4g fiber), 10g pro.

BAKED BLUEBERRY PANCAKE

For a quick breakfast, I make the pancake while I fix supper the night before, then cut it into squares. The next morning, I top the pieces with butter and syrup before placing them in the microwave. This innovative way to make pancakes takes most of the fuss out of making breakfast.
—Norna Detig, Lindenwood, IL

TAKES: 20 MIN. • **MAKES:** 6 SERVINGS

  2 **cups pancake mix**
1½ **cups fat-free milk**
  1 **large egg**
  1 **Tbsp. canola oil**
  1 **tsp. ground cinnamon**
  1 **cup fresh or frozen blueberries**
    Butter and maple syrup

1. In a large bowl, combine the pancake mix, milk, egg, oil and cinnamon just until blended (batter will be lumpy). Fold in blueberries.
2. Spread into a greased 15x10x1-in. baking pan. Bake at 400° until golden brown, 10-12 minutes. Serve with butter and syrup.
Note: If using frozen blueberries, use without thawing to avoid discoloring the batter.
1 serving: 200 cal., 4g fat (1g sat. fat), 36mg chol., 527mg sod., 34g carb. (6g sugars, 3g fiber), 7g pro. **Diabetic exchanges:** 2 starch, 1 fat.

MIGAS BREAKFAST TACOS

Unless you grew up in the Southwest or visit there often, you might be hearing of migas for the first time. Think of them as the best scrambled eggs ever. The secret ingredient? Corn tortillas. I think they really make my migas tacos extra special!
—Stephen Exel, Des Moines, IA

TAKES: 30 MIN. • **MAKES:** 3 SERVINGS

¼ **cup finely chopped onion**
 1 **jalapeno pepper, seeded and chopped**
 1 **Tbsp. canola oil**
 2 **corn tortillas (6 in.), cut into thin strips**
 4 **large eggs**
¼ **tsp. salt**
⅛ **tsp. pepper**
½ **cup crumbled queso fresco or shredded Monterey Jack cheese**
¼ **cup chopped seeded tomato**
 6 **flour tortillas (6 in.), warmed**
    Optional toppings: Refried beans, sliced avocado, sour cream and minced fresh cilantro

1. In a large skillet, saute onion and jalapeno in oil until tender. Add tortilla strips; cook 3 minutes longer. In a small bowl, whisk the eggs, salt and pepper. Add to skillet; cook and stir until almost set. Stir in cheese and tomato.
2. Serve in flour tortillas with toppings of your choice.
Note: Wear disposable gloves when cutting hot peppers; the oils can burn skin. Avoid touching your face.
2 each: 424 cal., 21g fat (5g sat. fat), 295mg chol., 821mg sod., 39g carb. (2g sugars, 1g fiber), 21g pro.

FRUITY WAFFLE PARFAITS

This recipe satisfied all of my cravings for breakfast when I was pregnant. I knew I was getting plenty of nutrition in each serving and it tasted wonderful.
—Penelope Wyllie, San Francisco, CA

TAKES: 10 MIN. • **MAKES:** 4 SERVINGS

- 4 frozen low-fat multigrain waffles
- ½ cup almond butter or creamy peanut butter
- 2 cups strawberry yogurt
- 2 large bananas, sliced
- 2 cups sliced fresh strawberries
  Toasted chopped almonds, optional
  Maple syrup, optional

1. Toast waffles according to package directions. Spread each waffle with 2 Tbsp. almond butter. Cut waffles into bite-sized pieces.
2. Layer half the yogurt, bananas, strawberries and waffle pieces into 4 parfait glasses. Repeat layers. If desired, top with toasted almonds and maple syrup. Serve immediately.

1 serving: 469 cal., 20g fat (4g sat. fat), 6mg chol., 337mg sod., 65g carb. (39g sugars, 8g fiber), 15g pro.

CRANBERRY-WALNUT OATMEAL

My family loves cranberries, but we can get them fresh only during the holiday season. This recipe lets us enjoy the tartness of cranberry with the comfort of oatmeal all year long.
—Teena Petrus, Johnstown, PA

TAKES: 15 MIN. • **MAKES:** 4 SERVINGS

- 3½ cups water
- ¼ tsp. salt
- 2 cups quick-cooking oats
- 3 Tbsp. sugar
- 1 tsp. vanilla extract
- 2 tsp. cinnamon-sugar
- ½ cup whole-berry cranberry sauce
- ¼ cup chopped walnuts, toasted

1. In a large saucepan, bring water and salt to a boil. Stir in oats. Cook 1 minute over medium heat, stirring occasionally.

2. Remove from heat; stir in sugar and vanilla. Top servings with cinnamon-sugar, cranberry sauce and walnuts.
Note: To toast nuts, bake in a shallow pan in a 350° oven for 5-10 minutes or cook in a skillet over low heat until nuts are lightly browned, stirring occasionally.
1 cup: 293 cal., 8g fat (1g sat. fat), 0 chol., 156mg sod., 53g carb. (21g sugars, 5g fiber), 7g pro.

WAFFLE MONTE CRISTOS

Adults love the sweet, smoky flavor of this recipe. I use frozen waffles to save time, but have at it if you want to put your waffle iron to good use.
—Kelly Reynolds, Urbana, IL

TAKES: 20 MIN. • **MAKES:** 4 SERVINGS

- ½ cup apricot preserves
- 8 frozen waffles
- 4 slices deli turkey
- 4 slices deli ham
- 4 slices Havarti cheese (about 3 oz.)
- 4 bacon strips, cooked
- 2 Tbsp. butter, softened
  Maple syrup

1. Preheat griddle over medium heat. Spread preserves over 4 waffles. Layer with turkey, ham, cheese and bacon; top with remaining waffles. Lightly spread outsides of waffles with butter.
2. Place on griddle and cook 4-5 minutes on each side or until golden brown and heated through. Serve with syrup for dipping.
1 sandwich: 511 cal., 23g fat (10g sat. fat), 70mg chol., 1163mg sod., 57g carb. (22g sugars, 2g fiber), 21g pro.

RASPBERRY WHITE CHOCOLATE PANCAKES

We grow raspberries in the summer and I'm always looking for new ways to incorporate them into our meals. I created these pancakes on a whim, and my husband—who's not a big fan of raspberries—thought they were great! Semisweet chocolate chips can easily be substituted for the white baking chips if that's what you have on hand.
—Sue Gronholz, Beaver Dam, WI

TAKES: 30 MIN. • **MAKES:** 4 SERVINGS

- 1½ cups all-purpose flour
- 2 Tbsp. sugar
- 1½ tsp. baking powder
- ½ tsp. salt
- ⅛ tsp. ground nutmeg
- 2 large eggs, room temperature
- ¾ cup 2% milk
- ¾ cup plain Greek yogurt
- 2 Tbsp. canola oil
- ¼ tsp. almond extract
- 1 cup fresh or frozen raspberries
- ¼ cup white baking chips
  Optional: additional fresh raspberries and baking chips

1. Preheat a griddle over medium heat. In a large bowl, combine flour, sugar, baking powder, salt and nutmeg. In a small bowl, combine eggs, milk, yogurt, oil and extract; stir into dry ingredients just until moistened. Fold in raspberries and baking chips.

2. Lightly grease griddle. Pour batter by ¼ cupfuls onto griddle; cook until bubbles on top begin to pop and bottoms are golden brown. Turn; cook until second sides are golden brown. Serve with additional raspberries and baking chips.

Freeze option: Freeze cooled pancakes between layers of waxed paper in freezer containers. To use, place pancakes on an ungreased baking sheet, cover with foil and reheat in a preheated 375° oven until heated through, 5-10 minutes. Or, place a stack of 3 pancakes on a microwave-safe plate and microwave on high until heated through, 45-90 seconds.

3 pancakes: 439 cal., 19g fat (7g sat. fat), 110mg chol., 569mg sod., 56g carb. (18g sugars, 3g fiber), 12g pro.

QUINOA BREAKFAST BOWL

Quinoa has been around for a while, but I'm just now jumping on the quinoa breakfast bowl bandwagon. I've made it several times as a savory side or salad but never as a warm breakfast cereal. I finally gave it a try last weekend and loved it!
—Erica Schmidt, Kansas City, KS

TAKES: 20 MIN. • **MAKES:** 4 SERVINGS

- 2 cups 2% or coconut milk
- 1 cup quinoa, rinsed
  Optional: Ground cinnamon, vanilla Greek yogurt, sugar substitute blend, honey, brown sugar, raisins, fresh blueberries, chopped apple, chia seeds and fresh mint leaves

In a large saucepan, bring milk to a boil over medium heat, stirring occasionally. Add quinoa. Reduce heat; simmer, covered, until liquid is absorbed, 12-15 minutes. Remove from heat; fluff with a fork. If desired, stir in any combination of optional ingredients.

0.750 cup: 217 cal., 5g fat (2g sat. fat), 10mg chol., 59mg sod., 33g carb. (6g sugars, 3g fiber), 10g pro. **Diabetic exchanges:** 1½ starch, ½ reduced-fat milk.

SAUSAGE, EGG & CHEDDAR FARMER'S BREAKFAST

This hearty combination of sausage, hash browns and eggs will warm you up on a cold winter morning.
—Bonnie Roberts, Newaygo, MI

TAKES: 30 MIN. • **MAKES:** 4 SERVINGS

- 6 large eggs
- ⅓ cup 2% milk
- ½ tsp. dried parsley flakes
- ¼ tsp. salt
- 6 oz. bulk pork sausage
- 1 Tbsp. butter
- 1½ cups frozen cubed hash brown potatoes, thawed
- ¼ cup chopped onion
- 1 cup shredded cheddar cheese

1. Whisk eggs, milk, parsley and salt; set aside. In a 9-in. cast-iron or other heavy skillet, cook sausage over medium heat until no longer pink; remove and drain. In same skillet, heat butter over medium heat. Add potatoes and onion; cook and stir until tender, 5-7 minutes. Return sausage to pan.
2. Add egg mixture; cook and stir until almost set. Sprinkle with cheese. Cover and cook until cheese is melted, 1-2 minutes.

1 cup: 330 cal., 24g fat (11g sat. fat), 364mg chol., 612mg sod., 9g carb. (3g sugars, 1g fiber), 20g pro.

TEST KITCHEN TIP

If you don't have frozen hash brown potatoes handy, use parcooked cubed potatoes instead.

2 Tbsp. butter
2 medium sweet potatoes, peeled and shredded (about 4 cups)
1 garlic clove, minced
½ tsp. salt, divided
⅛ tsp. dried thyme
2 cups fresh baby spinach
4 large eggs
⅛ tsp. coarsely ground pepper

1. In a large cast-iron or other heavy skillet, heat the butter over low heat. Add sweet potatoes, garlic, ¼ tsp. salt and thyme; cook, covered, until potatoes are almost tender, 4-5 minutes, stirring occasionally. Stir in spinach just until wilted, 2-3 minutes.

2. With the back of a spoon, make 4 wells in potato mixture. Break an egg into each well. Sprinkle eggs with pepper and remaining salt. Cook, covered, over medium-low heat until egg whites are completely set and yolks begin to thicken but are not hard, 5-7 minutes.

1 serving: 224 cal., 11g fat (5g sat. fat), 201mg chol., 433mg sod., 24g carb. (10g sugars, 3g fiber), 8g pro. **Diabetic exchanges:** 1½ starch, 1½ fat, 1 medium-fat meat.

SWEET POTATO & EGG SKILLET

I try to incorporate nutritious sweet potatoes in my meals as often as possible, especially with breakfast! This recipe originated with the purpose of feeding my family a healthy, hearty breakfast... and it worked!
—Jeanne Larson, Rancho Santa Margarita, CA

TAKES: 25 MIN. • **MAKES:** 4 SERVINGS

TEST KITCHEN TIP

If you like your eggs sunny-side up, leave the pan uncovered while they cook. Break the eggs into a small dish before adding to the pan. It's easier to remove stray shell pieces if they get into the egg.

SAUSAGE BREAKFAST BURRITOS

Breakfast routine in a rut? Shake things up with these speedy savory wraps.
—Brenda Spann, Granger, IN

TAKES: 20 MIN. • **MAKES:** 8 SERVINGS

- 1 **lb. bulk pork sausage**
- 1 **small onion, chopped**
- ½ **green pepper, chopped**
- 1 **can (4 oz.) mushroom stems and pieces, drained**
- 1 **Tbsp. butter**
- 6 **large eggs, beaten**
- 8 **flour tortillas (8 in.), warmed**
- 1 **cup shredded cheddar cheese**
   Salsa, optional

1. In a large skillet, brown sausage. Drain, reserving 2 Tbsp. drippings. Saute the onion, green pepper and mushrooms in the drippings until the vegetables are tender.
2. In another skillet, melt butter over medium-high heat. Add eggs; cook and stir until set.
3. Divide the sausage mixture among the tortillas; top with eggs and cheese. Fold bottom of tortilla over filling and roll up. Serve with salsa if desired.

1 burrito: 429 cal., 25g fat (9g sat. fat), 188mg chol., 778mg sod., 30g carb. (1g sugars, 2g fiber), 19g pro.

PECAN CHOCOLATE WAFFLES

If you like waffles and chocolate, this recipe is for you. These tender but crunchy waffles are good for breakfast, brunch or an after-dinner dessert. Instead of chocolate, top with berries and whipped cream or simply sprinkle with powdered sugar.
—Agnes Golian, Garfield Heights, OH

TAKES: 25 MIN.
MAKES: 4 ROUND WAFFLES

- 2 **cups pancake mix**
- 2 **large eggs, room temperature**
- 1½ **cups 2% milk**
- ½ **cup chocolate syrup**
- ¼ **cup canola oil**
- ⅔ **cup chopped pecans**

CHOCOLATE BUTTER
- ½ **cup butter, softened**
- ½ **cup confectioners' sugar**
- 2 **Tbsp. baking cocoa**

1. Place pancake mix in a bowl. In another bowl, whisk eggs, milk, chocolate syrup and oil. Stir into pancake mix just until combined. Stir in pecans.
2. Bake in a preheated round Belgian waffle maker according to manufacturer's directions until golden brown. Meanwhile, in a small bowl, beat chocolate butter ingredients until smooth. Serve with waffles.

Freeze option: Cool waffles on wire racks. Freeze between layers of waxed paper in a resealable freezer container. Reheat waffles in a toaster on a medium setting. Or microwave each waffle on high for 30-60 seconds or until heated through.

1 waffle with 2 Tbsp. chocolate butter: 322 cal., 17g fat (2g sat. fat), 57mg chol., 415mg sod., 36g carb. (18g sugars, 3g fiber), 7g pro.

PB&J FRENCH TOAST

My grandpa made an awesome breakfast for us grandkids: French toast that started on the griddle as a peanut butter and jelly sandwich.
—Lindsey Folsom, Dorsey, IL

TAKES: 15 MIN. • **MAKES:** 4 SERVINGS

- ¼ cup creamy peanut butter
- ¼ cup grape jelly or jelly of your choice
- 8 slices sandwich bread
- 2 large eggs
- ¼ cup 2% milk
- 2 Tbsp. butter
  Sliced fresh strawberries and chopped salted peanuts, optional
  Confectioners' sugar or maple syrup

1. Spread peanut butter and jelly over 4 slices of bread. Top with remaining bread. In a shallow bowl, whisk eggs and milk until blended.
2. On a griddle, melt butter over medium heat. Dip both sides of sandwiches in egg mixture. Place on griddle; toast 2-3 minutes on each side or until golden brown. If desired, top with strawberries and peanuts. Dust with confectioners' sugar or serve with syrup.

1 sandwich: 370 cal., 19g fat (7g sat. fat), 109mg chol., 416mg sod., 40g carb. (18g sugars, 2g fiber), 11g pro.

SAUSAGE-SWEET POTATO HASH & EGGS

When I first began making this dish for breakfast I served it with fried eggs on top. Now I sometimes make it for supper and serve it without eggs. It's perfect when I want a dish I can make quickly, with minimal cleanup.
—Nancy Murphy, Mount Dora, FL

TAKES: 25 MIN. • **MAKES:** 4 SERVINGS

- ½ lb. Italian turkey sausage links, casings removed
- 2 medium sweet potatoes, peeled and cut into ¼-in. cubes
- 2 medium Granny Smith apples, chopped
- ¼ cup dried cranberries
- ¼ cup chopped pecans
- ¼ tsp. salt
- 4 green onions, sliced
- 4 large eggs

1. In a large nonstick skillet coated with cooking spray, cook sausage and sweet potatoes over medium-high heat 8-10 minutes or until sausage is no longer pink, breaking up sausage into crumbles.
2. Add apples, cranberries, pecans and salt; cook and stir 4-6 minutes longer or until potatoes are tender. Remove from pan; sprinkle with green onions. Keep warm.
3. Wipe skillet clean and coat with cooking spray; place skillet over medium-high heat. Break 1 egg at a time into pan. Reduce heat to low. Cook to desired doneness, turning after whites are set if desired. Serve with hash.

1 serving: 338 cal., 14g fat (3g sat. fat), 207mg chol., 465mg sod., 42g carb. (23g sugars, 6g fiber), 15g pro. **Diabetic exchanges:** 2 starch, 2 medium-fat meat, ½ fruit.

BLACK FOREST OATMEAL

I'm always looking for healthier ways to incorporate my chocolate addiction into every meal. I've made this with peanut butter chips with bananas, and white chocolate and mint chocolate chips with raspberries.
—Rachel Strong, Moseley, VA

TAKES: 25 MIN. • **MAKES:** 4 SERVINGS

- 3¾ cups water, divided
- ¼ tsp. salt
- 2 cups old-fashioned oats
- ¼ cup toasted wheat germ
- ½ cup baking cocoa
- ⅓ cup sugar
- 2 tsp. vanilla extract
- 1 cup dried cherries plus additional cherries
  Miniature semisweet chocolate chips, optional
  Sweetened whipped cream, optional

1. In a large saucepan, bring 3¼ cups water and ¼ tsp. salt to a boil. Stir in oats and wheat germ; reduce heat and simmer mixture, uncovered, until water is absorbed, about 5 minutes.
2. Meanwhile, combine cocoa, sugar, vanilla and remaining ½ cup water; stir until smooth. Add chocolate mixture and cherries to oats; stir until well combined and heated through. Serve topped with additional cherries and, if desired, miniature chocolate chips and sweetened whipped cream.
1¼ cups: 410 cal., 5g fat (1g sat. fat), 0 chol., 153mg sod., 86g carb. (45g sugars, 8g fiber), 10g pro.

NUTMEG WAFFLES

Bake an extra batch of these tender, golden waffles on the weekend. Freeze them in packages of two so you can pop in the toaster and reheat on hurried mornings. Nutmeg adds to their warm, feel-good flavor!
—James Christensen, St Anthony, ID

TAKES: 15 MIN. • **MAKES:** 8 WAFFLES

- 1¼ cups all-purpose flour
- 1 tsp. baking powder
- 1 tsp. ground cinnamon
- ½ tsp. salt
- ½ tsp. ground nutmeg
- ¼ tsp. baking soda
- 1 egg, lightly beaten
- 1 cup fat-free milk
- 1 tsp. canola oil
- 1 tsp. vanilla extract
  Butter and maple syrup, optional

1. In a small bowl, combine the flour, baking powder, cinnamon, salt, nutmeg and baking soda. In another bowl, combine the egg, milk, oil and vanilla; stir into dry ingredients until smooth.
2. Bake in a preheated waffle iron according to manufacturer's directions until golden brown. Serve with butter and syrup if desired.

Freeze option: Serve desired amount of waffles with syrup. Arrange remaining waffles in a single layer on sheet pans. Freeze overnight or until frozen. Transfer to a freezer container. Pour remaining syrup into a freezer container. Waffles and syrup may be frozen for up to 2 months. To use, reheat frozen waffles in a toaster. Serve with butter and syrup if desired.
2 waffles: 196 cal., 3g fat (1g sat. fat), 54mg chol., 518mg sod., 34g carb. (4g sugars, 1g fiber), 8g pro. **Diabetic exchanges:** 2 starch, ½ fat.

HASH BROWN QUICHE CUPS

Quiche cups are my showstopper potluck dish. Hash browns and Asiago cheese make up the crusts. Eggs, spinach and bacon do the rest.
—Nicole Stone, Gilbertville, IA

TAKES: 30 MIN. • **MAKES:** 4 SERVINGS

- 1 **large egg**
- ¼ **tsp. salt**
- ⅛ **tsp. pepper**
- 2 **cups frozen shredded hash brown potatoes, thawed**
- ¼ **cup shredded Asiago cheese**

FILLING
- 3 **large eggs**
- 1 **Tbsp. minced fresh chives**
- ⅓ **cup shredded Colby-Monterey Jack cheese**
- ⅓ **cup fresh baby spinach, thinly sliced**
- 2 **bacon strips, cooked and crumbled**

1. Preheat oven to 400°. Grease 8 muffin cups.
2. In a bowl, whisk egg, salt and pepper until blended; stir in potatoes and Asiago cheese. To form crusts, press about ¼ cup potato mixture onto bottom and up side of each prepared muffin cup. Bake until light golden brown, 14-17 minutes.
3. For filling, in a small bowl, whisk eggs and chives until blended; stir in cheese and spinach. Spoon into crusts; top with bacon. Bake until a knife inserted in the center comes out clean, 6-8 minutes.

Freeze option: Freeze cooled baked tarts for up to 3 months. To use, reheat tarts on a baking sheet in a preheated 350° oven until heated through, 5-10 minutes.
2 mini quiches: 180 cal., 11g fat (5g sat. fat), 205mg chol., 375mg sod., 8g carb. (1g sugars, 0 fiber), 12g pro.
Diabetic exchanges: 2 medium-fat meat, ½ starch.

TEST KITCHEN TIP

Get creative with these cups. Add your favorite cheese or switch the bacon with chopped mushrooms or onions or last night's taco meat.

SOUPS & SAMMIES

These recipes prove that hot soups and hearty sandwiches
make the ultimate combo, particularly when time is tight!

DILL CHICKEN SOUP

I could eat soup for every meal of the day, all year long. I particularly like cooking with dill and spinach—they add a brightness to this healthy soup.
—Robin Haas, Hyde Park, MA

TAKES: 30 MIN.
MAKES: 6 SERVINGS (2 QT.)

- 1 Tbsp. canola oil
- 2 medium carrots, chopped
- 1 small onion, coarsely chopped
- 2 garlic cloves, minced
- ½ cup uncooked whole wheat orzo pasta
- 1½ cups coarsely shredded rotisserie chicken
- 6 cups reduced-sodium chicken broth
- 1½ cups frozen peas (about 6 oz.)
- 8 oz. fresh baby spinach (about 10 cups)
- 2 Tbsp. chopped fresh dill or 1 Tbsp. dill weed
- 2 Tbsp. lemon juice
  Coarsely ground pepper, optional

1. In a 6-qt. stockpot, heat oil over medium heat. Add carrots, onion and garlic; saute until carrots are tender, 4-5 minutes.
2. Stir in orzo, chicken and broth; bring to a boil. Reduce heat; simmer, uncovered, 5 minutes. Stir in peas, spinach and dill; return to a boil. Reduce heat; simmer, uncovered, until orzo is tender, 3-4 minutes. Stir in lemon juice.
3. If desired, top each serving with coarsely ground pepper.
1⅓ cups: 198 cal., 6g fat (1g sat. fat), 31mg chol., 681mg sod., 20g carb. (4g sugars, 5g fiber), 18g pro. **Diabetic exchanges:** 2 lean meat, 1 starch, 1 vegetable, 0.500 fat.

BISTRO TURKEY SANDWICH

As a turkey lover who can't get enough during fall and winter, I was inspired to come up with a restaurant-worthy sandwich. I love it with a soft, rich cheese such as Brie.
—Grace Voltolina, Westport, CT

TAKES: 30 MIN. • **MAKES:** 4 SERVINGS

- 2 Tbsp. butter, divided
- 1 large Granny Smith or Honeycrisp apple, cut into ¼-in. slices
- ½ tsp. sugar
- ¼ tsp. ground cinnamon
- ½ medium sweet onion, sliced
- ¼ cup whole-berry or jellied cranberry sauce
- 4 ciabatta rolls, split
- 1 lb. cooked turkey, sliced
- 8 slices Camembert or Brie cheese (about 8 oz.)
- 3 cups arugula (about 2 oz.)

1. Preheat broiler. In a large skillet, heat 1 Tbsp. butter over medium heat; saute apple with sugar and cinnamon until crisp-tender, 3-4 minutes. Remove from pan.
2. In same pan, melt remaining butter over medium heat; saute the onion until lightly browned, 3-4 minutes. Remove from heat; stir in sauteed apple.
3. Spread cranberry sauce onto cut side of bottom portion of rolls; layer with turkey, apple mixture and cheese. Place on a baking sheet alongside roll tops, cut side up.
4. Broil 3-4 in. from heat until cheese begins to melt and roll tops are golden brown, 45-60 seconds. Add arugula; close sandwiches.
1 sandwich: 797 cal., 28g fat (14g sat. fat), 171mg chol., 1196mg sod., 87g carb. (16g sugars, 6g fiber), 55g pro.

ITALIAN JOES ON TEXAS TOAST

This is toasty-good for a weeknight on the go. If you double the crushed tomatoes, meat and wine, you'll have enough sauce to freeze.
—Ashely Armstrong, Kingsland, GA

TAKES: 30 MIN. • **MAKES:** 8 SERVINGS

- 1 lb. ground beef
- 1 small green pepper, finely chopped
- 1 medium onion, finely chopped
- 3 garlic cloves, minced
- ½ cup dry red wine or beef broth
- 1 can (14½ oz.) diced tomatoes, undrained
- ¼ cup tomato paste
- ¼ tsp. salt
- ⅛ tsp. pepper
- 1 pkg. (11¼ oz.) frozen garlic Texas toast
- 8 slices part-skim mozzarella cheese

1. Preheat oven to 425°. In a large skillet, cook beef with green pepper, onion and garlic over medium-high heat until meat is no longer pink, 5-7 minutes; crumble beef; drain. Stir in wine and bring to a boil; cook until wine is reduced by half, about 2 minutes. Stir in the tomatoes, tomato paste, salt and pepper; return to a boil. Reduce heat; simmer, uncovered, until mixture is thickened, 2-3 minutes, stirring occasionally.
2. Meanwhile, place Texas toast on a foil-lined 15x10x1-in. pan; bake until lightly browned, 8-10 minutes.
3. Spoon beef mixture onto toast; top with cheese. Bake until the cheese is melted, 3-4 minutes. Serve immediately.

1 open-faced sandwich: 353 cal., 19g fat (7g sat. fat), 58mg chol., 626mg sod., 25g carb. (5g sugars, 2g fiber), 22g pro.

FRUITY CHICKEN SALAD PITAS

I found this handwritten recipe tucked into an old community cookbook that I bought at a garage sale more than 40 years ago. I made a few changes to suit my family's tastes.
—Kristine Chayes, Smithtown, NY

TAKES: 15 MIN. • **MAKES:** 2 SERVINGS

- 1 cup cubed rotisserie chicken
- ½ cup chopped apple
- ½ cup chopped celery
- ½ cup unsweetened crushed pineapple, well drained
- ¼ cup dried cranberries
- ¼ cup mayonnaise
- 1 tsp. lemon juice
- ¼ tsp. onion powder
- ⅛ tsp. salt
- 4 pita pocket halves

Combine the first 9 ingredients. Fill pita halves with chicken mixture.

2 filled pita halves: 588 cal., 26g fat (5g sat. fat), 64mg chol., 670mg sod., 63g carb. (28g sugars, 4g fiber), 26g pro.

GRILLED BEEF & BLUE CHEESE SANDWICHES

Roast beef, red onion and blue cheese really amp up this deluxe grilled sandwich. If you like a little heat, mix some horseradish into the spread.
—Bonnie Hawkins, Elkhorn, WI

TAKES: 25 MIN. • **MAKES:** 4 SERVINGS

- 2 oz. cream cheese, softened
- 2 oz. crumbled blue cheese
- 8 slices sourdough bread
- ¾ lb. thinly sliced deli roast beef
- ½ small red onion, thinly sliced
- ¼ cup olive oil

1. In a small bowl, mix cream cheese and blue cheese until blended. Spread over bread slices. Layer 4 of the slices with roast beef and onion; top with the remaining bread slices.
2. Brush outsides of sandwiches with oil. In a large skillet, toast sandwiches over medium heat 4-5 minutes on each side or until golden brown.

1 sandwich: 471 cal., 27g fat (9g sat. fat), 72mg chol., 1021mg sod., 31g carb. (4g sugars, 1g fiber), 27g pro.

ASIAN LONG NOODLE SOUP

This flavorful soup is perfect when you want something warm and filling in a hurry. If you can't find long noodles, angel hair pasta is a good substitute.
—Carol Emerson, Aransas Pass, TX

TAKES: 30 MIN.
MAKES: 6 SERVINGS (2 QT.)

- 6 oz. uncooked Asian lo mein noodles
- 1 pork tenderloin (¾ lb.), cut into thin strips
- 2 Tbsp. soy sauce, divided
- ⅛ tsp. pepper
- 2 Tbsp. canola oil, divided
- 1½ tsp. minced fresh gingerroot
- 1 garlic clove, minced
- 1 carton (32 oz.) chicken broth
- 1 celery rib, thinly sliced
- 1 cup fresh snow peas, halved diagonally
- 1 cup coleslaw mix
- 2 green onions, sliced diagonally
  Fresh cilantro leaves, optional

1. Cook noodles according to package directions. Drain and rinse with cold water; drain well.
2. Meanwhile, toss pork with 1 Tbsp. soy sauce and pepper. In a 6-qt. stockpot, heat 1 Tbsp. oil over medium-high heat; saute pork until lightly browned, 2-3 minutes. Remove from pot.
3. In same pot, heat the remaining 1 Tbsp. oil over medium-high heat; saute ginger and garlic until fragrant, 20-30 seconds. Stir in broth and remaining 1 Tbsp. soy sauce; bring to a boil. Add celery and snow peas; return to a boil. Simmer, uncovered, until crisp-tender, 2-3 minutes.
4. Stir in pork and coleslaw mix; cook just until cabbage begins to wilt. Add noodles; remove from heat. Top with green onions and, if desired, cilantro.

1⅓ cups: 227 cal., 7g fat (1g sat. fat), 35mg chol., 1078mg sod., 23g carb. (2g sugars, 1g fiber), 16g pro.

TEST KITCHEN TIP

Enjoy this delightful Asian noodle soup as a meal, or serve it alongside spring rolls, a no-fuss salad or your favorite type of Asian dumpling.

INSTANT POT®
CHILI CON CARNE

Although multicookers can't replace every tool in the kitchen, they sure are coming close. Chili con carne is one of our favorite dishes to re-create in them. This cooks up fast but tastes as if it simmered all day!
—*Taste of Home* Test Kitchen

TAKES: 30 MIN. • **MAKES:** 7 CUPS

- 1 can (16 oz.) pinto beans, rinsed and drained
- 1 can (14½ oz.) Mexican diced tomatoes, undrained
- 1 can (8 oz.) tomato sauce
- 1 medium green pepper, chopped
- 1 medium onion, chopped
- 1 cup beef broth
- 1 jalapeno pepper, seeded and minced
- 2 Tbsp. chili powder
- ¼ tsp. salt
- ¼ tsp. pepper
- 1½ lbs. lean ground beef (90% lean)
  Optional: Sour cream and sliced jalapeno

1. Combine the first 10 ingredients in a 6-qt. electric pressure cooker. Crumble beef over top; stir to combine. Lock lid; close pressure-release valve. Adjust to pressure-cook on high for 5 minutes.
2. Allow pressure to naturally release for 10 minutes, then quick-release any remaining pressure. Stir chili. If desired, serve with sour cream and additional jalapenos.
1 cup: 248 cal., 9g fat (3g sat. fat), 61mg chol., 687mg sod., 18g carb. (5g sugars, 5g fiber), 24g pro. **Diabetic exchanges:** 3 lean meat, 1 starch.

///

AIR-FRYER
PORTOBELLO MELTS

We're always looking for satisfying vegetarian meals, and this one tops the list. These melts are especially delicious in the summer when we have tons of homegrown tomatoes.
—Amy Smalley, Morehead, KY

TAKES: 25 MIN. • **MAKES:** 2 SERVINGS

- 2 large portobello mushrooms (4 oz. each), stems removed
- ¼ cup olive oil
- 2 Tbsp. balsamic vinegar
- ½ tsp. salt
- ½ tsp. dried basil
- 4 tomato slices
- 2 slices mozzarella cheese
- 2 slices Italian bread (1 in. thick)
  Chopped fresh basil

1. Place mushrooms in a shallow bowl. Mix oil, vinegar, salt and dried basil; brush onto both sides of mushrooms. Let stand 5 minutes. Reserve remaining marinade. Preheat air fryer to 400°.
2. Place mushrooms on greased tray in air-fryer basket, stem side down. Cook until tender, about 3-4 minutes per side. Remove from basket. Top stem sides with tomato and cheese; secure with toothpicks. Cook until cheese is melted, about 1 minute. Remove and keep warm; discard toothpicks.
3. Place bread on tray in air-fryer basket; brush with the reserved marinade. Cook until lightly toasted, 2-3 minutes. Top with mushrooms. Sprinkle with chopped basil.

1 open-faced sandwich: 427 cal., 30g fat (4g sat. fat), 4mg chol., 864mg sod., 33g carb. (8g sugars, 4g fiber), 8g pro.

TEST KITCHEN TIP

If you don't have an air fryer, you can make this recipe in an oven.

1 Tbsp. olive oil
3 garlic cloves, minced
¾ cup uncooked arborio rice
1 carton (32 oz.) vegetable broth
¾ tsp. dried basil
½ tsp. dried thyme
¼ tsp. dried oregano
1 pkg. (16 oz.) frozen broccoli-cauliflower blend
1 can (15 oz.) cannellini beans, rinsed and drained
2 cups fresh baby spinach
Lemon wedges, optional

1. In a large saucepan, heat oil over medium heat; saute garlic 1 minute. Add rice; cook and stir 2 minutes. Stir in broth and herbs; bring to a boil. Reduce heat; simmer, covered, until rice is al dente, 10 minutes.
2. Stir in frozen vegetables and beans; cook, covered, over medium heat until heated through and the rice is tender, 8-10 minutes, stirring occasionally. Stir in the spinach until wilted. If desired, serve with lemon wedges.

1¾ cups: 303 cal., 4g fat (1g sat. fat), 0 chol., 861mg sod., 52g carb. (2g sugars, 6g fiber), 9g pro.

HEALTH TIP

Neutral flavor and tender skin make white beans a versatile addition to any soup or stew. They add almost 4 grams of fiber per serving in this recipe.

ARBORIO RICE & WHITE BEAN SOUP

Soup is the ultimate comfort food. This hearty, satisfying soup with arborio rice is low in fat and comes together in about 30 minutes.
—Deanna Wolfe, Muskegon, MI

TAKES: 30 MIN. • **MAKES:** 4 SERVINGS

ASIAN CHICKEN CRUNCH WRAPS

My kids love all kinds of wraps and Asian foods. This is an easy go-to in our house that works for everyone.
—Mary Lou Timpson, Colorado City, AZ

TAKES: 25 MIN. • **MAKES:** 4 SERVINGS

- 8 frozen breaded chicken tenders (about 10 oz.)
- 2 cups coleslaw mix
- ½ cup sweet chili sauce
- 2 green onions, chopped
- 2 Tbsp. chopped fresh cilantro
- 1 tsp. soy sauce
- 4 flour tortillas (8 in.), warmed
- ½ cup dry roasted peanuts, chopped

1. Bake chicken tenders according to package directions. Meanwhile, in a large bowl, toss coleslaw mix with chili sauce, green onions, cilantro and soy sauce.
2. Arrange chicken down center of each tortilla; top with coleslaw mixture and peanuts. Fold sides of tortillas over filling and roll up. Cut each diagonally in half.

1 wrap: 519 cal., 21g fat (3g sat. fat), 13mg chol., 1250mg sod., 66g carb. (19g sugars, 7g fiber), 19g pro.

TURKEY & VEGETABLE BARLEY SOUP

Using ingredients on hand, I stirred up this turkey and veggie-packed soup. If you have them, corn, beans and celery are great here, too.
—Lisa Wiger, St Michael, MN

TAKES: 30 MIN.
MAKES: 6 SERVINGS (2 QT.)

- 1 Tbsp. canola oil
- 5 medium carrots, chopped
- 1 medium onion, chopped
- ⅔ cup quick-cooking barley
- 6 cups reduced-sodium chicken broth
- 2 cups cubed cooked turkey breast
- 2 cups fresh baby spinach
- ½ tsp. pepper

1. In a large saucepan, heat oil over medium-high heat. Add carrots and onion; cook and stir until carrots are crisp-tender, 4-5 minutes.

2. Stir in barley and broth; bring to a boil. Reduce heat; simmer, covered, until carrots and barley are tender, 10-15 minutes. Stir in turkey, spinach and pepper; heat through.

1⅓ cups: 208 cal., 4g fat (1g sat. fat), 37mg chol., 662mg sod., 23g carb. (4g sugars, 6g fiber), 21g pro.
Diabetic exchanges: 2 lean meat, 1 starch, 1 vegetable, ½ fat.

MUSTARD BARBECUE SHAVED HAM SANDWICHES

This recipe makes enough ham rolls to feed a crowd and is so easy to put together. Have your butcher slice the ham very thin. I like to make this on the stovetop and serve it from my slow cooker.
—Joyce Moynihan, Lakeville, MN

TAKES: 30 MIN. • **MAKES:** 20 SERVINGS

- 1 cup cider vinegar
- 1 cup yellow mustard
- 1 cup ketchup
- ⅓ cup packed brown sugar
- ¼ cup butter, cubed
- 1 Tbsp. Worcestershire sauce
- 2 tsp. onion powder
- 1 tsp. garlic powder
- ½ tsp. cayenne pepper
- ½ tsp. pepper
- 5 lbs. shaved deli ham
- 20 sandwich rolls, split

In a Dutch oven, combine the first 10 ingredients. Cook and stir over medium heat until the butter is melted. Bring to a boil; reduce heat. Simmer, covered, for 15 minutes. Add ham; heat through. Serve on rolls.

1 sandwich: 382 cal., 10g fat (2g sat. fat), 57mg chol., 1761mg sod., 46g carb. (15g sugars, 2g fiber), 29g pro.

VEGGIE THAI CURRY SOUP

My go-to Thai restaurant inspired this curry soup. Shiitake mushrooms are my favorite, but any fresh mushroom will work. Fresh basil and lime add a burst of bright flavors.

—Tre Balchowsky, Sausalito, CA

TAKES: 30 MIN. • **MAKES:** 6 SERVINGS

- 1 pkg. (8.8 oz.) thin rice noodles or uncooked angel hair pasta
- 1 Tbsp. sesame oil
- 2 Tbsp. red curry paste
- 1 cup light coconut milk
- 1 carton (32 oz.) reduced-sodium chicken broth or vegetable broth
- 1 Tbsp. reduced-sodium soy sauce or fish sauce
- 1 pkg. (14 oz.) firm tofu, drained and cubed
- 1 can (8¾ oz.) whole baby corn, drained and cut in half
- 1 can (5 oz.) bamboo shoots, drained
- 1½ cups sliced fresh shiitake mushrooms
- ½ medium sweet red pepper, cut into thin strips
  Torn fresh basil leaves and lime wedges

1. Prepare noodles according to package directions.
2. Meanwhile, in a 6-qt. stockpot, heat oil over medium heat. Add curry paste; cook until aromatic, about 30 seconds. Gradually whisk in coconut milk until blended. Stir in broth and soy sauce; bring to a boil.
3. Add the tofu and vegetables to stockpot; cook until vegetables are crisp-tender, 3-5 minutes. Drain the noodles; add to the soup. Top each serving with basil; serve with lime wedges.
1⅔ cups: 289 cal., 9g fat (3g sat. fat), 0 chol., 772mg sod., 41g carb. (3g sugars, 2g fiber), 11g pro. **Diabetic exchanges:** 2½ starch, 1 medium-fat meat, ½ fat.

CHEESEBURGER QUESADILLAS

I created these fun cheeseburger quesadilla mashups in honor of my family's two favorite foods. They are so yummy and easy to make!

—Jennifer Stowell, Deep River, IA

TAKES: 25 MIN. • **MAKES:** 4 SERVINGS

- 1 lb. ground beef
- 1 cup ketchup
- ⅓ cup prepared mustard
- 4 bacon strips, cooked and crumbled
- 2 Tbsp. Worcestershire sauce
- ⅔ cup mayonnaise
- 2 Tbsp. 2% milk
- 2 Tbsp. dill pickle relish
- ¼ tsp. pepper
- 8 flour tortillas (8 in.)
- 1 cup shredded cheddar cheese
  Optional: Shredded lettuce and chopped tomatoes

1. In a large skillet, cook beef over medium heat until no longer pink, 6-8 minutes; crumble meat; drain. Stir in ketchup, mustard, bacon and Worcestershire sauce; bring to a boil. Reduce heat; simmer, uncovered, until slightly thickened, 5-7 minutes, stirring occasionally.
2. Meanwhile, in a small bowl, combine mayonnaise, milk, relish and pepper.
3. Preheat griddle over medium heat. Sprinkle 4 tortillas with cheese; top with beef mixture and remaining tortillas. Place on griddle; cook until golden brown and cheese is melted, 1-2 minutes on each side. Serve with sauce and, if desired, lettuce and tomatoes.
1 quesadilla with about ¼ cup sauce: 1002 cal., 60g fat (17g sat. fat), 110mg chol., 2115mg sod., 75g carb. (18g sugars, 4g fiber), 39g pro.

BUFFALO TOFU WRAP

My family loves the tofu filling in this wrap! For parties, we often serve it as a dip with tortilla chips or pita bread. My husband requests these wraps often, and it's super easy to double the recipe if needed.
—Deanna Wolfe, Muskegon, MI

TAKES: 20 MIN. • **MAKES:** 6 SERVINGS

- 1   cup shredded dairy-free cheddar-flavored cheese
- ½   cup vegan mayonnaise
- ¼   cup finely chopped onion
- ¼   cup finely chopped celery
- 3   Tbsp. Louisiana-style hot sauce
- 1   Tbsp. lemon juice
- ½   tsp. garlic powder
- ¼   tsp. salt
- ¼   tsp. pepper
- 1   pkg. (16 oz.) extra-firm tofu, drained
- 6   spinach tortillas (8 in.)
- 1½ cups fresh baby spinach

In a large bowl, combine the first 9 ingredients. Crumble tofu into bowl; mix well. Spoon about ½ cup tofu mixture down center of each tortilla; top with spinach. Fold bottom and sides of tortilla over filling and roll up.

1 wrap: 452 cal., 29g fat (7g sat. fat), 0 chol., 1066mg sod., 38g carb. (1g sugars, 2g fiber), 11g pro.

TEST KITCHEN TIP

You can make these tasty wraps even faster. The tofu portion of this recipe can be prepared ahead and chilled for a few hours or overnight.

GRILLED CHEESE, HAM & APPLE SANDWICH

In this stepped-up version of a ham and cheese sandwich, melty cheeses, crispy apples and smoky ham are the ultimate combination.
—Josh Rink, Milwaukee, WI

TAKES: 25 MIN. • **MAKES:** 4 SERVINGS

- 6   Tbsp. butter, softened, divided
- 8   slices sourdough bread
- 3   Tbsp. mayonnaise
- 3   Tbsp. finely shredded Manchego or Parmesan cheese
- ⅛   tsp. onion powder
- ½   cup shredded sharp white cheddar cheese
- ½   cup shredded Monterey Jack cheese
- ½   cup shredded Gruyere cheese
- 4   oz. Brie cheese with rind removed, sliced
- 12 slices deli ham
- 1   tart apple, thinly sliced

1. Spread 3 Tbsp. butter on 1 side of bread slices. Toast the bread, butter side down, in a large skillet or electric griddle over medium-low heat until golden brown, roughly 2-3 minutes; remove. In a small bowl, mix together mayonnaise, Manchego cheese, onion powder and remaining 3 Tbsp. butter. In another bowl, combine cheddar, Monterey Jack and Gruyere.
2. To assemble sandwiches, top toasted side of 4 bread slices with sliced Brie. Sprinkle cheddar cheese mixture evenly over Brie. Layer ham and apple slices over Brie; top with remaining bread slices, toasted side facing inward. Spread mayonnaise mixture on the outsides of each sandwich. Place in same skillet and cook until bread is golden brown and cheese is melted, 5-6 minutes on each side. Serve immediately.

1 sandwich: 725 cal., 50g fat (27g sat. fat), 141mg chol., 1415mg sod., 37g carb. (9g sugars, 2g fiber), 32g pro.

SUPREME PIZZA SOUP

A local restaurant serves a delicious baked tomato soup that tastes like a cheese pizza! I am taking it a step further and adding all the fixin's of a supreme pizza. You can add your own favorite pizza toppings as long as you include the ooey, gooey, melty cheese on top. It's like eating a supreme pizza with a spoon. Add your favorite pizza toppings to make it your own. If you can't find the tomato and sweet basil soup, use canned tomato bisque soup and add Italian seasoning.
—Susan Bickta, Kutztown, PA

TAKES: 30 MIN.
MAKES: 6 SERVINGS (2 QT.)

- 6 slices frozen garlic Texas toast
- 2 oz. bulk Italian sausage
- ¼ cup chopped onion
- ¼ cup chopped green pepper
- ⅓ cup sliced pepperoni, chopped
- 3 containers (15½ oz. each) ready-to-serve tomato-basil soup, such as Campbell's
- 1 cup whole milk
- 2 plum tomatoes, peeled and chopped
- 12 slices provolone cheese
- 18 slices pepperoni
- 6 Tbsp. grated Parmesan cheese

1. Prepare Texas toast according to package directions. Meanwhile, in a large saucepan, cook sausage, onion and green pepper over medium-high heat until sausage is no longer pink and vegetables are tender, about 5 minutes, breaking up sausage into crumbles. Add chopped pepperoni; cook 3 minutes longer. Stir in soup, milk and tomatoes; heat through.

2. Place six 10-oz. broiler-safe bowls or ramekins on a baking sheet. Ladle with soup; top each with 1 toast, 2 slices cheese and 3 pepperoni slices; sprinkle with Parmesan. Broil 4 in. from heat until cheese is melted.
1⅓ cups: 576 cal., 32g fat (14g sat. fat), 60mg chol., 1548mg sod., 51g carb. (18g sugars, 3g fiber), 24g pro.

TOASTED CHICKEN SALAD SANDWICHES

I love chicken salad sandwiches. In this recipe, I use a rotisserie chicken from the supermarket and toss it with avocado oil mayonnaise, capers and dill relish, then layer it on crusty bread with sliced radishes and butter lettuce. You can easily vary the flavor by adding herbs or even some finely diced roasted red peppers.
—David Ross, Spokane Valley, WA

TAKES: 30 MIN. • **MAKES:** 10 SERVINGS

- 4 cups cubed rotisserie chicken
- ¾ cup chopped celery
- ½ cup chopped green onions
- ½ cup reduced-fat mayonnaise or avocado oil mayonnaise
- 2 Tbsp. capers, drained and chopped
- 2 Tbsp. caper juice
- 2 Tbsp. dill pickle relish
- ½ tsp. salt
- ½ tsp. pepper
- 20 slices French bread (½ in. thick)
- 3 Tbsp. butter, softened
- 10 Bibb or Boston lettuce leaves
- 1 cup thinly sliced radishes

1. Place chicken in a food processor; pulse until finely chopped. Transfer to a large bowl; stir in celery, green onions, mayonnaise, capers and juice, relish, salt and pepper.
2. Brush 1 side of each bread slice with butter. In a large skillet, toast bread, buttered side down, in batches, over medium heat until golden brown. To assemble sandwiches, place 10 slices bread toasted side down. Layer with lettuce, radishes and chicken salad; top with remaining toast slices.
1 sandwich: 249 cal., 12g fat (4g sat. fat), 63mg chol., 507mg sod., 15g carb. (1g sugars, 1g fiber), 19g pro.

CAROLINA SHRIMP SOUP

Fresh shrimp from the Carolina coast is one of our favorite foods. We add kale, garlic, red peppers and black-eyed peas to complete this wholesome, filling soup.
—Mary Leverette, Columbia, SC

TAKES: 25 MIN. • **MAKES:** 6 SERVINGS

- 4 tsp. olive oil, divided
- 1 lb. uncooked shrimp (31-40 per lb.), peeled and deveined
- 5 garlic cloves, minced
- 1 bunch kale, trimmed and coarsely chopped (about 16 cups)
- 1 medium sweet red pepper, cut into ¾-in. pieces
- 3 cups reduced-sodium chicken broth
- 1 can (15½ oz.) black-eyed peas, rinsed and drained
- ¼ tsp. salt
- ¼ tsp. pepper
   Minced fresh chives, optional

1. In a 6-qt. stockpot, heat 2 tsp. oil over medium-high heat. Add shrimp; cook and stir 2 minutes. Add garlic; cook just until shrimp turn pink, 1-2 minutes longer. Remove from pot.
2. In same pot, heat remaining 2 tsp. oil over medium-high heat. Stir in kale and red pepper; cook, covered, until kale is tender, stirring occasionally, 8-10 minutes. Add broth; bring to a boil. Stir in peas, salt, pepper and shrimp; heat through. If desired, sprinkle servings with chives.

1 cup: 188 cal., 5g fat (1g sat. fat), 92mg chol., 585mg sod., 18g carb. (2g sugars, 3g fiber), 19g pro.
Diabetic exchanges: 2 lean meat, 2 vegetable, ½ starch, ½ fat.

HEALTH TIP

This soup's colorful mix of veggies means you're getting a variety of nutrients. Aim for lots of color when planning meals through the day.

- ⅛ tsp. onion powder
- ½ cup shredded sharp white cheddar cheese
- ½ cup shredded Monterey Jack cheese
- ½ cup shredded Gruyere cheese
- 4 oz. Brie cheese, rind removed and sliced

1. Spread 3 Tbsp. butter on 1 side of bread slices. Toast bread, butter side down, in a large skillet or an electric griddle over medium-low heat until they are golden brown, 2-3 minutes; remove. In a small bowl, mix together mayonnaise, Manchego cheese, onion powder and remaining 3 Tbsp. butter. In another bowl, combine cheddar, Monterey Jack and Gruyere.

2. To assemble sandwiches, top toasted side of 4 bread slices with sliced Brie. Sprinkle cheddar cheese mixture evenly over Brie. Top with remaining bread slices, toasted side facing inward. Spread the mayonnaise mixture on the outsides of each sandwich. Place in same skillet and cook until bread is golden brown and cheese is melted, 5-6 minutes on each side. Serve immediately.

1 sandwich: 659 cal., 49g fat (27g sat. fat), 122mg chol., 1017mg sod., 30g carb. (3g sugars, 1g fiber), 24g pro.

TEST KITCHEN TIP

Even though it creates an extra step, toasting the bread on both sides makes a big difference!

THE BEST EVER GRILLED CHEESE SANDWICH

Spreading a mixture of mayo and butter on the bread creates a delightfully crispy crust with the well-loved, wonderful flavor of butter that one expects from a grilled cheese sandwich.
—Josh Rink, Milwaukee, WI

TAKES: 25 MIN. • **MAKES:** 4 SERVINGS

- 6 Tbsp. butter, softened, divided
- 8 slices sourdough bread
- 3 Tbsp. mayonnaise
- 3 Tbsp. finely shredded Manchego or Parmesan cheese

🌱 VEGAN CARROT SOUP

Yukon Gold potatoes—instead of cream—make a smooth carrot soup vegan and add a mild sweetness. If you don't have Yukon Golds on hand, russet potatoes will work, too.
—*Taste of Home* Test Kitchen

TAKES: 30 MIN. • **MAKES:** 6 SERVINGS

- 1   medium onion, chopped
- 2   celery ribs, chopped
- 1   Tbsp. canola oil
- 4   cups vegetable broth
- 1   lb. carrots, sliced
- 2   large Yukon Gold potatoes, peeled and cubed
- 1   tsp. salt
- ¼   tsp. pepper
  Fresh cilantro leaves, optional

1. In a large saucepan, saute onion and celery in oil until tender. Add the broth, carrots and potatoes; bring to a boil. Reduce heat; cover and simmer for 15-20 minutes or until vegetables are tender. Remove from the heat; cool slightly.
2. Transfer to a blender; cover and process until blended. Return to pan; stir in salt and pepper. Heat through. If desired, sprinkle with cilantro leaves.

1 cup: 176 cal., 3g fat (0 sat. fat), 0 chol., 710mg sod., 35g carb. (7g sugars, 4g fiber), 4g pro. **Diabetic exchanges:** 2 starch, ½ fat.

EASY MEXICAN BEAN SOUP

It never hurts to have a few meals that you can whip up in very little time, and this hearty soup is one of my busy-day favorites. Green chiles and chili powder give it some oomph.
—Colleen Delawder, Herndon, VA

TAKES: 20 MIN. • **MAKES:** 4 SERVINGS

- 1   can (16 oz.) butter beans, rinsed and drained
- 1   can (15½ oz.) small white beans or navy beans, rinsed and drained
- 1   can (14½ oz.) no-salt-added diced tomatoes, undrained
- 1   can (4 oz.) chopped green chiles
- 1   Tbsp. minced fresh cilantro
- 1½ tsp. chili powder
- ½   tsp. onion powder
- 1½ cups vegetable stock
  Optional: Crumbled queso fresco and additional cilantro

In a large saucepan, combine first 8 ingredients; bring to a boil. Reduce heat; simmer, covered, until flavors are blended, 10 minutes. If desired, top with cheese and additional cilantro.

1⅓ cups: 214 cal., 1g fat (0 sat. fat), 0 chol., 893mg sod., 45g carb. (4g sugars, 12g fiber), 14g pro.

QUICK PEPPERONI CALZONES

Take your calzones to the next level by topping them with Parmesan and herbs.
—Shannon Norris, Cudahy, WI

TAKES: 30 MIN. • **MAKES:** 4 SERVINGS

- 1   cup chopped pepperoni
- ½   cup pasta sauce with meat
- ¼   cup shredded part-skim mozzarella cheese
- 1   loaf (1 lb.) frozen bread dough, thawed
- 1   to 2 Tbsp. 2% milk
- 1   Tbsp. grated Parmesan cheese
- ½   tsp. Italian seasoning, optional

1. Preheat oven to 350°. In a small bowl, mix pepperoni, pasta sauce and mozzarella cheese.
2. On a lightly floured surface, divide dough into 4 portions. Roll each into a 6-in. circle; top each with a scant ⅓ cup pepperoni mixture. Fold dough over filling; pinch edges to seal. Place on a greased baking sheet.
3. Brush milk over tops; sprinkle with Parmesan cheese and, if desired, Italian seasoning. Bake until golden brown, 20-25 minutes.

1 calzone: 540 cal., 23g fat (8g sat. fat), 36mg chol., 1573mg sod., 59g carb. (7g sugars, 5g fiber), 21g pro.

TURKEY SANDWICH WITH RASPBERRY-MUSTARD SPREAD

My hearty sandwich has different yet complementary flavors and textures. It is filled with flavor and nutrients, without all the unhealthy fats, sodium and added sugar that so many other sandwiches have. And it's absolutely delicious as well!
—Sarah Savage, Buena Vista, VA

TAKES: 25 MIN. • **MAKES:** 2 SERVINGS

- 1 Tbsp. honey
- 1 Tbsp. spicy brown mustard
- 1 tsp. red raspberry preserves
- ¼ tsp. mustard seed
- 1 Tbsp. olive oil
- 4 oz. fresh mushrooms, thinly sliced
- 1 cup fresh baby spinach, coarsely chopped
- 1 garlic clove, minced
- ½ tsp. chili powder
- 4 slices multigrain bread, toasted
- 6 oz. sliced cooked turkey breast
- ½ medium ripe avocado, sliced

1. Combine the honey, mustard, preserves and mustard seed. In a large skillet, heat oil over medium-high heat. Add mushrooms; cook and stir until tender, 4-5 minutes. Add the spinach, garlic and chili powder; cook and stir until the spinach is wilted, 3-4 minutes.
2. Spread half the mustard mixture over 2 slices of toast. Layer with turkey, mushroom mixture and avocado. Spread remaining mustard mixture over remaining toast; place over top.
1 sandwich: 449 cal., 16g fat (3g sat. fat), 68mg chol., 392mg sod., 40g carb. (14g sugars, 7g fiber), 35g pro.

EASY TORTELLINI SPINACH SOUP

This is the easiest soup you will ever make—take it from me! I always keep the ingredients on hand so if I'm feeling under the weather or just plain busy, I can throw together this comforting soup in a flash.
—Angela Lively, Conroe, TX

TAKES: 20 MIN.
MAKES: 8 SERVINGS (3 QT.)

- 16 frozen fully cooked Italian meatballs (about 1 lb.)
- 1 can (14½ oz.) fire-roasted diced tomatoes, undrained
- ¼ tsp. Italian seasoning
- ¼ tsp. pepper
- 2 cartons (32 oz. each) chicken stock
- 2 cups frozen cheese tortellini (about 8 oz.)
- 3 oz. fresh baby spinach (about 4 cups)
  Shredded Parmesan cheese, optional

1. Place the first 5 ingredients in a 6-qt. stockpot; bring to a boil. Reduce heat; simmer, covered, 10 minutes.
2. Return to a boil. Add tortellini; cook, uncovered, until meatballs are heated through and tortellini are tender, 3-5 minutes, stirring occasionally. Stir in spinach until wilted. Serve immediately. If desired, top with cheese.
1½ cups: 177 cal., 8g fat (4g sat. fat), 18mg chol., 949mg sod., 14g carb. (3g sugars, 1g fiber), 12g pro.

TEST KITCHEN TIP

One 9-oz. package refrigerated cheese tortellini may be substituted for 2 cups frozen tortellini. Plan on serving the soup soon after adding the tortellini and spinach for the best pasta texture.

BEER-CHEESE VELVET SOUP

This soup was a hit with a group of German exchange teachers who visited our high school. I usually serve it with soft pretzels or crusty bread, and it's also a treat with slices of cooked bratwurst or kielbasa stirred into it.
—Paula Zsiray, Logan, UT

TAKES: 25 MIN.
MAKES: 8 SERVINGS (1½ QT.)

- ¾   cup butter, cubed
- ¾   cup all-purpose flour
- 1   bottle (12 oz.) light beer
- 4   cups chicken or vegetable stock, divided
- 2   tsp. Worcestershire sauce
- 1   tsp. ground mustard
- ½   tsp. salt
- ¼   tsp. pepper
- ¼   tsp. cayenne pepper
- 4   cups shredded cheddar cheese
  Optional: Bread bowls, crumbled bacon and shredded cheddar cheese

1. In a large saucepan, melt butter over medium heat. Stir in flour until blended; gradually whisk in beer until smooth. Whisk in stock, Worcestershire sauce, mustard, salt, pepper and cayenne.
2. Bring to a boil, stirring constantly; cook and stir until thickened, about 1-2 minutes. Reduce heat. Gradually stir in the cheese until melted. If desired, serve soup in bread bowls and top with crumbled bacon and shredded cheese.
¾ cup: 450 cal., 36g fat (22g sat. fat), 102mg chol., 925mg sod., 12g carb. (1g sugars, 0 fiber), 17g pro.

CUBAN SLIDERS

Bake till these wonderful little rolls are lightly toasted and the cheese melts. The leftovers keep really well in the fridge, and they make a great snack when served cold. Followers of my blog, houseofyumm.com, go nuts for these sliders!
—Serene Herrera, Dallas, TX

TAKES: 30 MIN. • **MAKES:** 2 DOZEN

- 2   pkg. (12 oz. each) Hawaiian sweet rolls
- 1¼   lbs. thinly sliced deli ham
- 9   slices Swiss cheese (about 6 oz.)
- 24   dill pickle slices
- TOPPING
- ½   cup butter, cubed
- 2   Tbsp. finely chopped onion
- 2   Tbsp. Dijon mustard

1. Preheat oven to 350°. Without separating rolls, cut each package of rolls in half horizontally; arrange bottom halves in a greased 13x9-in. baking pan. Layer with the ham, cheese and pickles; replace top halves of rolls.
2. In a microwave, melt butter; stir in onion and mustard. Drizzle over rolls. Bake, covered, 10 minutes. Uncover; bake until golden brown and heated through, 5-10 minutes longer.
1 slider: 191 cal., 10g fat (5g sat. fat), 42mg chol., 532mg sod., 17g carb. (6g sugars, 1g fiber), 10g pro.

TEST KITCHEN TIP

Hawaiian sweet rolls are tender and slightly sweet. If they're not in your store, use egg or potato rolls, which are softer and richer than the regular dinner rolls.

SPICY PEANUT BUTTER & PORK SANDWICH

A little spicy, a little sweet, with just a hint of curry, this flavor combo is something you just have to try.
—James Schend, Pleasant Prairie, WI

TAKES: 10 MIN. • **MAKES:** 1 SERVING

1 Tbsp. creamy peanut butter
1 slice crusty white bread
2 Tbsp. shredded cooked pork
1 tsp. Sriracha chili sauce
  Curry powder
  Thinly sliced jalapeno pepper

Spread peanut butter over bread. Layer with pork and chili sauce. Sprinkle with curry powder; top with jalapeno.

1 open-faced sandwich: 215 cal., 11g fat (2g sat. fat), 16mg chol., 381mg sod., 20g carb. (5g sugars, 2g fiber), 11g pro.

QUICK & HEALTHY TURKEY VEGGIE SOUP

I freeze our leftover turkey at the holidays so we can enjoy meals like this year-round. This soup is especially delicious on a chilly fall or winter day. If you're looking for a dish that's more filling, add some cooked pasta.
—Joan Hallford, North Richland Hills, TX

TAKES: 30 MIN.
MAKES: 9 SERVINGS (3 QT.)

2 Tbsp. butter
1 medium onion, chopped
1 celery rib, chopped
2 garlic cloves, minced
5 cups reduced-sodium chicken broth
3 medium carrots, julienned
¼ tsp. pepper
1 lb. zucchini or yellow summer squash, julienned (about 6 cups)
3 medium tomatoes, chopped
1 can (15½ oz.) hominy, rinsed and drained
2½ cups frozen lima beans (about 12 oz.), thawed
2 cups cubed cooked turkey
1½ tsp. minced fresh basil or ½ tsp. dried basil
  Shredded Parmesan cheese

In a Dutch oven, heat butter over medium-high heat. Add onion, celery and garlic; cook and stir until tender, 5-8 minutes. Add broth, carrots and pepper. Bring to a boil; reduce heat. Simmer, uncovered, 5 minutes. Add zucchini, tomatoes, hominy, lima beans and turkey. Cook until the zucchini is tender, 5-8 minutes. Top with basil; serve with Parmesan cheese.

1⅓ cups: 187 cal., 4g fat (2g sat. fat), 38mg chol., 614mg sod., 22g carb. (5g sugars, 5g fiber), 16g pro. **Diabetic exchanges:** 2 lean meat, 1½ starch, ½ fat.

DID YOU KNOW?

Hominy is actually field corn that has been processed in such a manner as to give it a puffy and meaty texture.

QUICK & EASY STROMBOLI

Sandwich fixings get rolled into this dinner favorite, thanks to refrigerated pizza dough. Use any combo of cheese, deli meat and veggies that you like or whatever you have on hand.
—Catherine Cassidy, Milwaukee, WI

TAKES: 30 MIN. • **MAKES:** 8 SERVINGS

- 1 **tube (13.8 oz.) refrigerated pizza crust**
- ½ **lb. thinly sliced deli turkey**
- ½ **lb. thinly sliced Muenster cheese**
- ¼ **cup pickled pepper rings**
- 2 **tsp. yellow mustard**
- 2 **tsp. minced fresh herbs or ½ tsp. dried herbs**
- 1 **large egg**
- 1 **Tbsp. water**

1. Preheat oven to 350°. Unroll pizza dough onto the bottom of a greased 15x10x1-in. baking pan. Layer with turkey, cheese and peppers. Spread with mustard; sprinkle with herbs.
2. Roll dough into a log; pinch ends to seal. In a small bowl, combine egg and water; brush over dough. Bake until crust is lightly browned, 20-25 minutes. Slice and serve.

1 piece: 271 cal., 11g fat (6g sat. fat), 42mg chol., 965mg sod., 25g carb. (3g sugars, 1g fiber), 19g pro.

HASSELBACK TOMATO CLUBS

This no-fuss, no-bread riff on a classic is perfect during tomato season. Make it for lunch or pair with pasta salad for a light dinner.
—*Taste of Home* Test Kitchen

TAKES: 15 MIN. • **MAKES:** 2 SERVINGS

- 4 **plum tomatoes**
- 2 **slices Swiss cheese, quartered**
- 4 **cooked bacon strips, halved**
- 4 **slices deli turkey**
- 4 **Bibb lettuce leaves**
- ½ **medium ripe avocado, peeled and cut into 8 slices**
   Cracked pepper

Cut 4 crosswise slices in each tomato, leaving them intact at the bottom. Fill each slice with cheese, bacon, turkey, lettuce and avocado. Sprinkle with pepper.

2 stuffed tomatoes: 272 cal., 17g fat (5g sat. fat), 48mg chol., 803mg sod., 9g carb. (3g sugars, 4g fiber), 21g pro.

SHORTCUT MEATBALL & TORTELLINI MINESTRONE SOUP

This hearty soup is quick to prepare with shortcut ingredients and ready in less than an hour. Add a basic salad and a warm crusty loaf of bread or breadsticks to round out the meal.
—Joan Hallford, North Richland Hills, TX

TAKES: 30 MIN.
MAKES: 8 SERVINGS (2¾ QT.)

- 2 **cans (14½ oz. each) beef broth**
- 1 **jar (24 oz.) marinara sauce**
- 3 **cups frozen mixed vegetables, thawed**
- 1 **can (15½ oz.) navy beans, rinsed and drained**
- 24 **frozen fully cooked Italian meatballs, thawed**
- 5 **oz. frozen chopped spinach, thawed and squeezed dry (about ½ cup)**
- 1 **pkg. (9 oz.) refrigerated cheese tortellini**
   Shredded Parmesan cheese

In a Dutch oven, combine broth, marinara sauce and mixed vegetables. Bring to a boil; add beans, meatballs and spinach. Simmer, uncovered, for 5 minutes. Stir in tortellini; cook 7 minutes longer. Serve with shredded Parmesan cheese.

1⅓ cups: 384 cal., 15g fat (6g sat. fat), 36mg chol., 1467mg sod., 44g carb. (7g sugars, 9g fiber), 21g pro.

MEATY ENTREES

Looking for a game-changing meal that's big on comfort and short on time? These beefed-up recipes are always a cut above the rest.

PIEROGI BEEF SKILLET

Hearty and thick with beef, veggies and potatoes, this is a complete meal in one.
—*Taste of Home* Test Kitchen

TAKES: 25 MIN. • **MAKES:** 4 SERVINGS

- 1   lb. ground beef
- ½   cup chopped onion
- ¼   cup all-purpose flour
- ½   tsp. Italian seasoning
- ½   tsp. pepper
- ⅛   tsp. salt
- 1   can (14½ oz.) beef broth
- 1   pkg. (16 oz.) frozen cheese and potato pierogi, thawed
- 2   cups frozen mixed vegetables (about 10 oz.), thawed and drained
- ½   cup shredded cheddar cheese

1. In a large cast-iron or other heavy skillet, cook and crumble beef with onion over medium heat until no longer pink, 5-7 minutes; drain, reserving 3 Tbsp. drippings. Stir in flour and seasonings until blended. Gradually stir in broth; bring to a boil. Cook and stir until thickened, 1-2 minutes.

2. Stir in pierogi and vegetables. Cook, uncovered, until heated through, about 5 minutes, stirring occasionally. Sprinkle with cheese.

1¾ cups: 654 cal., 31g fat (12g sat. fat), 102mg chol., 1157mg sod., 57g carb. (12g sugars, 7g fiber), 34g pro.

STOVETOP CHEESEBURGER PASTA

Cheeseburgers are delicious in any form, but I'm partial to this creamy pasta dish that seriously tastes just like the real thing. It's weeknight comfort in a bowl.
—Tracy Avis, Peterborough, ON

TAKES: 30 MIN. • **MAKES:** 8 SERVINGS

- 1   pkg. (16 oz.) penne pasta
- 1   lb. ground beef
- ¼   cup butter, cubed
- ½   cup all-purpose flour
- 2   cups 2% milk
- 1¼ cups beef broth
- 1   Tbsp. Worcestershire sauce
- 3   tsp. ground mustard
- 2   cans (14½ oz. each) diced tomatoes, drained
- 4   green onions, chopped
- 3   cups shredded Colby-Monterey Jack cheese, divided
- ⅔   cup grated Parmesan cheese, divided

1. Cook pasta according to package directions; drain.

2. Meanwhile, in a Dutch oven, cook beef over medium heat until no longer pink, 5-7 minutes, breaking it into crumbles. Remove from pan with a slotted spoon; pour off drippings.

3. In same pan, melt butter over low heat; stir in flour until smooth. Cook and stir until lightly browned, 2-3 minutes (do not burn). Gradually whisk in milk, broth, Worcestershire sauce and mustard. Bring to a boil, stirring constantly; cook and stir until thickened, 1-2 minutes. Stir in tomatoes; return to a boil. Reduce heat; simmer, covered, 5 minutes.

4. Stir in green onions, pasta and beef; heat through. Stir in half the cheeses until melted. Sprinkle with remaining cheese; remove from heat. Let stand, covered, until melted.

1½ cups: 616 cal., 29g fat (17g sat. fat), 98mg chol., 727mg sod., 56g carb. (7g sugars, 3g fiber), 33g pro.

TEST KITCHEN TIP

The Parmesan cheese may seem a bit out of character for this cheeseburger pasta—but, trust us, it adds a perfect punch of salty flavor.

STEAK & MUSHROOM STROGANOFF

This homey recipe of steak and egg noodles in a creamy sauce is just like what we had at my gran's house when we visited. It's one of my favorite memory meals, as I call them.
—Janelle Shank, Omaha, NE

TAKES: 30 MIN. • **MAKES:** 6 SERVINGS

6 cups uncooked egg noodles (about 12 oz.)
1 beef top sirloin steak (1½ lbs.), cut into 2x½-in. strips
1 Tbsp. canola oil
½ tsp. salt
½ tsp. pepper
2 Tbsp. butter
1 lb. sliced fresh mushrooms
2 shallots, finely chopped
½ cup beef broth
1 Tbsp. snipped fresh dill
1 cup sour cream

1. Cook the noodles according to package directions; drain.
2. Meanwhile, toss the beef with oil, salt and pepper. Place a large skillet over medium-high heat; saute half the beef until browned, 2-3 minutes. Remove from pan; repeat with remaining beef.
3. In the same pan, heat the butter over medium-high heat; saute the mushrooms until lightly browned, 4-6 minutes. Add shallots; cook and stir until tender, 1-2 minutes. Stir in the broth, dill and beef; heat through. Reduce heat to medium; stir in sour cream until blended. Serve with noodles.
1 serving: 455 cal., 19g fat (10g sat. fat), 115mg chol., 379mg sod., 34g carb. (4g sugars, 2g fiber), 34g pro.

SIRLOIN STIR-FRY WITH RAMEN NOODLES

I created this recipe when I was craving good Chinese food. The leftovers taste just as yummy when they are reheated the next day.
—Annette Hemsath, Sutherlin, OR

TAKES: 30 MIN. • **MAKES:** 4 SERVINGS

2 pkg. (3 oz. each) beef ramen noodles
2 Tbsp. cornstarch
2 cups beef broth, divided
1 lb. beef top sirloin steak, cut into thin strips
2 Tbsp. canola oil
2 Tbsp. reduced-sodium soy sauce
2 cans (14 oz. each) whole baby corn, rinsed and drained
2 cups fresh broccoli florets
1 cup diced sweet red pepper
1 cup shredded carrots
4 green onions, cut into 1-in. pieces
½ cup unsalted peanuts

1. Set aside seasoning packets from noodles. Cook noodles according to package directions.
2. Meanwhile, in a small bowl, combine cornstarch and ¼ cup broth until smooth; set aside. In a large skillet or wok, stir-fry beef in oil until no longer pink. Add the soy sauce; cook until liquid has evaporated, 3-4 minutes. Remove beef and keep warm.
3. Add corn, broccoli, red pepper, carrots, onions and remaining broth to the pan. Sprinkle with contents of seasoning packets. Stir-fry until vegetables are crisp-tender, 5-7 minutes.
4. Stir cornstarch mixture and add to skillet. Bring to a boil; cook and stir until thickened, about 2 minutes. Drain noodles. Add beef and noodles to pan; heat through. Garnish with peanuts.
1½ cups: 593 cal., 28g fat (8g sat. fat), 46mg chol., 2022mg sod., 49g carb. (8g sugars, 8g fiber), 38g pro.

SPICY LASAGNA SKILLET DINNER

This shortcut lasagna always bails me out when I'm in a frenzy to serve dinner. A leafy salad and buttery garlic toast round out the meal.
—Donna Booth, Tomahawk, KY

TAKES: 30 MIN. • **MAKES:** 6 SERVINGS

- 1   pkg. (6.4 oz.) lasagna dinner mix
- 1   lb. lean ground beef (90% lean)
- 1   large onion, chopped
- 1   medium green pepper, chopped
- 1   garlic clove, minced
- 1   jar (14 oz.) meatless spaghetti sauce
- ½   cup chunky salsa
- 1   tsp. garlic powder
- 1   tsp. Italian seasoning
- ½   tsp. dried thyme
- ½   tsp. ground cumin
- ¼   tsp. salt
- ¼   tsp. crushed red pepper flakes
- 1   cup shredded mozzarella and provolone cheese blend

1. Fill a large saucepan three-fourths full with water; bring to a boil. Add pasta from lasagna dinner; cook, uncovered, for 10-12 minutes or until tender.
2. Meanwhile, in a large skillet, cook beef, onion, green pepper and garlic over medium heat 6-8 minutes or until the beef is no longer pink and vegetables are tender, breaking beef into crumbles; drain.
3. Stir in spaghetti sauce, salsa, seasonings and contents of seasoning packet from lasagna dinner. Bring to a boil. Reduce the heat; simmer, uncovered, 5 minutes. Remove from heat.

4. Drain pasta. Add to tomato mixture; toss to coat. Sprinkle with cheese; let stand, covered, until cheese is melted.
Freeze option: Freeze cooled pasta mixture and cheese in separate freezer containers. To use, partially thaw in refrigerator overnight. Heat through in a skillet, stirring occasionally; add a little water if necessary. Remove from heat. Sprinkle with cheese; let stand, covered, until cheese is melted.
1 cup: 319 cal., 11g fat (5g sat. fat), 60mg chol., 1403mg sod., 31g carb. (7g sugars, 3g fiber), 24g pro.

TEST KITCHEN TIP

When at the grocery store, you'll find packages of lasagna dinner mix with the boxed skillet dinners or pasta/noodle dinners.

BASIL-BUTTER STEAKS WITH ROASTED POTATOES

A few ingredients and 30 minutes are all you need for this incredibly satisfying meal. A simple basil butter gives these steaks a very special flavor.
—*Taste of Home* Test Kitchen

TAKES: 30 MIN. • **MAKES:** 4 SERVINGS

- 1 pkg. (15 oz.) frozen Parmesan and roasted garlic red potato wedges
- 4 beef tenderloin steaks (1¼ in. thick and 6 oz. each)
- ½ tsp. salt
- ½ tsp. pepper
- 5 Tbsp. butter, divided
- 2 cups grape tomatoes
- 1 Tbsp. minced fresh basil

1. Bake potato wedges according to package directions.
2. Meanwhile, sprinkle steaks with salt and pepper. In a 10-in. cast-iron or other ovenproof skillet, brown steaks in 2 Tbsp. butter. Add tomatoes to skillet. Bake, uncovered, at 425° until meat reaches desired doneness, 15-20 minutes (for medium-rare, a thermometer should read 135°; medium, 140°; medium-well, 145°).
3. In a small bowl, combine basil and remaining butter. Spoon over steaks and serve with potatoes.

1 serving: 538 cal., 29g fat (13g sat. fat), 112mg chol., 740mg sod., 27g carb. (2g sugars, 3g fiber), 41g pro.

BEEF FILETS WITH PORTOBELLO SAUCE

These tasty steaks seem special, but they are fast enough for an everyday dinner. We enjoy the mushroom-topped filets with crusty French bread, a mixed salad and a light lemon dessert.
—Christel Stein, Tampa, FL

TAKES: 20 MIN. • **MAKES:** 2 SERVINGS

- 2 beef tenderloin steaks (4 oz. each)
- 1¾ cups sliced baby portobello mushrooms (about 4 oz.)
- ½ cup dry red wine or reduced-sodium beef broth
- 1 tsp. all-purpose flour
- ½ cup reduced-sodium beef broth
- 1 tsp. ketchup
- 1 tsp. steak sauce
- 1 tsp. Worcestershire sauce
- ½ tsp. ground mustard
- ¼ tsp. pepper
- ⅛ tsp. salt
- 1 Tbsp. minced fresh chives, optional

1. Place a large skillet coated with cooking spray over medium-high heat; brown steaks on both sides. Remove from pan.
2. Add mushrooms and wine to pan; bring to a boil over medium heat, stirring to loosen browned bits from pan. Cook until liquid is reduced by half, 2-3 minutes. Mix flour and broth until smooth; stir into pan. Stir in all remaining ingredients except chives; bring to a boil.
3. Return steaks to pan; cook, uncovered, until meat reaches desired doneness (for medium-rare, a thermometer should read 135°; medium, 140°), 1-2 minutes per side. If desired, sprinkle with minced chives.

1 steak with ⅓ cup sauce: 247 cal., 7g fat (3g sat. fat), 51mg chol., 369mg sod., 7g carb. (3g sugars, 1g fiber), 27g pro. **Diabetic exchanges:** 3 lean meat, 1 vegetable.

1 jalapeno pepper, seeded and finely chopped
1½ cups uncooked instant rice
1 can (14½ oz.) diced tomatoes with mild green chiles
1½ cups beef broth
1 tsp. ground cumin
¼ tsp. salt
¼ tsp. pepper
1 cup shredded Mexican cheese blend

1. In a large skillet, cook the beef, onion, green pepper and jalapeno over medium heat until meat is no longer pink and vegetables are tender, 8-10 minutes, breaking beef into crumbles; drain.

2. Add rice, tomatoes, broth and seasonings. Bring to a boil, then reduce heat. Simmer, covered, until liquid is absorbed, about 5 minutes. Fluff with a fork. Remove from heat; sprinkle with the cheese. Let stand, covered, until cheese is melted.

1½ cups: 482 cal., 19g fat (8g sat. fat), 96mg chol., 962mg sod., 41g carb. (5g sugars, 4g fiber), 33g pro.

HEALTH TIP

Use instant brown rice instead of white, switch to reduced-sodium broth, skip the added salt and sprinkle with just ¼ cup sharp cheddar instead of 1 cup of the mild blend. The result: 400 calories, 13g fat and 540mg sodium per serving.

SOUTHWESTERN BEEF & RICE SKILLET

I like to serve this kicked-up skillet dish with warm flour tortillas and a side of guacamole. If you like things a little spicier, add more jalapeno and enjoy the heat!
—Pat Hockett, Ocala, FL

TAKES: 30 MIN. • **MAKES:** 4 SERVINGS

1 lb. lean ground beef (90% lean)
1 medium onion, chopped
1 medium green pepper, chopped

ASPARAGUS BEEF SAUTE

I love filet mignon, but I'm not crazy about its price, so I came up with a recipe for more affordable beef tenderloin. Now I cook it once a week. My husband loves the leftovers, too.
—Linda Flynn, Ellicott City, MD

TAKES: 30 MIN. • **MAKES:** 4 SERVINGS

- 1 lb. beef tenderloin or top sirloin steak, cut into ¾-in. cubes
- ½ tsp. salt
- ¼ tsp. pepper
- 1 Tbsp. canola oil
- 2 garlic cloves, minced
- 1 green onion, sliced
- ¼ cup butter, cubed
- 1 lb. fresh asparagus, trimmed and cut into 2-in. pieces
- ½ lb. sliced fresh mushrooms
- 1 Tbsp. reduced-sodium soy sauce
- 1½ tsp. lemon juice
  Hot cooked rice

1. Toss beef with salt and pepper. In a large skillet, heat the oil over medium-high heat; saute beef 2 minutes. Add garlic and green onion; cook and stir until beef is browned, 2-3 minutes. Remove from pan.
2. In same skillet, heat the butter over medium-high heat; saute asparagus and mushrooms until asparagus is crisp-tender. Add beef, soy sauce and lemon juice; heat through, tossing to combine. Serve with rice.

1¼ cups beef mixture: 328 cal., 22g fat (10g sat. fat), 80mg chol., 540mg sod., 5g carb. (2g sugars, 2g fiber), 28g pro.

GROUND BEEF SPAGHETTI SKILLET

I remember my grandma making this stovetop supper many times—we always loved Granny's spaghetti! My husband and I now enjoy making this for our dinner. You can easily substitute ground turkey for the ground beef if that's what you have on hand.
—Jill Thomas, Washington, IN

TAKES: 30 MIN. • **MAKES:** 4 SERVINGS

- 1 lb. ground beef
- 1 medium green pepper, chopped
- 1 small onion, chopped
- 2 garlic cloves, minced
- 1½ cups water
- 1 can (14½ oz.) diced tomatoes, undrained
- 1 can (8 oz.) tomato sauce
- 1 Tbsp. chili powder
- 1 Tbsp. grape jelly
- ½ tsp. salt
- 6 oz. uncooked thin spaghetti, halved

1. In a Dutch oven, cook the beef, green pepper, onion and garlic over medium heat until beef is no longer pink and vegetables are tender, 8-10 minutes, breaking beef into crumbles; drain.
2. Add water, tomatoes, tomato sauce, chili powder, jelly and salt. Bring to a boil. Stir in the spaghetti. Reduce heat; simmer, covered, until spaghetti is tender, 6-8 minutes.

1½ cups: 431 cal., 15g fat (5g sat. fat), 70mg chol., 843mg sod., 47g carb. (10g sugars, 5g fiber), 28g pro.

TEST KITCHEN TIP

The chili powder adds a subtle southwestern flavor to this spaghetti dish. Garnish each serving with your favorite taco toppings—maybe a dollop of sour cream and chopped green onions.

CHEESEBURGER CUPS

A recipe for moms with young kids and busy lives, this simple, inexpensive dish is made with handy ingredients and takes just a short time. Best of all, kids will go absolutely crazy for these darling dinner bites.
—Jeri Millhouse, Ashland, OH

TAKES: 30 MIN. • **MAKES:** 5 SERVINGS

- 1 lb. ground beef
- ½ cup ketchup
- 2 Tbsp. brown sugar
- 1 Tbsp. prepared mustard
- 1½ tsp. Worcestershire sauce
- 1 tube (12 oz.) refrigerated buttermilk biscuits
- ½ cup cubed Velveeta

1. In a large skillet, cook beef over medium heat until no longer pink, breaking it into crumbles; drain. Stir in ketchup, brown sugar, mustard and Worcestershire sauce. Remove from heat; set aside.
2. Press each biscuit onto the bottom and up the sides of a greased muffin cup. Spoon the beef mixture into the cups; top with cheese cubes. Bake at 400° for 14-16 minutes or until cups are golden brown.

Freeze option: Freeze cooled pastries in a freezer container, separating layers with waxed paper. To use, thaw pastries in the refrigerator for 8 hours. Reheat on a baking sheet in a preheated 375° oven until heated through.

2 cheeseburger cups: 440 cal., 16g fat (7g sat. fat), 78mg chol., 1142mg sod., 45g carb. (13g sugars, 0 fiber), 27g pro.

EASY STUFFED POBLANOS

My partner adores these saucy stuffed peppers—and I love how quickly they come together. Top with low-fat sour cream and your favorite salsa.
—Jean Erhardt, Portland, OR

TAKES: 25 MIN. • **MAKES:** 4 SERVINGS

- ½ lb. Italian turkey sausage links, casings removed
- ½ lb. lean ground beef (90% lean)
- 1 pkg. (8.8 oz.) ready-to-serve Spanish rice
- 4 large poblano peppers
- 1 cup enchilada sauce
- ½ cup shredded Mexican cheese blend
  Minced fresh cilantro, optional

1. Preheat broiler. In a large skillet, cook the turkey and beef over medium heat until no longer pink, 5-7 minutes, breaking into crumbles; drain.
2. Prepare rice according to package directions. Add rice to meat mixture.
3. Cut peppers lengthwise in half; remove seeds. Place on a foil-lined 15x10x1-in. baking pan, cut side down. Broil 4 in. from heat until skins blister, about 5 minutes. With tongs, turn peppers.
4. Fill with turkey mixture; top with enchilada sauce and sprinkle with cheese. Broil until cheese is melted, 1-2 minutes longer. If desired, top with cilantro.

2 stuffed pepper halves: 312 cal., 13g fat (4g sat. fat), 63mg chol., 1039mg sod., 27g carb. (5g sugars, 2g fiber), 22g pro.

TEST KITCHEN TIP

Prepared Spanish rice adds so much flavor with so little effort! If you have leftover Spanish rice, use about 2 cups cooked rice for the filling.

AIR-FRYER STEAK FAJITAS

Zesty salsa, bright avocado and tender strips of steak make these traditional fajitas extra special.
—Rebecca Baird, Salt Lake City, UT

TAKES: 30 MIN. • **MAKES:** 6 SERVINGS

- 2 **large tomatoes, seeded and chopped**
- ½ **cup diced red onion**
- ¼ **cup lime juice**
- 1 **jalapeno pepper, seeded and minced**
- 3 **Tbsp. minced fresh cilantro**
- 2 **tsp. ground cumin, divided**
- ¾ **tsp. salt, divided**
- 1 **beef flank steak (about 1½ lbs.)**
- 1 **large onion, halved and sliced**
- 6 **whole wheat tortillas (8 in.), warmed**
  Optional: Sliced avocado and lime wedges

1. For the salsa, place the first 5 ingredients in a small bowl; stir in 1 tsp. cumin and ¼ tsp. salt. Let stand until serving.
2. Preheat air fryer to 400°. Sprinkle steak with the remaining cumin and salt. Place on greased tray in air-fryer basket. Cook until meat reaches desired doneness (for medium-rare, a thermometer should read 135°; medium, 140°; medium-well, 145°), 6-8 minutes per side. Remove from basket and let stand 5 minutes.
3. Meanwhile, place the onion on tray in air-fryer basket. Cook until crisp-tender, 2-3 minutes, stirring once. Slice steak thinly across the grain; serve in tortillas with onion and salsa. If desired, serve with avocado and lime wedges.

1 fajita: 309 cal., 9g fat (4g sat. fat), 54mg chol., 498mg sod., 29g carb. (3g sugars, 5g fiber), 27g pro. **Diabetic exchanges:** 4 lean meat, 2 starch.

MEATBALL SUBMARINE CASSEROLE

We were hosting a bunch of friends, and after a comedy of errors, I had to come up with a plan B for dinner. I realized that much-loved meatball subs are even better as a hearty casserole—so delicious!
—Rick Friedman, Palm Springs, CA

TAKES: 30 MIN. • **MAKES:** 4 SERVINGS

- 1 **pkg. (12 oz.) frozen fully cooked Italian meatballs**
- 4 **slices sourdough bread**
- 1½ **tsp. olive oil**
- 1 **garlic clove, halved**
- 1½ **cups pasta sauce with mushrooms**
- ½ **cup shredded part-skim mozzarella cheese, divided**
- ½ **cup grated Parmesan cheese, divided**

1. Preheat broiler. Microwave the meatballs, covered, on high until heated through, 4-6 minutes. Meanwhile, place bread on an ungreased baking sheet; brush 1 side of bread with oil. Broil 4-6 in. from heat until golden brown, 1-2 minutes. Rub bread with cut surface of garlic; discard garlic. Tear bread into bite-sized pieces; transfer to a greased 11x7-in. baking dish. Reduce oven setting to 350°.
2. Add pasta sauce, ¼ cup mozzarella cheese and ¼ cup Parmesan cheese to meatballs; toss to combine. Pour mixture over bread pieces; sprinkle with the remaining cheeses. Bake, uncovered, until cheeses are melted, 15-18 minutes.

1 serving: 417 cal., 28g fat (13g sat. fat), 59mg chol., 1243mg sod., 22g carb. (8g sugars, 3g fiber), 23g pro.

BEEF & SPINACH LO MEIN

If you like a good stir-fry, this dish will definitely satisfy. I discovered the recipe at an international luncheon, and it's now a favorite go-to meal.
—Denise Patterson, Bainbridge, OH

TAKES: 30 MIN. • **MAKES:** 5 SERVINGS

- ¼ cup hoisin sauce
- 2 Tbsp. soy sauce
- 1 Tbsp. water
- 2 tsp. sesame oil
- 2 garlic cloves, minced
- ¼ tsp. crushed red pepper flakes
- 1 lb. beef top round steak, thinly sliced
- 6 oz. uncooked spaghetti
- 4 tsp. canola oil, divided
- 1 can (8 oz.) sliced water chestnuts, drained
- 2 green onions, sliced
- 1 pkg. (10 oz.) fresh spinach, coarsely chopped
- 1 red chili pepper, seeded and thinly sliced

1. In a small bowl, mix the first 6 ingredients. Remove ¼ cup mixture to a large bowl; add beef and toss to coat. Marinate at room temperature 10 minutes.
2. Cook the spaghetti according to package directions. Meanwhile, in a large skillet, heat 1½ tsp. canola oil. Add half the beef mixture; stir-fry 1-2 minutes or until no longer pink. Remove from pan. Repeat with an additional 1½ tsp. oil and remaining beef mixture.
3. Stir-fry water chestnuts and green onions in remaining canola oil 30 seconds. Stir in spinach and remaining hoisin mixture; cook until spinach is wilted. Return beef to pan; heat through.

4. Drain spaghetti; add to beef mixture and toss to combine. Sprinkle with chili pepper.
Note: Wear disposable gloves when cutting hot peppers; the oils can burn skin. Avoid touching your face.
1⅓ cups: 358 cal., 10g fat (2g sat. fat), 51mg chol., 681mg sod., 40g carb. (6g sugars, 4g fiber), 28g pro.
Diabetic exchanges: 3 lean meat, 2 vegetable, 1½ starch, 1 fat.

TEST KITCHEN TIP

Whole wheat or other multigrain spaghetti can be wonderful in Asian dishes. Besides being more nutritious than regular spaghetti, either gives a more robust and toothsome texture.

BEEF & BACON GNOCCHI SKILLET

This gnocchi dish tastes like bacon cheeseburgers. Go ahead and top it as you would a burger—with ketchup, mustard and pickles.
—Ashley Lecker, Green Bay, WI

TAKES: 30 MIN. • **MAKES:** 6 SERVINGS

- 1 pkg. (16 oz.) potato gnocchi
- 1¼ lbs. lean ground beef (90% lean)
- 1 medium onion, chopped
- 8 cooked bacon strips, crumbled and divided
- 1 cup water
- ½ cup heavy whipping cream
- 1 Tbsp. ketchup
- ¼ tsp. salt
- ¼ tsp. pepper
- 1½ cups shredded cheddar cheese
- ½ cup chopped tomatoes
- 2 green onions, sliced

1. Preheat broiler. Cook the gnocchi according to package directions; drain.
2. Meanwhile, in a large cast-iron or other ovenproof skillet, cook beef and onion over medium heat until beef is no longer pink, 4-6 minutes, breaking meat into crumbles. Drain.
3. Stir in half the bacon; add the gnocchi, water, cream and ketchup. Bring to a boil. Cook and stir over medium heat until sauce has thickened, 3-4 minutes. Add salt and pepper. Sprinkle with cheese.
4. Broil 3-4 in. from heat until cheese has melted, 1-2 minutes. Top with tomatoes, green onions and remaining bacon.

Note: Look for potato gnocchi in the pasta or frozen foods section.
1 cup: 573 cal., 31g fat (16g sat. fat), 136mg chol., 961mg sod., 35g carb. (7g sugars, 2g fiber), 36g pro.

ONE-SKILLET LASAGNA

This is hands-down one of the best skillet lasagna recipes our testing panel has ever tasted. And with classic flavors and cheesy layers, it's definitely kid-friendly.
—*Taste of Home* Test Kitchen

TAKES: 30 MIN. • **MAKES:** 6 SERVINGS

- ¾ lb. ground beef
- 2 garlic cloves, minced
- 1 can (14½ oz.) diced tomatoes with basil, oregano and garlic, undrained
- 2 jars (14 oz. each) spaghetti sauce
- ⅔ cup condensed cream of onion soup, undiluted
- 2 large eggs, lightly beaten
- 1¼ cups 1% cottage cheese
- ¾ tsp. Italian seasoning
- 9 no-cook lasagna noodles
- ½ cup shredded Colby-Monterey Jack cheese
- ½ cup shredded part-skim mozzarella cheese

1. In a large skillet, cook beef and garlic over medium heat until meat is no longer pink, breaking beef into crumbles; drain. Stir in tomatoes and spaghetti sauce; heat through. Transfer to a large bowl.
2. In a small bowl, combine soup, eggs, cottage cheese and Italian seasoning.
3. Return 1 cup meat sauce to the skillet; spread evenly. Layer with 1 cup cottage cheese mixture, 1½ cups meat sauce and half the noodles, breaking to fit. Repeat layers of cottage cheese mixture, meat sauce and noodles. Top with remaining meat sauce. Bring to a boil. Reduce heat; cover and simmer for 15-17 minutes or until noodles are tender.
4. Remove from heat. Sprinkle with shredded cheeses; cover and let stand for 2 minutes or until cheese is melted.
1 serving: 478 cal., 20g fat (8g sat. fat), 128mg chol., 1552mg sod., 43g carb. (15g sugars, 4g fiber), 31g pro.

1 lb. ground beef
2 tsp. canola oil
1 cup mayonnaise
⅓ cup salsa
4 flour tortillas (12 in.)
4 slices pepper jack or
   cheddar cheese
4 tostada shells

1. Gently shape the beef into
4 balls, shaping just enough to
keep together (do not compact). In
a large skillet, heat oil over medium
heat. Working in batches, add beef.
With a heavy metal spatula, flatten
meat to ¼- to ½-in. thickness.
Cook until edges start to brown,
about 1½ minutes. Turn burgers;
cook until well browned and a
thermometer reads at least 160°,
about 1 minute. Repeat with the
remaining beef. Remove from
skillet; wipe skillet clean.
2. Combine the mayonnaise and
salsa; reserve half for serving.
Spread the remaining mixture
over tortillas. On the center of
each tortilla, place 1 slice cheese,
1 burger and 1 tostada shell. Fold
the sides of tortilla over burger;
fold top and bottom to close,
pleating as you go.
3. In batches, place wraps in skillet,
seam side down. Cook on medium
heat 1-2 minutes on each side or
until golden brown. Serve with
remaining sauce.
1 wrap: 912 cal., 69g fat (17g sat. fat),
93mg chol., 1144mg sod., 41g carb.
(2g sugars, 5g fiber), 31g pro.

CRUNCHY BURGER QUESADILLAS

*We adore burgers—all kinds! We
also love quesadillas and tacos. I
combined all of the above to make a
scrumptious and very filling burger
that my whole family enjoys.*
—Ann Marie Eberhart, Gig Harbor, WA

TAKES: 30 MIN. • **MAKES:** 4 SERVINGS

DILL PICKLE HAMBURGER PIZZA

My husband's favorite foods are pizza and cheeseburgers, so I combined the two in a pizza with mayo and dill pickle juice topping. People who try it start laughing because it's so good.
—Angie Zimmerman, Eureka, IL

TAKES: 30 MIN. • **MAKES:** 6 SERVINGS

- ½ lb. ground beef
- 1 prebaked 12-in. pizza crust
- ½ cup ketchup
- ¼ cup prepared mustard
- 1½ cups shredded cheddar cheese
- 2 cups shredded lettuce
- ½ cup chopped dill pickle
- ¼ cup chopped onion
- ½ cup mayonnaise
- 2 to 3 Tbsp. dill pickle juice

1. Preheat oven to 425°. In a large skillet, cook beef over medium heat until no longer pink, 3-4 minutes, breaking it into crumbles; drain.
2. Meanwhile, place crust on an ungreased baking sheet or pizza pan. Mix ketchup and mustard; spread over crust. Add ground beef; bake 5 minutes. Sprinkle with cheese; bake until cheese is bubbly and crust is lightly browned, 8-10 minutes longer.
3. Top with the lettuce, pickle and onion. Whisk the mayonnaise and enough pickle juice to reach desired consistency; drizzle over pizza.

1 slice: 521 cal., 32g fat (10g sat. fat), 59mg chol., 1192mg sod., 36g carb. (7g sugars, 2g fiber), 21g pro.

🟠 CHICKEN-FRIED STEAK & GRAVY

As a child, I learned from my grandmother how to make these easy chicken-fried steaks. I taught my daughters, and when my granddaughters are older, I'll show them, too.
—Donna Cater, Fort Ann, NY

TAKES: 30 MIN. • **MAKES:** 4 SERVINGS

- 1¼ cups all-purpose flour, divided
- 2 large eggs
- 1½ cups 2% milk, divided
- 4 beef cubed steaks (6 oz. each)
- 1¼ tsp. salt, divided
- 1 tsp. pepper, divided
  Oil for frying
- 1 cup water

1. Place 1 cup flour in a shallow bowl. In a separate shallow bowl, whisk eggs and ½ cup milk until blended. Sprinkle the steaks with ¾ tsp. each salt and pepper. Dip in flour to coat both sides; shake off excess. Dip in egg mixture, then again in flour.
2. In a large cast-iron or other heavy skillet, heat ¼ in. oil over medium heat. Add the steaks; cook until golden brown and a thermometer reads 160°, 4-6 minutes on each side. Remove from pan; drain on paper towels. Keep warm.
3. Remove all but 2 Tbsp. oil from pan. Stir in the remaining ¼ cup flour, ½ tsp. salt and ¼ tsp. pepper until smooth; cook and stir over medium heat until golden brown, 3-4 minutes. Gradually whisk in water and remaining milk. Bring to a boil, stirring constantly; cook and stir until thickened, 1-2 minutes. Serve with steaks.

1 steak with ⅓ cup gravy: 563 cal., 28g fat (5g sat. fat), 148mg chol., 839mg sod., 29g carb. (4g sugars, 1g fiber), 46g pro.

15-MINUTE MEAT LOAF

I combined a few awesome-tasting meat loaf recipes to create this flavorful version, which my husband loves. And because it's made in the microwave, the entree is ideal for busy nights.
—Deb Thompson, Lincoln, NE

TAKES: 15 MIN. • **MAKES:** 4 SERVINGS

- 1 large egg, lightly beaten
- 5 Tbsp. ketchup, divided
- 2 Tbsp. prepared mustard
- ½ cup dry bread crumbs
- 2 Tbsp. onion soup mix
- ¼ tsp. salt
- ¼ tsp. pepper
- 1 lb. ground beef
- ¼ cup sugar
- 2 Tbsp. brown sugar
- 2 Tbsp. cider vinegar

1. In a large bowl, combine egg, 2 Tbsp. ketchup, mustard, bread crumbs, dry soup mix, salt and pepper. Crumble beef over the mixture and mix well. Shape into an oval loaf.
2. Place loaf in a shallow 1-qt. microwave-safe dish. Cover and microwave on high for 10-12 minutes or until no pink remains and a thermometer reads 160°; drain.
3. Meanwhile, in a small bowl, combine the sugars, vinegar and remaining ketchup; drizzle over meat loaf. Cover and microwave on high for 2-3 minutes longer or until heated through. Let stand for 10 minutes before slicing.
Note: This recipe was tested in a 1,100-watt microwave.
4 oz.: 375 cal., 13g fat (5g sat. fat), 94mg chol., 960mg sod., 38g carb. (0 sugars, 1g fiber), 27g pro. **Diabetic exchanges:** 3 lean meat, 2½ starch.

INDIAN-SPICED BEEFY LETTUCE WRAPS

Since I love the flavors of Indian food, I almost always have coconut milk, a jar of mango chutney and garam masala seasoning in my pantry. This recipe is one of my go-tos when I am short on time but want something that tastes spectacular. If you'd like to give this a different style of Asian flair, use hoisin sauce in place of the chutney and Chinese five-spice powder in place of the garam masala.
—Noelle Myers, Grand Forks, ND

TAKES: 30 MIN. • **MAKES:** 4 SERVINGS

- 1 lb. ground beef
- 1 medium onion, finely chopped
- 2 garlic cloves, minced
- ⅓ cup mango chutney
- 2 Tbsp. soy sauce
- 1 tsp. garam masala
- 1 pkg. (12.70 oz.) Asian crunch salad mix
- ¼ cup canned coconut milk
- 12 Bibb or Boston lettuce leaves
- 1 medium mango, peeled and sliced

1. In a large skillet, cook beef, onion and garlic over medium heat until beef is no longer pink and onion is tender, 6-8 minutes, breaking beef into crumbles; drain. Stir in chutney, soy sauce and garam masala; heat through. Add salad mix (reserve packets); cook and stir until slightly wilted, about 5 minutes.
2. Combine coconut milk and reserved dressing packet until smooth. Spoon beef mixture into lettuce leaves; sprinkle with contents from reserved toppings packet. Drizzle with coconut milk mixture and top with mango.
3 filled lettuce wraps: 493 cal., 22g fat (8g sat. fat), 74mg chol., 957mg sod., 48g carb. (33g sugars, 5g fiber), 24g pro.

TANGY SWEET-AND-SOUR MEATBALLS

A fabulous sauce, green pepper and pineapple chunks transform premade meatballs into something special. Serving them over rice makes for a satisfying main dish.
—Ruth Andrewson, Leavenworth, WA

TAKES: 30 MIN. • **MAKES:** 6 SERVINGS

- 1   can (20 oz.) pineapple chunks
- ⅓   cup water
- 3   Tbsp. vinegar
- 1   Tbsp. soy sauce
- ½   cup packed brown sugar
- 3   Tbsp. cornstarch
- 30   frozen fully cooked Italian meatballs (about 15 oz.)
- 1   large green pepper, cut into 1-in. pieces
      Hot cooked rice

1. Drain pineapple, reserving juice. Set pineapple aside. Add water to juice if needed to measure 1 cup; pour liquid into a large skillet. Add ⅓ cup water, vinegar, soy sauce, brown sugar and cornstarch; stir mixture until smooth.
2. Cook over medium heat until thick, stirring constantly. Add the pineapple, meatballs and green pepper.
3. Simmer, uncovered, until heated through, about 20 minutes. Serve with rice.

5 meatballs: 389 cal., 19g fat (8g sat. fat), 30mg chol., 682mg sod., 47g carb. (36g sugars, 2g fiber), 11g pro.

KOREAN BEEF & RICE

A friend raved about Korean bulgogi, which is beef cooked in soy sauce and ginger, so I tried it. It's delicious! You'll dazzle the table with this tasty version of beef and rice.
—Elizabeth King, Duluth, MN

TAKES: 15 MIN. • **MAKES:** 4 SERVINGS

- 1   lb. lean ground beef (90% lean)
- 3   garlic cloves, minced
- ¼   cup packed brown sugar
- ¼   cup reduced-sodium soy sauce
- 2   tsp. sesame oil
- ¼   tsp. ground ginger
- ¼   tsp. crushed red pepper flakes
- ¼   tsp. pepper
- 2⅔   cups hot cooked brown rice
- 3   green onions, thinly sliced

1. In a large skillet, cook beef and garlic over medium heat 6-8 minutes or until beef is no longer pink, breaking beef into crumbles. Meanwhile, in a small bowl, mix brown sugar, soy sauce, oil and seasonings.
2. Stir sauce into beef; heat through. Serve with cooked rice. Sprinkle with green onions.
Freeze option: Freeze cooled meat mixture in freezer containers. To use, partially thaw in refrigerator overnight. Heat through in a saucepan, stirring occasionally.
½ cup beef mixture with ⅔ cup rice: 413 cal., 13g fat (4g sat. fat), 71mg chol., 647mg sod., 46g carb. (14g sugars, 3g fiber), 27g pro.
Diabetic exchanges: 3 starch, 3 lean meat, ½ fat.

TEST KITCHEN TIP

Dark brown sugar contains more molasses than light or golden brown sugar. The types are interchangeable in recipes, but if you prefer a bolder flavor, choose dark brown sugar.

LEMONY GREEK BEEF & VEGETABLES

I love the lemon in this recipe— the latest addition to my collection of quick, healthy dinners. I'm sensitive to cow's milk, so I use goat cheese crumbles on my portion instead of Parmesan.
—Alice Neff, Lake Worth, FL

TAKES: 30 MIN. • **MAKES:** 4 SERVINGS

- 1   bunch baby bok choy
- 1   lb. ground beef
- 1   Tbsp. olive oil
- 5   medium carrots, sliced
- 3   garlic cloves, minced
- ¼   cup plus 2 Tbsp. white wine, divided
- 1   can (15 to 16 oz.) navy beans, rinsed and drained
- 2   Tbsp. minced fresh oregano or 2 tsp. dried oregano
- ¼   tsp. salt
- 2   Tbsp. lemon juice
- ½   cup shredded Parmesan cheese

1. Trim and discard root end of bok choy. Coarsely chop leaves. Cut stalks into 1-in. pieces. Set aside.
2. In a large skillet, cook beef over medium-high heat until no longer pink, 5-7 minutes, breaking beef into crumbles; drain. Remove from skillet and set aside.
3. In same skillet, heat oil over medium-high heat. Add carrots and bok choy stalks; cook and stir until crisp-tender, 5-7 minutes. Stir in garlic, bok choy leaves and ¼ cup wine. Cook, stirring to loosen browned bits from pan, until greens wilt, 3-5 minutes.
4. Stir in the ground beef, beans, oregano, salt and enough remaining wine to keep mixture moist. Reduce heat; simmer about 3 minutes. Stir in lemon juice; sprinkle with Parmesan cheese.
1½ cups: 478 cal., 21g fat (7g sat. fat), 77mg chol., 856mg sod., 36g carb. (7g sugars, 10g fiber), 36g pro.

TEST KITCHEN TIP

Can't find bok choy? Any hearty greens, like kale or collards, will be just as delicious. And if you don't have white wine on hand, simply use beer, water or broth instead.

1   lb. ground beef
½   cup chopped onion
3   cups frozen chopped broccoli
1   cup shredded part-skim
    mozzarella cheese
½   cup sour cream
¼   tsp. salt
¼   tsp. pepper
2   tubes (8 oz. each) refrigerated
    crescent rolls

1. Preheat oven to 350°. In a large skillet, cook beef and onion over medium heat 6-8 minutes or until beef is no longer pink, breaking beef into crumbles; drain. Stir in broccoli, cheese, sour cream, salt and pepper; heat through.
2. Unroll 1 tube of crescent dough onto a greased baking sheet; form into a 12x8-in. rectangle, pressing perforations to seal. Spoon half the beef mixture lengthwise down center of rectangle.
3. On each long side, cut 1-in.-wide strips at an angle, about 3 in. into the center. Fold 1 strip from each side over filling and pinch ends together; repeat.
4. Repeat with the remaining ingredients to make second braid. Bake 15-20 minutes or until golden brown.
1 serving: 396 cal., 23g fat (6g sat. fat), 48mg chol., 644mg sod., 29g carb. (8g sugars, 2g fiber), 20g pro.

BROCCOLI BEEF BRAIDS
Each slice of this fast-to-fix, golden bread is like a hot sandwich packed with beef, broccoli and mozzarella.
—Penny Lapp, North Royalton, OH

TAKES: 30 MIN.
MAKES: 2 LOAVES (4 SERVINGS EACH)

SPICY SHEPHERD'S PIE

Taco seasoning adds zip to this hearty main dish. It's easy to top with instant mashed potatoes, which I stir up while browning the beef.
—Mary Malchow, Neenah, WI

TAKES: 30 MIN. • **MAKES:** 6 SERVINGS

- 3 cups mashed potato flakes
- 1 lb. ground beef
- 1 medium onion, chopped
- 1 can (14½ oz.) diced tomatoes, undrained
- 1 can (11 oz.) Mexicorn, drained
- 1 can (2¼ oz.) sliced ripe olives, drained
- 1 envelope taco seasoning
- 1½ tsp. chili powder
- ½ tsp. salt
- ⅛ tsp. garlic powder
- 1 cup shredded cheddar cheese, divided

1. Prepare mashed potatoes according to package directions. Meanwhile, in a large skillet, cook beef and onion over medium heat until the meat is no longer pink, breaking beef into crumbles; drain. Add tomatoes, corn, olives, taco seasoning, chili powder, salt and garlic powder. Bring to a boil; cook and stir for 1-2 minutes.

2. Transfer to a greased 2½-qt. baking dish. Top with ¾ cup cheese. Spread mashed potatoes over the top; sprinkle with the remaining cheese. Bake, uncovered, at 350° for 12-15 minutes or until cheese is melted.

Note: You may substitute 4½ cups hot homemade mashed potatoes for the instant potatoes if desired.

1 serving: 516 cal., 25g fat (13g sat. fat), 90mg chol., 1337mg sod., 49g carb. (10g sugars, 5g fiber), 24g pro.

BEEF TENDERLOIN IN MUSHROOM SAUCE

When our kids are visiting Grandma, I make this recipe for just my husband and myself. It's a recipe my mother-in-law has been using for more than 30 years. I especially look forward to preparing it as part of a special Valentine's Day menu.
—Denise McNab, Warminster, PA

TAKES: 25 MIN. • **MAKES:** 2 SERVINGS

- 4 Tbsp. butter, divided
- 1 tsp. canola oil
- 2 beef tenderloin steaks (1 in. thick and 4 oz. each)
- 1 cup sliced fresh mushrooms
- 1 Tbsp. chopped green onion
- 1 Tbsp. all-purpose flour
- ⅛ tsp. salt
  Dash pepper
- ⅔ cup chicken or beef broth
- ⅛ tsp. browning sauce, optional

1. In a large skillet, heat 2 Tbsp. butter and oil over medium-high heat; cook steaks to desired doneness (for medium-rare, a thermometer should read 135°; medium, 140°), 5-6 minutes per side. Remove from pan, reserving drippings; keep warm.

2. In same pan, heat drippings and remaining butter over medium-high heat; saute mushrooms and green onion until tender. Stir in flour, salt and pepper until blended; gradually stir in the broth and, if desired, browning sauce. Bring to a boil, stirring constantly; cook and stir until thickened, 1-2 minutes. Serve with steaks.

1 serving: 417 cal., 32g fat (17g sat. fat), 112mg chol., 659mg sod., 5g carb. (1g sugars, 1g fiber), 26g pro.

DID YOU KNOW?

Browning sauce is a blend of caramel color, vegetable concentrates and seasonings. Usually added to sauces and gravies, browning sauce works well in meaty recipes to deepen the flavor, and in soups and stews to darken the broth.

POULTRY FAVORITES

There's no meat as mouthwatering, versatile and economical as poultry. Turn to one of these chicken or turkey recipes for a classic meal that's sure to please.

STOVETOP ORANGE-GLAZED CHICKEN

I love a recipe that can put dinner on the table quickly without sacrificing flavor. This sweet and saucy dish does just that with ingredients you probably already have on hand!
—Kallee Krong-Mccreery, Escondido, CA

TAKES: 25 MIN. • **MAKES:** 2 SERVINGS

- ¼ cup orange juice
- 1 Tbsp. reduced-sodium soy sauce
- ½ tsp. cornstarch
- ½ tsp. Dijon mustard
- 2 Tbsp. orange marmalade
- 2 boneless skinless chicken breast halves (6 oz. each)
- ¼ tsp. garlic salt
- 1 Tbsp. olive oil

1. For glaze, whisk together the first 4 ingredients in a microwave-safe bowl; stir in marmalade. Microwave, covered, on high until thickened, 2½-3 minutes, stirring occasionally.

2. Pound the chicken breasts to ½-in. thickness; sprinkle with garlic salt. In a large skillet, heat oil over medium heat; cook chicken until a thermometer reads 165°, 5-6 minutes per side. Top with the glaze.

1 chicken breast half with about 2 Tbsp. glaze: 314 cal., 11g fat (2g sat. fat), 94mg chol., 656mg sod., 18g carb. (15g sugars, 0 fiber), 35g pro. **Diabetic exchanges:** 5 lean meat, 1½ fat, 1 starch.

SWEET POTATO & TURKEY COUSCOUS

We always have turkey and sweet potatoes left over after our big Thanksgiving feast. I combine them in this fast, easy and nutritious main dish that satisfies alongside a simple green salad.
—Roxanne Chan, Albany, CA

TAKES: 30 MIN. • **MAKES:** 6 SERVINGS

- 1 lb. sweet potatoes (about 2 medium), peeled and cut into ¾-in. cubes
- 1 Tbsp. canola oil
- 1 pkg. (8.8 oz.) uncooked pearl (Israeli) couscous
- ¼ cup chopped onion
- ¼ cup chopped celery
- ½ tsp. poultry seasoning
- ½ tsp. salt
- ½ tsp. pepper
- 2 cans (14½ oz. each) chicken broth
- 2 cups chopped cooked turkey
- ¼ cup dried cranberries
- 1 tsp. grated orange zest
  Chopped fresh parsley

1. Place sweet potatoes in a saucepan; add water to cover. Bring to a boil. Reduce heat; cook, uncovered, until tender, 8-10 minutes. Drain.

2. Meanwhile, in a large cast-iron or other heavy skillet, heat oil over medium-high heat; saute couscous, onion and celery until couscous is lightly browned. Stir in seasonings and broth; bring to a boil. Reduce heat; simmer, uncovered, until the couscous is tender, about 10 minutes.

3. Stir in turkey, cranberries, orange zest and potatoes. Cook, covered, over low heat until heated through. Sprinkle with parsley.

1 cup: 365 cal., 5g fat (1g sat. fat), 50mg chol., 848mg sod., 59g carb. (13g sugars, 3g fiber), 21g pro.

5i

CHICKEN PROVOLONE

Even though this is one of my simplest dishes, it is one of my husband's favorites. It is easy to prepare and looks fancy served on a dark plate with a garnish of fresh parsley or basil. Add buttered noodles for an easy side dish.
—Dawn Bryant, Thedford, NE

TAKES: 25 MIN. • **MAKES:** 4 SERVINGS

- 4 boneless skinless chicken breast halves (4 oz. each)
- ¼ tsp. pepper
  Butter-flavored cooking spray
- 8 fresh basil leaves
- 4 thin slices prosciutto or deli ham
- 4 slices provolone cheese

1. Sprinkle chicken with pepper. In a large skillet coated with cooking spray, cook chicken over medium heat until a thermometer reads 165°, 4-5 minutes on each side.
2. Transfer to an ungreased baking sheet; top with basil, prosciutto and cheese. Broil 6-8 in. from the heat until cheese is melted, 1-2 minutes.
1 chicken breast: 236 cal., 11g fat (6g sat. fat), 89mg chol., 435mg sod., 1g carb. (0 sugars, 0 fiber), 33g pro.
Diabetic exchanges: 4 lean meat.

5i

SWEET & SPICY CHICKEN

My husband and children love this tender chicken with its spicy sauce. Peach preserves add just a touch of sweetness, while taco seasoning and salsa give the dish some kick.
—Sheri White, Higley, AZ

TAKES: 20 MIN. • **MAKES:** 4 SERVINGS

- 3 Tbsp. taco seasoning
- 1 lb. boneless skinless chicken breasts, cut into ½-in. cubes
- 1 to 2 Tbsp. canola oil
- 1⅔ cups chunky salsa
- ½ cup peach preserves
  Hot cooked rice

1. Place taco seasoning in a large shallow dish; add chicken and stir to coat.
2. In a large skillet, brown chicken in oil until no longer pink.
3. Combine salsa and preserves; stir into skillet. Bring to a boil. Reduce heat; cover and simmer for 2-3 minutes or until heated through. Serve with rice.
1 cup: 301 cal., 6g fat (1g sat. fat), 63mg chol., 985mg sod., 37g carb. (27g sugars, 0 fiber), 23g pro.

5i

BLACKENED CHICKEN & BEANS

My husband loves any spicy food, and this is one quick-fix recipe we can both agree on. As the chicken cooks, whip up salads of lettuce, tomato, avocado and shredded cheddar cheese.
—Christine Zongker, Spring Hill, KS

TAKES: 20 MIN. • **MAKES:** 4 SERVINGS

- 2 tsp. chili powder
- ¼ tsp. salt
- ¼ tsp. pepper
- 4 boneless skinless chicken breast halves (4 oz. each)
- 1 Tbsp. canola oil
- 1 can (15 oz.) black beans, rinsed and drained
- 1 cup frozen corn
- 1 cup chunky salsa

1. Combine the chili powder, salt and pepper; rub over both sides of the chicken.
2. In a large nonstick skillet, cook chicken in oil over medium heat for 4-5 minutes on each side or until a thermometer reads 170°. Remove and keep warm.
3. Add the beans, corn and salsa to the pan; heat through. Serve with chicken.
1 chicken breast half with ¾ cup bean mixture: 297 cal., 7g fat (1g sat. fat), 63mg chol., 697mg sod., 26g carb. (4g sugars, 8g fiber), 29g pro. **Diabetic exchanges:** 3 lean meat, 1½ starch, 1 fat.

CRESCENT TURKEY CASSEROLE

How do you make a dinner of turkey and vegetables appealing to kids? You turn it into a pie, of course! My version tastes classic but doesn't take any time at all.
—Daniela Essman, Perham, MN

TAKES: 30 MIN. • **MAKES:** 4 SERVINGS

- ½ cup mayonnaise
- 2 Tbsp. all-purpose flour
- 1 tsp. chicken bouillon granules
- ⅛ tsp. pepper
- ¾ cup 2% milk
- 2 cups frozen mixed vegetables (about 10 oz.), thawed
- 1½ cups cubed cooked turkey breast
- 1 tube (4 oz.) refrigerated crescent rolls

1. Preheat oven to 375°. In a saucepan, mix first 4 ingredients until smooth; gradually stir in milk. Bring to a boil over medium heat; cook and stir until thickened, about 2 minutes. Add vegetables and turkey; cook and stir until heated through. Transfer to a greased 8-in. square baking pan.
2. Unroll the crescent dough and separate into 8 triangles; arrange over turkey mixture. Bake until casserole is heated through and the topping is golden brown, 15-20 minutes.
1 piece: 453 cal., 28g fat (6g sat. fat), 48mg chol., 671mg sod., 26g carb. (7g sugars, 3g fiber), 22g pro.

Turkey Biscuit Potpie: Thaw vegetables; combine in a bowl with turkey breast, one 10¾-oz. can condensed cream of chicken soup and ¼ tsp. dried thyme. Place in a deep-dish 9-in. pie plate. Mix 1 cup biscuit/baking mix, ½ cup milk and 1 egg; spoon over top. Bake at 400° for 25-30 minutes.

Turkey Asparagus Casserole: Thaw a 10-oz. package of frozen cut asparagus; combine in a bowl with turkey breast, one 10¾-oz. can condensed cream of chicken soup and ¼ cup water. Bake at 350° for 30 minutes, topping with a 2.8-oz. can of french-fried onions during last 5 minutes.

TEST KITCHEN TIP

Don't have crescent roll dough on hand? You can try this recipe with a tube of refrigerated pizza crust as well.

CHICKEN & GARLIC WITH FRESH HERBS

The key to this savory chicken is the combination of garlic, fresh rosemary and thyme. I like to serve it with mashed potatoes or crusty Italian bread.
—Jan Valdez, Lombard, IL

TAKES: 30 MIN. • **MAKES:** 6 SERVINGS

- 6 boneless skinless chicken thighs (about 1½ lbs.)
- ½ tsp. salt
- ¼ tsp. pepper
- 1 Tbsp. olive oil
- 10 garlic cloves, peeled and halved
- 2 Tbsp. brandy or chicken stock
- 1 cup chicken stock
- 1 tsp. minced fresh rosemary or ¼ tsp. dried rosemary, crushed
- ½ tsp. minced fresh thyme or ⅛ tsp. dried thyme
- 1 Tbsp. minced fresh chives

1. Sprinkle chicken with salt and pepper. In a large cast-iron or other heavy skillet, heat oil over medium-high heat. Brown chicken on both sides. Remove from pan.
2. Remove skillet from heat; add halved garlic cloves and brandy. Return to heat; cook and stir over medium heat until liquid is almost evaporated, 1-2 minutes.
3. Stir in the stock, rosemary and thyme; return chicken to pan. Bring to a boil. Reduce heat; simmer, uncovered, until a thermometer reads 170°, 6-8 minutes. Sprinkle with chives.

1 chicken thigh with 2 Tbsp. cooking juices: 203 cal., 11g fat (3g sat. fat), 76mg chol., 346mg sod., 2g carb. (0 sugars, 0 fiber), 22g pro. **Diabetic exchanges:** 3 lean meat, ½ fat.

SOUTHWEST SWEET POTATO SKILLET

One of the first things my husband made for me was a variation of this sweet potato skillet. Over the years, it's become a family favorite. Top with cheese, sour cream, avocado, lettuce or anything else your family likes.
—MacKenzie Wright, Eugene, OR

TAKES: 30 MIN. • **MAKES:** 4 SERVINGS

- 1 Tbsp. olive oil
- 2 medium sweet potatoes, cubed (about ½-in. cubes)
- ½ medium onion, finely chopped
- 1 garlic clove, minced
- 2 cups cubed cooked chicken
- 1 can (15 oz.) black beans, rinsed and drained
- 1 medium zucchini, chopped
- 1 cup reduced-sodium chicken broth
- 1 cup salsa
- ½ large sweet red pepper, chopped
- 1 tsp. ground cumin
- 1 tsp. chili powder
- ¼ tsp. salt
- ¼ tsp. pepper
  Optional: Sour cream and minced fresh cilantro

1. In a large skillet, heat oil over medium-high heat. Add sweet potatoes and onion; cook and stir until lightly browned, 5-8 minutes. Add garlic; cook 1 minute longer. Stir in the chicken, black beans, zucchini, broth, salsa, red pepper and seasonings.
2. Bring to a boil; reduce heat. Simmer, covered, until sweet potatoes are tender, 10-12 minutes. If desired, serve with sour cream and cilantro.

1½ cups: 392 cal., 9g fat (2g sat. fat), 62mg chol., 826mg sod., 47g carb. (15g sugars, 9g fiber), 29g pro.

4 cups fresh broccoli florets
1 cup chicken broth
1 Tbsp. all-purpose flour
1 Tbsp. snipped fresh dill
1 cup 2% milk

1. Sprinkle chicken with garlic salt and pepper. In a large skillet, heat oil over medium heat; brown chicken on both sides. Remove from pan.

2. Add broccoli and broth to same skillet; bring to a boil. Reduce heat; simmer, covered, until the broccoli is just tender, 3-5 minutes. Using a slotted spoon, remove broccoli from pan, reserving broth. Keep broccoli warm.

3. In a small bowl, mix the flour, dill and milk until smooth; stir into broth in pan. Bring to a boil, stirring constantly; cook and stir until thickened, 1-2 minutes. Add the chicken; cook, covered, over medium heat until a thermometer inserted in chicken reads 165°, 10-12 minutes. Serve with broccoli.

1 serving: 274 cal., 9g fat (2g sat. fat), 100mg chol., 620mg sod., 8g carb. (4g sugars, 2g fiber), 39g pro. **Diabetic exchanges:** 5 lean meat, 1 vegetable, 1 fat.

CHICKEN & BROCCOLI WITH DILL SAUCE

I've had this chicken and broccoli recipe for so many years, I don't remember when I first made it. Serve it with a side of couscous or rice for a complete meal, or add some sliced mushrooms or carrots for extra veggies.
—Kallee Krong-McCreery, Escondido, CA

TAKES: 30 MIN. • **MAKES:** 4 SERVINGS

4 boneless skinless chicken breast halves (6 oz. each)
½ tsp. garlic salt
¼ tsp. pepper
1 Tbsp. olive oil

TEST KITCHEN TIP

If you're buying whole broccoli stalks, don't throw out the stems! Peel away the tough outer portion and chop the center to use in soups and stir-fries or to add to salads and slaws.

CREAMY CURRIED CHICKEN

This is a big hit in our house. My young son and daughter gobble it up. With its irresistible blend of curry and sweet coconut milk, it'll become a favorite with your family, too.
—Tracy Simiele, Chardon, OH

TAKES: 30 MIN. • **MAKES:** 4 SERVINGS

- 1½ cups uncooked instant rice
- 1 lb. boneless skinless chicken breasts, cut into 1-in. pieces
- 2 tsp. curry powder
- ¾ tsp. salt
- ¼ tsp. pepper
- ½ cup chopped onion
- 1 Tbsp. canola oil
- 1 can (13.66 oz.) coconut milk
- 2 Tbsp. tomato paste
- 3 cups fresh baby spinach
- 1 cup chopped tomato

1. Cook rice according to the package directions. Meanwhile, sprinkle chicken with curry, salt and pepper. In a large skillet, saute chicken and onion in oil until the chicken is no longer pink.
2. Stir in coconut milk and tomato paste. Bring to a boil. Reduce heat; simmer, uncovered, for 5 minutes or until thickened.
3. Add spinach and tomato; cook 2-3 minutes longer or until the spinach is wilted. Serve with rice.
1 cup chicken mixture with ¾ cup rice: 508 cal., 27g fat (19g sat. fat), 63mg chol., 541mg sod., 39g carb. (6g sugars, 4g fiber), 29g pro.

AIR-FRYER CHICKEN CORDON BLEU

My son loves chicken cordon bleu, but I'm not a fan of store-bought versions. My recipe has all the yummy flavors in a 30-minute home-cooked meal. And the leftovers freeze well.
—Ronda Eagle, Goose Creek, SC

TAKES: 30 MIN. • **MAKES:** 4 SERVINGS

- 4 boneless skinless chicken breast halves (4 oz. each)
- ¼ tsp. salt
- ¼ tsp. pepper
- 4 slices deli ham
- 2 slices aged Swiss cheese, halved
- 1 cup panko bread crumbs
  Cooking spray

SAUCE
- 1 Tbsp. all-purpose flour
- ½ cup 2% milk
- ¼ cup dry white wine
- 3 Tbsp. finely shredded Swiss cheese
- ⅛ tsp. salt
  Dash pepper

1. Preheat air fryer to 365°. Sprinkle chicken breasts with salt and pepper. Place on greased tray in air-fryer basket. Cook for 10 minutes.
2. Top each chicken breast with 1 slice ham and ½ slice cheese, folding ham in half and covering chicken as much as possible. Sprinkle with bread crumbs. Carefully spritz crumbs with cooking spray. Cook until a thermometer inserted in chicken reads 165°, 5-7 minutes longer.
3. For the sauce, in a small saucepan, whisk flour and milk until smooth. Bring to a boil, stirring constantly; cook and stir 1-2 minutes or until thickened.
4. Reduce to medium heat. Stir in wine and cheese; cook and stir 2-3 minutes or until cheese is melted and sauce is thickened and bubbly.
5. Stir in salt and pepper. Keep warm over low heat until ready to serve. Serve with chicken.
1 chicken breast half with 3 Tbsp. sauce: 272 cal., 8g fat (3g sat. fat), 83mg chol., 519mg sod., 14g carb. (2g sugars, 1g fiber), 32g pro. **Diabetic exchanges:** 4 lean meat, 1 starch, 1 fat.

CHICKEN CORDON BLEU PIZZA

This recipe combines my two favorite foods—pizza and chicken cordon bleu. I've made this for my family and the teachers at my school. Now the teachers ask me to make it for them for lunch!
—Justin Rippel, Colgate, WI

TAKES: 30 MIN. • **MAKES:** 6 SERVINGS

- 1   tube (13.8 oz.) refrigerated pizza crust
- ½   cup Alfredo sauce
- ¼   tsp. garlic salt
- 1   cup shredded Swiss cheese
- 1½ cups cubed fully cooked ham
- 10 breaded chicken nuggets, thawed, cut into ½-in. pieces
- 1   cup shredded part-skim mozzarella cheese

1. Preheat oven to 425°. Unroll and press dough onto bottom of a greased 15x10x1-in. pan, pinching edges to form a rim if desired. Bake until the edges are light brown, 8-10 minutes.

2. Spread the crust with Alfredo sauce; sprinkle with garlic salt. Top with remaining ingredients. Bake until crust is golden brown and cheese is melted, 8-10 minutes.

1 serving: 438 cal., 20g fat (9g sat. fat), 65mg chol., 1386mg sod., 39g carb. (5g sugars, 2g fiber), 27g pro.

TURKEY BREAST TENDERLOINS WITH RASPBERRY SAUCE

Sweet and tangy raspberry sauce is a perfect complement to versatile turkey tenderloins. In fact, this sauce is so good, you'll be tempted to eat it with a spoon.
—Deirdre Cox, Kansas City, MO

TAKES: 30 MIN. • **MAKES:** 2 SERVINGS

- 2   turkey breast tenderloins (5 oz. each)
- ⅛   tsp. salt
- ⅛   tsp. pepper
- 2   tsp. olive oil
- 1   tsp. cornstarch
- ¼   cup cranberry-raspberry juice
- 2   Tbsp. Heinz 57 steak sauce
- 2   Tbsp. red raspberry preserves
- ½   tsp. lemon juice

1. Sprinkle turkey with salt and pepper. In a large nonstick skillet over medium heat, brown turkey in oil on all sides. Cover and cook until a thermometer reads 165°, 10-12 minutes. Remove and keep warm.

2. Combine cornstarch and juice until smooth; add to pan. Stir in the steak sauce, preserves and lemon juice. Bring to a boil; cook and stir until thickened, about 1 minute. Slice turkey; serve with sauce.

1 tenderloin with ¼ cup sauce: 275 cal., 6g fat (1g sat. fat), 69mg chol., 425mg sod., 22g carb. (19g sugars, 0 fiber), 33g pro.

DID YOU KNOW?

Turkey breast tenderloins are strips cut from either side of the center breast bone. Because they're so lean, they're vulnerable to overcooking, so they're ideal for a quick meal.

QUINOA UNSTUFFED PEPPERS

This deconstructed stuffed pepper dish packs a wallop of flavor. I truly make it all the time, and I make sure my freezer is stocked with single-serve portions to take to work.
—Rebecca Ende, Phoenix, NY

TAKES: 30 MIN. • **MAKES:** 4 SERVINGS

- 1½ cups vegetable stock
- ¾ cup quinoa, rinsed
- 1 lb. Italian turkey sausage links, casings removed
- 1 medium sweet red pepper, chopped
- 1 medium green pepper, chopped
- ¾ cup chopped sweet onion
- 1 garlic clove, minced
- ¼ tsp. garam masala
- ¼ tsp. pepper
- ⅛ tsp. salt

1. In a small saucepan, bring stock to a boil. Add quinoa. Reduce heat; simmer, covered, until liquid is absorbed, 12-15 minutes. Remove from heat.
2. In a large skillet, cook and crumble sausage with peppers and onion over medium-high heat until meat is no longer pink, 8-10 minutes. Add garlic and seasonings; cook and stir for 1 minute. Stir in quinoa.
Freeze option: Place cooled quinoa mixture in freezer containers. To use, partially thaw in refrigerator overnight. Microwave, covered, on high in a microwave-safe dish until heated through, stirring occasionally.
1 cup: 261 cal., 9g fat (2g sat. fat), 42mg chol., 760mg sod., 28g carb. (3g sugars, 4g fiber), 17g pro.
Diabetic exchanges: 2 starch, 2 medium-fat meat.

PARMESAN BOW TIE PASTA WITH CHICKEN

On lazy summer weekends, we enjoy chicken and yellow squash tossed with bow tie pasta. Fresh grated Parmesan adds a Sunday touch.
—Sarah Smiley, Bangor, ME

TAKES: 30 MIN. • **MAKES:** 6 SERVINGS

- 1 pkg. (16 oz.) bow tie pasta
- 5 Tbsp. butter, divided
- 1 lb. boneless skinless chicken breasts, cut into 1-in. pieces
- 1 tsp. salt, divided
- 1 tsp. pepper, divided
- 2 medium yellow summer squash or zucchini, cut into 1-in. pieces
- 3 Tbsp. all-purpose flour
- 2 garlic cloves, minced
- 1½ cups fat-free milk
- ¾ cup grated Parmesan cheese

1. In a 6-qt. stockpot, cook pasta according to package directions.
2. In a large cast-iron or other heavy skillet, heat 1 Tbsp. butter over medium heat. Add chicken; cook and stir until no longer pink, 7-9 minutes. Add ¼ tsp. each salt and pepper; remove from pan.
3. In same pan, heat 1 Tbsp. butter over medium heat. Add squash; cook and stir until tender, 3-5 minutes. Remove from heat.
4. In a small saucepan, melt the remaining 3 Tbsp. butter over medium heat. Stir in flour and garlic until blended; gradually whisk in milk. Bring to a boil, stirring constantly until thickened, 1-2 minutes. Remove from heat; stir in cheese and the remaining ¾ tsp. each salt and pepper.
5. Drain pasta; return to pot. Add chicken, squash and sauce; heat through, stirring to combine.
1½ cups: 528 cal., 16g fat (9g sat. fat), 77mg chol., 690mg sod., 64g carb. (7g sugars, 4g fiber), 33g pro.

SOUTHWEST CHICKEN DINNER

My family loves to takeout order gigantic Tex-Mex burritos, but they can be expensive and we always have leftovers. I created a lighter, no-guilt, no-tortilla alternative with the flavors my family loves.
—Marquisha Turner, Denver, CO

TAKES: 30 MIN. • **MAKES:** 4 SERVINGS

- 2 cups water
- 2 Tbsp. olive oil, divided
- ½ tsp. salt
- ¼ tsp. pepper
- 1 cup uncooked long grain rice
- 1 Tbsp. taco seasoning
- 4 boneless skinless chicken breast halves (4 oz. each)
- 1 cup canned black beans or pinto beans, rinsed and drained
- ¼ cup chopped fresh cilantro
- 1 tsp. grated lime zest
- 2 Tbsp. lime juice
  Optional: Pico de gallo, shredded Mexican cheese blend, sour cream, avocado, shredded lettuce and/or lime wedges

1. In a large saucepan, combine water, 1 Tbsp. oil, and the salt and pepper; bring to a boil. Stir in rice. Reduce heat; simmer, covered, 15-17 minutes or until liquid is absorbed and rice is tender.
2. Meanwhile, sprinkle taco seasoning over both sides of chicken. In a large skillet, heat the remaining 1 Tbsp. oil over medium heat. Add chicken; cook 4-5 minutes on each side or until a thermometer reads 165°.

3. In a microwave, heat beans until warmed. To serve, gently stir cilantro, lime zest and lime juice into rice; divide among 4 bowls. Cut chicken into slices. Place chicken and beans over rice; top as desired.
1 serving: 398 cal., 7g fat (1g sat. fat), 63mg chol., 678mg sod., 52g carb. (1g sugars, 3g fiber), 30g pro.

CHICKEN ENCHILADAS FOR FOUR

These chicken enchiladas add a little zip to any menu. The rolled tortillas are filled with a hearty mixture of cheese, chicken and green chiles, and then topped with a creamy sauce and more cheese. I sometimes use leftover turkey instead of chicken.
—Karen Bourne, Magrath, AB

TAKES: 30 MIN. • **MAKES:** 4 SERVINGS

- 2 Tbsp. butter
- ¼ cup all-purpose flour
- 2½ cups chicken broth
- 1 tsp. dried coriander
- 1 can (4 oz.) chopped green chiles, divided
- 2 cups cubed cooked chicken
- 1 cup shredded Monterey Jack cheese
- 8 flour tortillas (8 in.), warmed
- 1 cup shredded cheddar cheese

1. Preheat oven to 375°. In a large saucepan, melt butter; stir in flour until smooth. Gradually add the broth. Bring to a boil; cook and stir for 2 minutes or until thickened. Stir in the coriander and half the chiles.
2. In a large bowl, combine the chicken, Monterey Jack cheese and the remaining chiles.
3. Spoon ⅓ cup chicken mixture onto each tortilla; roll up. Place seam side down in an ungreased 13x9-in. baking dish. Pour sauce over enchiladas. Sprinkle with cheddar cheese.
4. Bake, uncovered, 15-18 minutes or until heated through and cheese is melted.
2 enchiladas: 767 cal., 36g fat (18g sat. fat), 134mg chol., 1654mg sod., 64g carb. (1g sugars, 4g fiber), 44g pro.

SPAGHETTI & MEATBALL SKILLET SUPPER

I developed this one-skillet spaghetti and meatball dish to cut down on cooking time on busy nights. The beans, artichokes and tomatoes bump up the nutrition factor, while the lemon and parsley make it pop with brightness.
—Roxanne Chan, Albany, CA

TAKES: 30 MIN. • **MAKES:** 6 SERVINGS

- 1 Tbsp. olive oil
- 12 oz. frozen fully cooked Italian turkey meatballs
- 1 can (28 oz.) whole tomatoes, undrained, broken up
- 1 can (15 oz.) cannellini beans, rinsed and drained
- 1 can (14 oz.) water-packed quartered artichoke hearts, drained
- ½ tsp. Italian seasoning
- 1 can (14½ oz.) reduced-sodium chicken broth
- 4 oz. uncooked spaghetti, broken into 2-in. pieces (about 1⅓ cups)
- ¼ cup chopped fresh parsley
- 1 Tbsp. lemon juice
  Grated Parmesan cheese

1. In a large skillet, heat oil over medium heat; add meatballs and cook until browned slightly, turning occasionally.
2. Add tomatoes, beans, artichoke hearts, Italian seasoning and broth; bring to a boil. Stir in spaghetti; return to a boil. Reduce heat; simmer, covered, until spaghetti is tender, 10-12 minutes, stirring occasionally.
3. Stir in parsley and lemon juice. Serve with cheese.

1⅓ cups: 330 cal., 10g fat (2g sat. fat), 43mg chol., 1051mg sod., 38g carb. (5g sugars, 6g fiber), 20g pro.

TEST KITCHEN TIPS

Because they are a major part of this recipe, high-quality crushed tomatoes are a must. It's worth splurging on San Marzano. If your kiddos are squeamish about tomatoes, switch to two 14-oz. cans of diced tomatoes so the pieces are smaller.

6 boneless skinless
   chicken thighs (about 1½ lbs.)
½ tsp. seasoned salt
½ tsp. pepper
1½ tsp. olive oil
4 shallots, thinly sliced
⅓ cup white wine or
   reduced-sodium
   chicken broth
1 pkg. (10 oz.) fresh spinach,
   trimmed
¼ tsp. salt
¼ cup reduced-fat sour cream

1. Sprinkle chicken with seasoned salt and pepper. In a large nonstick skillet, heat the oil over medium heat. Add the chicken; cook until a thermometer reads 170°, about 6 minutes on each side. Remove from pan; keep warm.
2. In same pan, cook and stir shallots until tender. Add wine; bring to a boil. Cook until wine is reduced by half. Add spinach and salt; cook and stir just until spinach is wilted. Stir in sour cream; serve with chicken.
Freeze option: Before adding sour cream, cool the chicken and spinach mixture. Freeze in freezer containers. To use, partially thaw in refrigerator overnight. Heat through slowly in a covered skillet, stirring occasionally, until a thermometer inserted in chicken reads 170°. Stir in sour cream.
1 chicken thigh with ¼ cup spinach mixture: 223 cal., 10g fat (3g sat. fat), 77mg chol., 360mg sod., 7g carb. (2g sugars, 1g fiber), 23g pro. **Diabetic exchanges:** 3 lean meat, 1½ fat, 1 vegetable.

CHICKEN THIGHS WITH SHALLOTS & SPINACH

What could be better than an entree that comes with its own creamy vegetable side? This healthy supper goes together in no time flat and makes an eye-catching presentation.
—Genna Johannes, Wrightstown, WI

TAKES: 30 MIN. • **MAKES:** 6 SERVINGS

SMOTHERED CHICKEN

I top tender chicken breasts with mushrooms, bacon, green onions and cheese for a quick, comforting meal that's become a staple in our house.
—Penny Walton, Westerville, OH

TAKES: 20 MIN. • **MAKES:** 4 SERVINGS

- 4 **boneless skinless chicken breast halves (5 oz. each)**
- ¼ **tsp. seasoned salt**
- ¼ **tsp. garlic powder**
- 3 **tsp. canola oil, divided**
- 1 **cup sliced fresh mushrooms**
- 1 **cup shredded Mexican cheese blend**
- 4 **green onions, chopped**
- 6 **bacon strips, cooked and chopped**

1. Pound the chicken breasts to ¼-in. thickness. Sprinkle with seasoned salt and garlic powder.
2. In a large nonstick skillet, heat 1 tsp. oil over medium-high heat; saute the mushrooms until tender, 2-3 minutes. Remove from pan.
3. In same pan, cook chicken in remaining 2 tsp. oil until bottoms are browned, about 4 minutes. Turn chicken; top with the mushrooms and remaining ingredients. Cook, covered, until chicken is no longer pink, 4-5 minutes.

1 chicken breast half: 363 cal., 21g fat (7g sat. fat), 116mg chol., 555mg sod., 3g carb. (1g sugars, 1g fiber), 40g pro.

CHICKEN QUESADILLAS

Leftover chicken gets Mexican flair from cumin in this fun main dish. The chicken quesadilla recipe has an impressive look and taste yet requires little preparation.
—Linda Wetzel, Woodland Park, CO

TAKES: 30 MIN. • **MAKES:** 6 SERVINGS

- 2½ **cups shredded cooked chicken**
- ⅔ **cup salsa**
- ⅓ **cup sliced green onions**
- ¾ **to 1 tsp. ground cumin**
- ½ **tsp. salt**
- ½ **tsp. dried oregano**
- 6 **flour tortillas (8 in.)**
- ¼ **cup butter, melted**
- 2 **cups shredded Monterey Jack cheese Sour cream and guacamole**

1. Preheat oven to 375°. In a large skillet, combine the first 6 ingredients. Cook, uncovered, over medium heat until heated through, about 10 minutes, stirring occasionally.
2. Brush 1 side of each tortilla with butter; place tortillas buttered side down on a lightly greased baking sheet. Spoon ⅓ cup chicken mixture over half of each tortilla; sprinkle with ⅓ cup cheese.
3. Fold plain side of each tortilla over filling and cheese. Bake until tortillas are crisp and golden brown, 9-11 minutes. Cut into wedges; serve with sour cream and guacamole.

1 serving: 477 cal., 26g fat (13g sat. fat), 106mg chol., 901mg sod., 27g carb. (1g sugars, 1g fiber), 31g pro.

DID YOU KNOW?

A Monterey, California, businessman named David Jacks made Monterey Jack cheese popular in the late 1800s by shipping it to San Francisco and other areas of the United States.

SWISS MUSHROOM CHICKEN

Everyone enjoys these golden chicken breasts topped with ham, melted Swiss cheese and fresh mushrooms. The entree is easy to prepare but looks and tastes special enough for company.
—Jan Baxter, Humarock, MA

TAKES: 20 MIN. • **MAKES:** 4 SERVINGS

- 4 **boneless skinless chicken breast halves (4 oz. each)**
- 1 **large egg**
- 1 **cup crushed butter-flavored crackers (about 25 crackers)**
- ¾ **tsp. salt**
- ½ **lb. fresh mushrooms, sliced**
- 2 **Tbsp. butter, divided**
- 4 **slices deli ham or thinly sliced hard salami**
- 4 **slices Swiss cheese**

1. Preheat broiler. Flatten chicken to ¼-in. thickness. In a shallow bowl, lightly beat the egg. Combine cracker crumbs and salt in another shallow bowl. Dip chicken in egg, then roll in crumbs; set aside.
2. In a large cast-iron or other ovenproof skillet, saute mushrooms in 1 Tbsp. butter until tender; remove and set aside. In same skillet, cook chicken over medium heat in remaining 1 Tbsp. butter until no longer pink, 3-4 minutes on each side.
3. Top each chicken breast half with a ham slice, mushrooms and a cheese slice. Broil 4-6 in. from the heat until cheese is melted, 1-2 minutes.
1 chicken breast half: 343 cal., 21g fat (10g sat. fat), 119mg chol., 956mg sod., 18g carb. (3g sugars, 1g fiber), 20g pro.

PRESSURE-COOKER INDIAN-STYLE CHICKEN & VEGETABLES

This easy Indian-influenced dish is one just about everyone will love. Feel free to add more or less sauce according to your taste.
—Erica Polly, Sun Prairie, WI

TAKES: 20 MIN. • **MAKES:** 8 SERVINGS

- 2 **lbs. boneless skinless chicken thighs, cubed**
- 2 **medium sweet potatoes, peeled and cut into 1½-in. pieces**
- 2 **medium sweet red peppers, cut into 1-in. pieces**
- 3 **cups fresh cauliflowerets**
- 2 **jars (15 oz. each) tikka masala curry sauce**
- ½ **cup water**
- ¾ **tsp. salt**
  Minced fresh cilantro, optional
  Naan flatbreads, warmed

In a 6-qt. electric pressure cooker, combine chicken and vegetables; add sauce, water and salt. Lock lid; close pressure-release valve. Adjust to pressure-cook on high for 3 minutes. Quick-release pressure. A thermometer inserted into a chicken cube should read at least 170°. If desired, top with cilantro; serve with warmed naan.

Freeze option: Omitting cilantro and naan, freeze cooled chicken and vegetable mixture in freezer containers. To use, partially thaw in refrigerator overnight. Microwave, covered, on high in a microwave-safe dish until heated through, stirring gently; add a little water if necessary. If desired, sprinkle with cilantro. Serve with warmed naan.
1¼ cups: 334 cal., 15g fat (4g sat. fat), 80mg chol., 686mg sod., 25g carb. (12g sugars, 5g fiber), 25g pro.
Diabetic exchanges: 3 lean meat, 2 fat, 1½ starch.

⑤ QUICK CHICKEN PICCATA

Laced with lemon and simmered in white wine, this stovetop piccata is super easy and elegant. Just add a side of veggies and bread to make it into a wonderful meal.
—Cynthia Heil, Augusta, GA

TAKES: 30 MIN. • **MAKES:** 4 SERVINGS

- ¼ cup all-purpose flour
- ½ tsp. salt
- ½ tsp. pepper
- 4 boneless skinless chicken breast halves (4 oz. each)
- ¼ cup butter, cubed
- ¼ cup white wine or chicken broth
- 1 Tbsp. lemon juice
  Minced fresh parsley, optional

1. In a shallow bowl, mix flour, salt and pepper. Pound chicken breasts with a meat mallet to ½-in. thickness. Dip chicken in flour mixture to coat both sides; shake off excess.

2. In a large skillet, heat butter over medium heat. Brown chicken on both sides. Add wine; bring to a boil. Reduce heat; simmer, uncovered, until the chicken is no longer pink, 12-15 minutes. Drizzle with lemon juice. If desired, sprinkle with parsley to serve.

1 chicken breast half with about 1 Tbsp. sauce: 265 cal., 14g fat (8g sat. fat), 93mg chol., 442mg sod., 7g carb. (0 sugars, 0 fiber), 24g pro.

PEANUTTY ASIAN LETTUCE WRAPS

This recipe packs so much flavor into a beautiful, healthy presentation. I usually serve it with a little extra hoisin sauce on the side.
—Mandy Rivers, Lexington, SC

TAKES: 30 MIN. • **MAKES:** 6 SERVINGS

- ⅓ cup reduced-sodium teriyaki sauce
- ¼ cup hoisin sauce
- 3 Tbsp. creamy peanut butter
- 1 Tbsp. rice vinegar
- 1 Tbsp. sesame oil
- 1½ lbs. lean ground turkey
- ½ cup shredded carrot
- 2 Tbsp. minced fresh gingerroot
- 4 garlic cloves, minced
- 1 can (8 oz.) whole water chestnuts, drained and chopped
- ½ cup chopped fresh snow peas
- 4 green onions, chopped
- 12 Bibb lettuce leaves
  Additional hoisin sauce, optional

1. Whisk together the first 5 ingredients until smooth. In a large skillet, cook and crumble turkey with carrot over medium-high heat until the turkey is no longer pink, 6-8 minutes; drain.

2. Add ginger and garlic; cook and stir for 1 minute. Stir in the sauce mixture, water chestnuts, snow peas and green onions; heat through.

3. Serve in lettuce leaves. If desired, drizzle with additional hoisin sauce.

2 wraps: 313 cal., 16g fat (4g sat. fat), 90mg chol., 613mg sod., 18g carb. (9g sugars, 3g fiber), 24g pro.

Diabetic exchanges: 3 lean meat, 2 vegetable, 2 fat, ½ starch.

PINEAPPLE-GINGER CHICKEN STIR-FRY

I found the original recipe for this dish on a can of pineapple slices in the 1980s. After making it for a number of years, I lightened the ingredients and adapted it to a quick skillet meal. My family gave it a big thumbs-up, and we've enjoyed it this way ever since!
—Sue Gronholz, Beaver Dam, WI

TAKES: 30 MIN. • **MAKES:** 4 SERVINGS

- 1 can (20 oz.) unsweetened pineapple chunks
- 1 Tbsp. cornstarch
- 3 Tbsp. reduced-sodium soy sauce
- 2 Tbsp. honey
- ¼ tsp. ground cinnamon
- 2 Tbsp. canola oil, divided
- 1 lb. boneless skinless chicken breasts, cut into 1-in. cubes
- 1 small onion, chopped
- 1 Tbsp. minced fresh gingerroot
- 2 garlic cloves, minced
   Hot cooked brown rice
   Minced fresh cilantro, optional

1. Drain pineapple, reserving juice. Mix cornstarch, soy sauce, honey, cinnamon and the reserved juice until smooth.

2. In a skillet, heat 1 Tbsp. oil over medium-high heat; saute chicken until lightly browned, 4-6 minutes. Remove from pan.

3. In the same pan, saute onion, ginger and garlic in the remaining 1 Tbsp. oil until crisp-tender, about 2 minutes. Stir cornstarch mixture; add it to pan with chicken and pineapple chunks. Bring to a boil, stirring constantly; cook and stir until sauce is thickened and chicken is cooked through, 5-7 minutes.

4. Serve with rice. If desired, sprinkle with cilantro.

1 cup chicken mixture: 316 cal., 10g fat (1g sat. fat), 63mg chol., 487mg sod., 31g carb. (26g sugars, 1g fiber), 25g pro. **Diabetic exchanges:** 3 lean meat, 1½ starch, 1½ fat, ½ fruit.

TEST KITCHEN TIP

Don't forget to stir the cornstarch mixture again before adding it to the hot pan. The cornstarch settles, sinking to the bottom over time, and will leave the sauce lumpy if it isn't remixed properly.

CURRIED CHICKEN SKILLET

This protein-packed skillet dish is loaded with bright flavor. A little curry and fresh ginger make the veggies, chicken and quinoa pop.
—Ruth Hartunian-Alumbaugh, Willimantic, CT

TAKES: 30 MIN. • **MAKES:** 4 SERVINGS

1⅓ cups plus ½ cup reduced-sodium chicken broth, divided
⅔ cup quinoa, rinsed
1 Tbsp. canola oil
1 medium sweet potato, diced
1 medium onion, chopped
1 celery rib, chopped
1 cup frozen peas
2 garlic cloves, minced
1 tsp. minced fresh gingerroot
3 tsp. curry powder
¼ tsp. salt
2 cups shredded cooked chicken

1. In a small saucepan, bring 1⅓ cups broth to a boil. Add quinoa. Reduce heat; simmer, covered, until liquid is absorbed, 12-15 minutes.
2. In a large skillet, heat oil over medium-high heat; saute sweet potato, onion and celery until potato is tender, 10-12 minutes.
3. Add peas, garlic, ginger and seasonings; cook and stir for 2 minutes. Stir in chicken and remaining ½ cup broth; heat through. Stir in quinoa.

2 cups: 367 cal., 11g fat (2g sat. fat), 62mg chol., 450mg sod., 39g carb. (8g sugars, 6g fiber), 29g pro. **Diabetic exchanges:** 3 lean meat, 2½ starch, ½ fat.

5i
SAUSAGE-STUFFED BUTTERNUT SQUASH

Load butternut squash shells with an Italian turkey sausage and squash mixture for a quick and easy meal. Even better, it's surprisingly low in calories.
—Katia Slinger, West Jordan, UT

TAKES: 30 MIN. • **MAKES:** 4 SERVINGS

1 medium butternut squash (about 3 lbs.)
1 lb. Italian turkey sausage links, casings removed
1 medium onion, finely chopped
4 garlic cloves, minced
½ cup shredded Italian cheese blend
Crushed red pepper flakes, optional

1. Preheat broiler. Cut squash lengthwise in half; discard seeds. Place squash in a large microwave-safe dish, cut side down; add ½ in. water. Microwave, covered, on high until soft, 20-25 minutes. Cool slightly.
2. Meanwhile, in a large nonstick skillet, cook and crumble sausage with onion over medium-high heat until meat is no longer pink, 5-7 minutes. Add garlic; cook and stir 1 minute.
3. Leaving ½-in.-thick shells, scoop flesh from squash; stir into sausage mixture. Place shells on a baking sheet; fill with sausage mixture. Sprinkle with shredded cheese.
4. Broil 4-5 in. from heat until the cheese is melted, 1-2 minutes. If desired, sprinkle with red pepper flakes. To serve, cut each half into 2 portions.

1 serving: 325 cal., 10g fat (4g sat. fat), 52mg chol., 587mg sod., 44g carb. (10g sugars, 12g fiber), 19g pro. **Diabetic exchanges:** 3 starch, 3 lean meat.

HEALTH TIP

Butternut squash is an excellent source of vitamin A in the form of beta carotene, which is important for normal vision and a healthy immune system. It also helps the heart, lungs and kidneys function properly.

PORK, HAM & MORE

Craving pork chops? What about tenderloin, bacon, sausage or ham? Everyone will go hog-wild for these tantalizing recipes that are ready in a hurry.

HERBED LEMON PORK CHOPS

You'll receive plenty of compliments on these tender and juicy pork chops. Mixed herbs and a final squeeze of lemon pack on the flavor in minutes!
—Billi Jo Sylvester, New Smyrna Beach, FL

TAKES: 20 MIN. • **MAKES:** 2 SERVINGS

- 1 tsp. salt-free garlic seasoning blend
- ½ tsp. dried basil
- ½ tsp. dried oregano
- ½ tsp. dried parsley flakes
- ¼ tsp. salt
- ¼ tsp. garlic powder
- ¼ tsp. dried rosemary, crushed
- 2 bone-in pork loin chops (6 oz. each)
- 1 tsp. olive oil
- 1 Tbsp. lemon juice

1. Mix seasonings; rub over both sides of chops. In a large nonstick skillet, heat oil over medium-high heat. Add the pork chops; cook until a thermometer reads 145°, 5-8 minutes per side.
2. Remove from heat; drizzle with lemon juice. Let stand, covered, 5 minutes before serving.

1 pork chop: 200 cal., 10g fat (3g sat. fat), 74mg chol., 350mg sod., 1g carb. (0 sugars, 0 fiber), 26g pro. **Diabetic exchanges:** 4 lean meat, ½ fat.

EGG ROLL NOODLE BOWL

We love Asian egg rolls, but they can be challenging to make. Simplify everything with this deconstructed egg roll made on the stovetop and served in a bowl.
—Courtney Stultz, Weir, KS

TAKES: 30 MIN. • **MAKES:** 4 SERVINGS

- 1 Tbsp. sesame oil
- ½ lb. ground pork
- 1 Tbsp. soy sauce
- 1 garlic clove, minced
- 1 tsp. ground ginger
- ½ tsp. salt
- ¼ tsp. ground turmeric
- ¼ tsp. pepper
- 6 cups shredded cabbage (about 1 small head)
- 2 large carrots, shredded (about 2 cups)
- 4 oz. rice noodles
- 3 green onions, thinly sliced
  Additional soy sauce, optional

1. In a large cast-iron or other heavy skillet, heat oil over medium-high heat; cook and crumble pork until browned, 4-6 minutes. Stir in soy sauce, garlic and seasonings. Add cabbage and carrots; cook until vegetables are tender, stirring occasionally, 4-6 minutes longer.
2. Cook rice noodles according to package directions; drain and immediately add to pork mixture, tossing to combine. Sprinkle with green onions. If desired, serve with additional soy sauce.

1½ cups: 302 cal., 12g fat (4g sat. fat), 38mg chol., 652mg sod., 33g carb. (2g sugars, 4g fiber), 14g pro. **Diabetic exchanges:** 2 medium-fat meat, 2 vegetable, 1½ starch, ½ fat.

TEST KITCHEN TIP

Meatless Monday? Try this with mushrooms, scrambled eggs or tofu instead of pork.

QUICK HAWAIIAN PIZZA

Our family never quite liked the taste of canned pizza sauce, so I tried mixing BBQ sauce into spaghetti sauce to add some sweetness. I've made my pizzas with this special and easy sauce ever since. My family loves it.
—Tonya Schieler, Carmel, IN

TAKES: 25 MIN. • **MAKES:** 6 SLICES

- 1   prebaked 12-in. thin whole wheat pizza crust
- ½   cup marinara sauce
- ¼   cup barbecue sauce
- 1   medium sweet yellow or red pepper, chopped
- 1   cup cubed fresh pineapple
- ½   cup chopped fully cooked ham
- 1   cup shredded part-skim mozzarella cheese
- ½   cup shredded cheddar cheese

1. Preheat oven to 425°. Place the crust on a baking sheet. Mix marinara and barbecue sauces; spread over crust.
2. Top with remaining ingredients. Bake until crust is browned and cheeses are melted, 10-15 minutes.
1 slice: 290 cal., 10g fat (5g sat. fat), 29mg chol., 792mg sod., 36g carb. (11g sugars, 5g fiber), 16g pro. **Diabetic exchanges:** 2 starch, 2 lean meat, ½ fat.

ANGEL HAIR PASTA WITH SAUSAGE & SPINACH

You won't miss the marinara once you taste this pasta dish flavored with chicken broth and Italian sausage. The sauce simmers away without much work on your part. My husband likes it so much that I make it twice a week.
—Daphine Smith, Baytown, TX

TAKES: 30 MIN. • **MAKES:** 4 SERVINGS

- 4   Italian sausage links (4 oz. each), sliced
- 1   medium onion, chopped
- 2   garlic cloves, minced
- 2   tsp. olive oil
- 2   cans (14½ oz. each) chicken broth
- 8   oz. uncooked angel hair pasta, broken in half
- 2   pkg. (9 oz. each) fresh spinach, trimmed and coarsely chopped
- 2   Tbsp. all-purpose flour
- ¼   tsp. pepper
- ⅓   cup heavy whipping cream

1. In a Dutch oven, cook sausage, onion and garlic in oil over medium heat until meat is no longer pink; drain. Add the broth; bring to a boil. Add the pasta; cook for 3 minutes, stirring frequently.
2. Gradually add spinach. Cook and stir until pasta is tender and spinach is wilted, 2-3 minutes. In a small bowl, combine the flour, pepper and cream until smooth; gradually stir into pasta mixture. Bring to a boil; cook and stir until thickened, 1-2 minutes.
1½ cups: 563 cal., 26g fat (10g sat. fat), 77mg chol., 1546mg sod., 57g carb. (6g sugars, 6g fiber), 25g pro.

OKTOBERFEST BRATS WITH MUSTARD SAUCE

I come from a town with a big German heritage, where we have a huge celebration each year for Oktoberfest. This recipe packs in all the traditional German flavors my whole family loves.
—Deborah Pennington, Falkville, AL

TAKES: 20 MIN. • **MAKES:** 4 SERVINGS

- ⅓ cup half-and-half cream
- 2 Tbsp. stone-ground mustard
- ½ tsp. dried minced onion
- ¼ tsp. pepper
  Dash paprika
- 4 fully cooked bratwurst links (about 12 oz.)
- 1 can (14 oz.) sauerkraut, rinsed and drained, warmed

1. For the sauce, mix the first 5 ingredients. Cut each bratwurst into thirds; thread onto 4 metal or soaked wooden skewers.
2. Grill brats, covered, over medium heat until golden brown and heated through, 7-10 minutes, turning occasionally. Serve with sauerkraut and sauce.

1 serving: 341 cal., 28g fat (10g sat. fat), 73mg chol., 1539mg sod., 9g carb. (3g sugars, 3g fiber), 14g pro.

HAM & BROCCOLI PASTA

It's hard to beat a meal that is created in one pan, takes 30 minutes and your kids will thank you for making. Sounds like a keeper in my book!
—Jana Cathey, Ada, MI

TAKES: 30 MIN. • **MAKES:** 6 SERVINGS

- 4½ cups uncooked bow tie pasta (12 oz.)
- 1 pkg. (16 oz.) frozen broccoli florets
- 3 cups cubed fully cooked ham
- 1 carton (8 oz.) spreadable chive and onion cream cheese

- ⅓ cup milk
- ¼ tsp. salt
- ½ tsp. pepper

1. In a Dutch oven, cook pasta according to package directions, adding broccoli during the last 5 minutes of cooking; drain and set aside.
2. In same pan, combine remaining ingredients; cook and stir over medium heat until heated through and cream cheese is melted. Return the pasta mixture to pan and toss to combine.

1¾ cups: 452 cal., 17g fat (10g sat. fat), 79mg chol., 1135mg sod., 48g carb. (6g sugars, 4g fiber), 26g pro.

5i
SAVORY BEER PORK CHOPS

These tender chops cooked in a savory sauce are perfect for hectic nights because they're so easy to prep. Try them with hot buttery noodles.
—Jana Christian, Farson, WY

TAKES: 20 MIN. • **MAKES:** 4 SERVINGS

- 4 boneless pork loin chops (4 oz. each)
- ½ tsp. salt
- ½ tsp. pepper
- 1 Tbsp. canola oil
- 3 Tbsp. ketchup
- 2 Tbsp. brown sugar
- ¾ cup beer or nonalcoholic beer

1. Sprinkle pork chops with salt and pepper. In a large skillet, heat oil over medium heat; brown chops on both sides.
2. Mix ketchup, brown sugar and beer; pour over chops. Bring to a boil. Reduce heat; simmer, uncovered, until a thermometer inserted in the pork reads 145°, 4-6 minutes. Let stand 5 minutes before serving.
Freeze option: Place pork chops in freezer containers; top with sauce. Cool and freeze. To use, partially thaw in refrigerator overnight. Heat through in a covered saucepan, gently stirring sauce; add a little water if necessary.
1 pork chop: 239 cal., 10g fat (3g sat. fat), 55mg chol., 472mg sod., 11g carb. (11g sugars, 0 fiber), 22g pro. **Diabetic exchanges:** 3 lean meat, 1 fat, ½ starch.

PENNE ALLA VODKA

This easy and impressive pasta is always on the menu when my husband and I invite first-time guests over for dinner. Many friends continue to ask me to make the recipe, even years after they first tried it.
—Cara Langer, Overland Park, KS

TAKES: 30 MIN. • **MAKES:** 6 SERVINGS

- 1 pkg. (16 oz.) penne pasta
- 3 Tbsp. butter
- 2 garlic cloves, minced
- 4 oz. thinly sliced prosciutto, cut into strips
- 1 can (28 oz.) whole plum tomatoes, drained and chopped
- ¼ cup vodka
- ½ tsp. salt
- ½ tsp. crushed red pepper flakes
- ½ cup heavy whipping cream
- ½ cup shredded Parmesan cheese

1. Cook the pasta according to package directions.
2. Meanwhile, in a large skillet, heat butter over medium-high heat. Add garlic; cook and stir 1 minute. Add prosciutto; cook 2 minutes longer. Stir in tomatoes, vodka, salt and pepper flakes. Bring to a boil. Reduce heat; simmer, uncovered, 5 minutes. Stir in cream; cook 2-3 minutes longer, stirring occasionally.
3. Drain pasta. Add pasta and cheese to sauce; toss to combine.
1⅓ cups: 504 cal., 19g fat (11g sat. fat), 64mg chol., 966mg sod., 62g carb. (6g sugars, 4g fiber), 19g pro.

TEST KITCHEN TIP

To keep pasta from sticking together when cooking, always use a large pot with plenty of water. Add a little cooking oil if desired (this also prevents boiling over).

½ lb. bulk Italian sausage
½ cup chopped red onion
1 medium fennel bulb, chopped
½ lb. baby portobello mushrooms, chopped
3 garlic cloves, minced
1 bunch Swiss chard, trimmed and chopped
½ tsp. salt
¼ tsp. pepper
¾ cup grated Parmesan cheese, divided
½ cup pine nuts or chopped walnuts, toasted

1. Cook pasta according to package directions for al dente. Meanwhile, in a large skillet, heat oil over medium heat. Cook sausage and red onion until no longer pink, 3-4 minutes, breaking meat into crumbles. Add fennel, mushrooms and garlic; cook until tender, 6-8 minutes. Add chopped Swiss chard; cook and stir until wilted, 4-5 minutes longer.
2. Drain pasta, reserving 1 cup pasta water. In a large bowl, combine pasta, sausage mixture, salt, pepper and ½ cup cheese, adding enough reserved pasta water to coat pasta and create a creamy texture. Serve with remaining cheese and pine nuts.
1⅓ cups: 487 cal., 25g fat (6g sat. fat), 34mg chol., 726mg sod., 51g carb. (5g sugars, 4g fiber), 19g pro.

SAUSAGE & SWISS CHARD PASTA

I whipped up lunch with fresh produce from the farmers market and the result was amazing.
—Kate Stiltner, Grand Rapids, MI

TAKES: 30 MIN. • **MAKES:** 6 SERVINGS

12 oz. uncooked orecchiette or small tube pasta (about 2½ cups)
1 Tbsp. olive oil

HEALTH TIP

Lighten this dish by using turkey Italian sausage, and add fiber with whole wheat orecchiette instead of white pasta.

PEAR, HAM & CHEESE PASTRY POCKETS

I came up with this simple recipe one night for a quick dinner. It's perfect with a cup of soup for a wonderfully comforting weeknight meal.
—Terri Crandall, Gardnerville, NV

TAKES: 30 MIN. • **MAKES:** 8 SERVINGS

- 1 pkg. (17.3 oz.) frozen puff pastry, thawed
- ¼ cup honey Dijon mustard
- 1 large egg, lightly beaten
- 8 slices deli ham
- 4 slices Muenster cheese, halved diagonally
- 1 medium red pear, very thinly sliced
- 1 small red onion, thinly sliced

1. Preheat oven to 400°. Unfold each sheet of puff pastry. Cut each into 4 squares. Spread 1½ tsp. mustard over each square to within ½ in. of edges. Brush egg over edges of pastry.
2. On 1 corner half of each square, layer ham, cheese, pear and onion. Fold opposite corner over filling, forming a triangle; press edges with a fork to seal. Transfer to ungreased baking sheets. Brush tops with remaining egg.
3. Bake 10-14 minutes or until golden brown. Serve warm.
Freeze option: Freeze cooled pockets in a freezer container, separating with waxed paper. To use, reheat pockets on a baking sheet in a preheated 400° oven until crisp and heated through.
1 pocket: 403 cal., 21g fat (6g sat. fat), 43mg chol., 540mg sod., 43g carb. (6g sugars, 6g fiber), 12g pro.

CINNAMON-APPLE PORK CHOPS

When I found this recipe online years ago, it quickly became a favorite. The ingredients are easy to keep on hand, and the one-pan cleanup is a bonus.
—Christina Price, Colorado Springs, CO

TAKES: 25 MIN. • **MAKES:** 4 SERVINGS

- 2 Tbsp. reduced-fat butter, divided
- 4 boneless pork loin chops (4 oz. each)
- 3 Tbsp. brown sugar
- 1 tsp. ground cinnamon
- ½ tsp. ground nutmeg
- ¼ tsp. salt
- 4 medium tart apples, thinly sliced
- 2 Tbsp. chopped pecans

1. In a large skillet, heat 1 Tbsp. butter over medium heat. Add pork chops; cook 4-5 minutes on each side or until a thermometer reads 145°. Meanwhile, in a small bowl, mix brown sugar, cinnamon, nutmeg and salt.
2. Remove chops; keep warm. Add apples, pecans, brown sugar mixture and remaining butter to pan; cook and stir until apples are tender. Serve with chops.
Note: This recipe was tested with Land O'Lakes light butter.
1 pork chop with ⅔ cup apple mixture: 316 cal., 12g fat (4g sat. fat), 62mg chol., 232mg sod., 31g carb. (25g sugars, 4g fiber), 22g pro.
Diabetic exchanges: 3 lean meat, 1 starch, 1 fruit, 1 fat.

TORTELLINI CARBONARA

Bacon, cream and Parmesan cheese make a classic pasta sauce that's absolutely heavenly. It's a delightful option for company!
—Cathy Croyle, Davidsville, PA

TAKES: 20 MIN. • **MAKES:** 4 SERVINGS

- 1 pkg. (9 oz.) refrigerated cheese tortellini
- 8 bacon strips, chopped
- 1 cup heavy whipping cream
- ½ cup grated Parmesan cheese
- ½ cup chopped fresh parsley

1. Cook the tortellini according to package directions; drain.
2. Meanwhile, in a large skillet, cook bacon over medium heat until crisp, stirring occasionally. Remove with a slotted spoon; drain on paper towels. Pour off drippings.
3. In same pan, combine cream, cheese, parsley and bacon; heat through over medium heat. Stir in tortellini. Serve immediately.
1 cup: 527 cal., 36g fat (20g sat. fat), 121mg chol., 728mg sod., 33g carb. (3g sugars, 2g fiber), 19g pro.

NO-FUSS PORK CHOPS

These tender chops taste like sweet-and-sour pork but require little attention or time. I prepare them year-round, whenever I'm on a tight schedule but still want something scrumptious.
—Sally Jones, Lancaster, NH

TAKES: 30 MIN. • **MAKES:** 4 SERVINGS

- ½ cup pineapple juice
- 2 Tbsp. brown sugar
- 2 Tbsp. cider vinegar
- ½ tsp. salt
- 2 Tbsp. olive oil, divided
- 4 boneless pork loin chops (5 oz. each)
- 2 medium onions, chopped
  Optional: Hot cooked noodles and sliced green onions

1. Mix first 4 ingredients. In a large skillet, heat 1 Tbsp. oil over medium heat; brown pork chops on both sides. Remove from pan.

2. In same pan, saute the onions in remaining oil over medium heat until tender. Add the juice mixture; bring to a boil. Reduce heat; simmer, covered, 10 minutes. Add pork chops; cook, covered, until a thermometer inserted in pork reads 145°, 2-3 minutes. Let stand, covered, 5 minutes before serving. If desired, serve over noodles and top with green onions.
1 pork chop: 315 cal., 15g fat (4g sat. fat), 68mg chol., 340mg sod., 16g carb. (12g sugars, 1g fiber), 28g pro.

PINEAPPLE CRANBERRY HAM

Tired of the same old meals for dinner? Try something new tonight! A sweet and tangy relish of cranberries and pineapple tops these hearty ham steaks, adding lots of flavor and color.
—Rita Brower, Exeter, CA

TAKES: 25 MIN. • **MAKES:** 4 SERVINGS

- 4 boneless fully cooked ham steaks (6 oz. each)
- 1½ tsp. canola oil
- ½ cup jellied cranberry sauce
- ½ cup undrained crushed pineapple
- 3 Tbsp. brown sugar
- ⅛ tsp. ground cloves

1. Cut each ham steak in half. In a large skillet over medium heat, cook ham in oil in batches until browned and heated through, 3-5 minutes on each side. Set aside and keep warm.
2. Meanwhile, in a small saucepan, mash the cranberry sauce; stir in the remaining ingredients. Bring to a boil; cook and stir until slightly thickened, 3-5 minutes. Serve with the ham.
1 serving: 405 cal., 16g fat (5g sat. fat), 90mg chol., 2186mg sod., 33g carb. (25g sugars, 1g fiber), 31g pro.

TENDERLOIN WITH HERB SAUCE

Tender pork is treated to a rich and creamy sauce with a slight red pepper kick. This hearty dish is very simple to prepare and is always a dinnertime winner at my home.
—Monica Shipley, Tulare, CA

TAKES: 25 MIN. • **MAKES:** 6 SERVINGS

- 2   pork tenderloins (1 lb. each)
- ½ tsp. salt
- 4   tsp. butter
- ⅔ cup half-and-half cream
- 2   Tbsp. minced fresh parsley
- 2   tsp. herbes de Provence
- 2   tsp. reduced-sodium soy sauce
- 1   tsp. beef bouillon granules
- ½ to ¾ tsp. crushed red pepper flakes

1. Cut each tenderloin into 12 slices; sprinkle with salt. In a large nonstick skillet, heat butter over medium heat; brown pork in batches, 3-4 minutes per side. Return all pork to pan.
2. Mix remaining ingredients; pour over pork. Cook, uncovered, over low heat until sauce is thickened and a thermometer inserted in pork reads 145°, 2-3 minutes, stirring occasionally. Let stand 5 minutes before serving.
Note: Look for herbes de Provence in the spice aisle.
4 oz. cooked pork: 238 cal., 10g fat (5g sat. fat), 104mg chol., 495mg sod., 2g carb. (1g sugars, 0 fiber), 31g pro.
Diabetic exchanges: 4 lean meat, 1 fat.

SWEET BARBECUED PORK CHOPS

I often prepare a double batch of these tangy chops, then freeze half to keep on hand for fast family dinners. They are so easy and taste so fresh, no one ever guesses my quick entree was frozen.
—Susan Holderman, Fostoria, OH

TAKES: 25 MIN. • **MAKES:** 8 SERVINGS

- 2   Tbsp. canola oil
- 8   boneless pork loin chops (¾ in. thick and 8 oz. each)
- ½ cup packed brown sugar
- ½ cup chopped sweet onion
- ½ cup each ketchup, barbecue sauce, French salad dressing and honey

1. In a large skillet, heat oil over medium heat. In batches, brown pork chops 2-3 minutes on each side. Return all to pan.
2. In a small bowl, mix remaining ingredients; pour over chops. Bring to a boil. Reduce heat; simmer, covered, 4-5 minutes or until a thermometer inserted in pork reads 145°. Let stand 5 minutes before serving.
Freeze option: Place pork chops in freezer containers; top with sauce. Cool and freeze. To use, partially thaw in refrigerator overnight. Heat through in a covered saucepan, gently stirring sauce; add a little water if necessary.
1 pork chop: 282 cal., 12g fat (3g sat. fat), 14mg chol., 533mg sod., 41g carb. (37g sugars, 1g fiber), 6g pro.

TEST KITCHEN TIP

You'll love this recipe's full-flavored sauce so much that you'll want to try it with chicken, too. Go ahead! Replace the pork with poultry for equally tasty results.

HAM PASTA TOSS

This is my favorite meal to make when I'm short on time. You can also use different meats or veggies depending on what you have on hand.
—Sharon Gerst, North Liberty, IA

TAKES: 25 MIN. • **MAKES:** 6 SERVINGS

- 12 oz. uncooked whole wheat spaghetti
- 3 Tbsp. butter
- 2 cups shredded or cubed fully cooked ham
- 2 garlic cloves, minced
- 3 cups frozen peas (about 12 oz.), thawed
- 2 Tbsp. minced fresh parsley
- ¼ cup grated Parmesan cheese

1. Cook the spaghetti according to package directions; drain. Meanwhile, in a large skillet, heat butter over medium heat. Add ham; cook and stir until browned, 2-4 minutes . Add garlic; cook 1 minute longer.
2. Stir in spaghetti, peas and parsley; heat through. Sprinkle with cheese; toss to combine.
1⅓ cups: 374 cal., 10g fat (5g sat. fat), 46mg chol., 738mg sod., 52g carb. (3g sugars, 10g fiber), 23g pro.

CHICKEN CORDON BLEU CRESCENT RING

A classic cordon bleu has chicken, cheese and ham. To change it up, roll everything inside crescent dough for a hand-held meal.
—Stella Culotta, Pasadena, MD

TAKES: 30 MIN. • **MAKES:** 6 SERVINGS

- 1 tube (8 oz.) refrigerated crescent rolls
- 2 cups shredded Swiss cheese
- 2 cups cubed cooked chicken
- ¾ cup mayonnaise
- ½ cup cubed fully cooked ham
- 2 Tbsp. honey mustard

1. Preheat oven to 375°. Unroll crescent dough and separate into triangles. On an ungreased 12-in. pizza pan, arrange triangles in a ring with points toward the outside and wide ends overlapping. Press overlapping dough to seal.
2. In a large bowl, mix remaining ingredients. Spoon across wide ends of triangles. Fold pointed ends of triangles over filling, tucking points under to form a ring (filling will be visible).
3. Bake 15-20 minutes or until golden brown and heated through.
1 slice: 603 cal., 45g fat (13g sat. fat), 91mg chol., 772mg sod.,19g carb. (6g sugars, 0 fiber), 29g pro.

GREEK SAUSAGE PITA PIZZAS

I turned my favorite sandwich into a pizza. It's perfect for lunch or dinner, but don't forget it when you're having a bunch of people over—it makes a fantastic appetizer, too.
—Marion McNeill, Mayfield Heights, OH

TAKES: 30 MIN. • **MAKES:** 4 SERVINGS

- 1   pkg. (19 oz.) Italian sausage links, casings removed
- 2   garlic cloves, minced
- 4   whole pita breads
- 2   plum tomatoes, seeded and chopped
- 1   medium ripe avocado, peeled and cubed
- ½   cup crumbled feta cheese
- 1   small cucumber, sliced
- ½   cup refrigerated tzatziki sauce

1. Preheat oven to 350°. In a large skillet, cook sausage and garlic over medium heat 6-8 minutes or until no longer pink, breaking sausage into large crumbles; drain.
2. Meanwhile, place pita breads on ungreased baking sheets. Bake 3-4 minutes on each side or until browned and almost crisp.
3. Top pita breads with sausage mixture, tomatoes, avocado and cheese. Bake 3-4 minutes longer or until heated through. Top with the cucumbers; drizzle with the tzatziki sauce.
1 pizza: 632 cal., 40g fat (12g sat. fat), 85mg chol., 1336mg sod., 43g carb. (3g sugars, 5g fiber), 25g pro.

HAM & SWISS STROMBOLI

This is an excellent dish to take to someone for dinner. It's also easy to change up the recipe with your favorite meats or cheeses.
—Tricia Bibb, Hartselle, AL

TAKES: 30 MIN. • **MAKES:** 6 SERVINGS

- 1   tube (11 oz.) refrigerated crusty French loaf
- 6   oz. sliced deli ham
- ¼   cup finely chopped onion
- 8   bacon strips, cooked and crumbled
- 6   oz. sliced Swiss cheese Honey mustard, optional

1. Preheat oven to 375°. Unroll dough on a baking sheet. Place ham down center third of dough to within 1 in. of edges; top with onion, bacon and cheese. Fold long sides of dough over filling, pinching seam and ends to seal; tuck ends under. Cut several slits in top.
2. Bake 20-25 minutes or until golden brown. Cut into slices. If desired, serve with honey mustard.
Freeze option: Securely wrap and freeze cooled unsliced stromboli in heavy-duty foil. To use, reheat stromboli on an ungreased baking sheet in a preheated 375° oven until heated through and a thermometer inserted in center reads 165°.
1 slice: 272 cal., 11g fat (5g sat. fat), 40mg chol., 795mg sod., 26g carb. (3g sugars, 1g fiber), 18g pro.

DID YOU KNOW?

You can also prepare this recipe with a tube of crescent roll dough or a tube of pizza crust dough.

¼ cup fat-free milk
¼ cup seasoned bread crumbs
¼ cup grated Parmesan cheese
¼ tsp. salt
¼ tsp. garlic powder
⅛ tsp. pepper
4 boneless pork loin chops
(4 oz. each)
Cooking spray

1. Preheat oven to 375°. Place milk in a shallow bowl. In another shallow bowl, toss bread crumbs with cheese and seasonings.
2. Dip pork chops in milk, then coat with crumb mixture. Place on a baking sheet coated with cooking spray; lightly spritz chops with cooking spray.
3. Bake 8-10 minutes on each side or until a thermometer reads 145°. Let stand 5 minutes before serving.
1 pork chop: 178 cal., 7g fat (3g sat. fat), 57mg chol., 207mg sod., 3g carb. (0 sugars, 0 fiber), 23g pro. **Diabetic exchanges:** 3 lean meat.

HEALTH TIP

Pair this healthy pork chop recipe with a low-cal side dish of butternut or acorn squash. You could also whip up a colorful blend of mushrooms, tomatoes and asparagus to quickly roast under the broiler.

BUSY-DAY PORK CHOPS

I created this recipe one day when I had pork chops and needed to find a simple way to make them. It was so easy and the response was a rave review! The chops are crispy outside, even though the preparation technique uses less fat.
—Dee Maltby, Wayne, OH

TAKES: 30 MIN. • **MAKES:** 4 SERVINGS

SPICED PORK MEDALLIONS WITH BOURBON SAUCE

I don't remember where I found this recipe, but it's become one of my favorite entrees to serve company. I usually prepare it with a side of roasted vegetables.
—Kathy Kantrud, Fenton, MI

TAKES: 25 MIN. • **MAKES:** 4 SERVINGS

- ½ cup bourbon or reduced-sodium chicken broth
- ¼ cup packed dark brown sugar
- 3 Tbsp. white vinegar
- 3 Tbsp. reduced-sodium soy sauce
- 2 garlic cloves, minced
- ½ tsp. pepper
- ½ tsp. chili powder
- ¼ tsp. ground cinnamon
- ⅛ tsp. salt
- ⅛ tsp. ground allspice
- 1 pork tenderloin (1 lb.), cut into 12 slices

1. In a small saucepan, combine bourbon, brown sugar, vinegar, soy sauce, garlic and pepper. Bring to a boil; cook until liquid is reduced to about ½ cup, stirring occasionally.
2. Meanwhile, combine chili powder, cinnamon, salt and allspice; rub over pork slices.
3. In a large skillet coated with cooking spray, cook pork over medium heat for 2-4 minutes on each side or until tender. Serve with the sauce.

3 oz. cooked pork: 221 cal., 4g fat (1g sat. fat), 63mg chol., 581mg sod., 15g carb. (13g sugars, 0 fiber), 23g pro. **Diabetic exchanges:** 3 lean meat, 1 starch.

EASY GINGER PORK STIR-FRY

An easy homemade stir-fry sauce is the perfect base for this weeknight dish. It comes together quickly but tastes impressive.
—Adeline Russell, Hartford, WI

TAKES: 20 MIN. • **MAKES:** 4 SERVINGS

- 2 Tbsp. cornstarch
- 1 cup beef broth
- 3 Tbsp. soy sauce
- 1 Tbsp. sugar
- 1½ tsp. ground ginger
- ½ tsp. garlic powder
- ½ tsp. crushed red pepper flakes
- 1 pork tenderloin (1 lb.), cut into 2-in. strips
- 2 Tbsp. canola oil, divided
- 1 pkg. (16 oz.) frozen sugar snap stir-fry vegetable blend, thawed
  Hot cooked rice
  Minced fresh cilantro, optional

1. In a small bowl, combine the cornstarch and broth until smooth. Stir in the soy sauce, sugar, ginger, garlic powder and pepper flakes; set aside.
2. In a wok or large skillet, stir-fry pork in 1 Tbsp. oil until juices run clear. Remove and keep warm. In the same pan, stir-fry vegetables in remaining oil until crisp-tender.
3. Stir broth mixture and add to the vegetables. Bring to a boil; cook and stir for 1 minute or until thickened. Return pork to the pan; heat through. Serve with rice and, if desired, sprinkle with cilantro.

1 cup: 278 cal., 11g fat (2g sat. fat), 63mg chol., 958mg sod., 16g carb. (7g sugars, 4g fiber), 27g pro.

Ginger-orange pork stir-fry: Omit first 7 ingredients. Combine 1 Tbsp. cornstarch with 1 cup orange juice and 2 Tbsp. soy sauce until smooth. Stir in 2 minced garlic cloves and ¾ tsp. ground ginger. Proceed as recipe directs.

HURRY-UP HAM & NOODLES

This rich-tasting dish is ready to serve in almost the time it takes to cook the noodles. I've made it for luncheons and potlucks, but mostly I make it on days when I'm in a hurry to get something on the table.
—Lucille Howell, Portland, OR

TAKES: 25 MIN. • **MAKES:** 4 SERVINGS

- 5   to 6 cups uncooked wide egg noodles
- ¼   cup butter, cubed
- 1   cup heavy whipping cream
- 1½ cups chopped fully cooked ham
- ½   cup grated Parmesan cheese
- ¼   cup thinly sliced green onions
- ¼   tsp. salt
- ⅛   tsp. pepper

1. Cook noodles according to package directions. Meanwhile, in a large skillet, melt butter over medium heat. Gradually whisk in cream. Bring to a boil, stirring constantly; cook and stir until thickened, about 2 minutes longer.
2. Add the ham, cheese, onions, salt and pepper; cook, uncovered, until heated through. Drain the noodles; add to ham mixture. Toss to coat; heat through.
1½ cups: 619 cal., 43g fat (25g sat. fat), 193mg chol., 1154mg sod., 38g carb. (3g sugars, 1g fiber), 22g pro.

ONE-POT RED BEANS & RICE

This is a one-pot meal that's ready in about 30 minutes. It is one of my husband's favorites and uses simple ingredients, so it's been a go-to recipe in our house for years.
—Janice Conklin, Stevensville, MT

TAKES: 30 MIN. • **MAKES:** 6 SERVINGS

- 1   Tbsp. olive oil
- 2   celery ribs, sliced
- 1   medium onion, chopped
- 1   medium green pepper, chopped
- 1   pkg. (14 oz.) smoked turkey sausage, sliced
- 1   carton (32 oz.) reduced-sodium chicken broth
- 1   can (16 oz.) kidney beans, rinsed and drained
- 1¼   cups uncooked converted rice
- ⅓   cup tomato paste
- 1   bay leaf
- 1½   tsp. Cajun seasoning
- ¼   tsp. cayenne pepper
      Hot pepper sauce, optional

1. In a Dutch oven, heat oil over medium-high heat. Add celery, onion and green pepper; cook and stir until crisp-tender, 3-4 minutes. Add sausage; cook until browned, 2-3 minutes.
2. Stir in broth, beans, rice, tomato paste, bay leaf, Cajun seasoning and cayenne pepper. Bring to a boil; reduce heat. Simmer, uncovered, until rice is tender and liquid is absorbed, 15-20 minutes, stirring occasionally. Discard bay leaf. If desired, serve with pepper sauce.
1⅓ cups: 347 cal., 6g fat (2g sat. fat), 41mg chol., 1272mg sod., 50g carb. (6g sugars, 5g fiber), 22g pro.

DID YOU KNOW?

Also called parboiled rice, converted rice is the unhulled grain that has been steam-pressured before milling. This process retains nutrients and makes fluffy separated grains of cooked rice. Converted rice takes slightly longer to cook than regular long grain rice.

HAM & VEGGIE CASSEROLE

I've paired ham with broccoli and cauliflower for years. To complete this casserole dinner, I pass around some dinner rolls.
—Sherri Melotik, Oak Creek, WI

TAKES: 30 MIN. • **MAKES:** 4 SERVINGS

- 1 pkg. (16 oz.) frozen broccoli florets
- 1 pkg. (16 oz.) frozen cauliflower
- 2 tsp. plus 2 Tbsp. butter, divided
- ¼ cup seasoned bread crumbs
- 2 Tbsp. all-purpose flour
- 1½ cups 2% milk
- ¾ cup shredded sharp cheddar cheese
- ½ cup grated Parmesan cheese
- 1½ cups cubed fully cooked ham (about 8 oz.)
- ¼ tsp. pepper

1. Preheat oven to 425°. Cook the broccoli and cauliflower according to package directions; drain.
2. Meanwhile, in a small skillet, melt 2 tsp. butter. Add the bread crumbs; cook and stir over medium heat until lightly toasted, 2-3 minutes. Remove from heat.
3. In a large saucepan, melt the remaining butter over medium heat. Stir in flour until smooth; gradually whisk in milk. Bring to a boil, stirring constantly; cook and stir until thickened, 1-2 minutes. Remove from heat; stir in cheeses until blended. Stir in ham, pepper and vegetables.
4. Transfer to a greased 8-in. square baking dish. Sprinkle with toasted crumbs. Bake, uncovered, until heated through, 10-15 minutes.
1½ cups: 420 cal., 23g fat (13g sat. fat), 89mg chol., 1233mg sod., 25g carb. (10g sugars, 6g fiber), 28g pro.

PUMPKIN & SAUSAGE PENNE

I once made this dish for my Italian father-in-law, who swears he'll eat pasta only with red sauce. He loved it!
—Karen Cambiotti, Stroudsburg, PA

TAKES: 30 MIN. • **MAKES:** 2 SERVINGS

- ¾ cup uncooked penne pasta
- 2 Italian sausage links, casings removed
- ½ cup chopped sweet onion
- 1 garlic clove, minced
- 1 tsp. olive oil
- ⅓ cup white wine or chicken broth
- 1 bay leaf
- ¾ cup chicken broth
- ⅓ cup canned pumpkin
- 3 tsp. minced fresh sage, divided
- ⅛ tsp. each salt, pepper and ground cinnamon Dash ground nutmeg
- 3 Tbsp. half-and-half cream
- 2 Tbsp. shredded Romano cheese

1. Cook pasta according to package directions. Meanwhile, in a large skillet, cook sausage over medium heat until no longer pink, breaking it into crumbles. Remove with a slotted spoon; drain on paper towels. Discard the drippings, reserving 1 tsp.
2. Cook and stir onion and garlic in oil and reserved drippings over medium-high heat until tender. Add wine and bay leaf. Bring to a boil; cook until liquid is reduced by half. Stir in the broth, pumpkin, 1½ tsp. sage and remaining seasonings; cook 1 minute longer. Add cream and sausage; heat through. Remove bay leaf.
3. Drain pasta; transfer to a large bowl. Add sausage mixture; toss to coat. Sprinkle with cheese and remaining sage.
1⅓ cups: 490 cal., 23g fat (9g sat. fat), 61mg chol., 950mg sod., 42g carb. (7g sugars, 4g fiber), 21g pro.

SAUSAGE-STUFFED ACORN SQUASH

Acorn squash gets the sweet and savory treatment when stuffed with sausage, onion, spinach and cranberries to make this cozy main dish. Cooking the squash in the microwave makes this quick enough for a busy weeknight.
—*Taste of Home* Test Kitchen

TAKES: 30 MIN. • **MAKES:** 4 SERVINGS

- 2 medium acorn squash
- 1 lb. bulk spicy pork sausage
- ½ cup chopped onion
- 1 cup fresh spinach, finely chopped
- ½ cup dried cranberries
- 1½ cups soft bread crumbs
- 1 large egg
- 2 Tbsp. 2% milk

1. Halve the squash lengthwise; discard seeds. Place the squash in a microwave-safe dish, cut side down. Microwave, covered, on high until tender, 10-12 minutes.
2. Meanwhile, in a large skillet, cook and crumble sausage with onion over medium heat until no longer pink, 5-7 minutes; drain. Remove from heat; stir in the spinach, cranberries and bread crumbs. In a small bowl, whisk together egg and milk; add to the sausage mixture and toss until moistened.
3. Turn over the squash; fill with the sausage mixture. Microwave, covered, until a thermometer inserted in stuffing reads 165°, 2-3 minutes.

1 stuffed squash half: 485 cal., 23g fat (8g sat. fat), 133mg chol., 843mg sod., 49g carb. (18g sugars, 5g fiber), 25g pro.

TEST KITCHEN TIP

To easily make soft bread crumbs, simply tear bread into pieces and place in a food processor or blender. Cover and pulse until crumbs form. One slice of bread yields ½-¾ cup crumbs.

MUFFULETTA PASTA

A friend gave me this recipe when she learned that I love muffuletta sandwiches. Very rich and filling, this easy skillet supper goes together quickly on a busy weeknight. Serve with some cheesy garlic bread.
—Jan Hollingsworth, Houston, MS

TAKES: 25 MIN. • **MAKES:** 8 SERVINGS

- 1 pkg. (16 oz.) bow tie pasta
- 1 bunch green onions, chopped
- 2 tsp. plus ¼ cup butter, divided
- 1 Tbsp. minced garlic
- 1 pkg. (16 oz.) cubed fully cooked ham
- 1 jar (12.36 oz.) tapenade or ripe olive bruschetta topping, drained
- 1 pkg. (3½ oz.) sliced pepperoni
- 1 cup heavy whipping cream
- 2 cups shredded Italian cheese blend

1. Cook pasta according to package directions. Meanwhile, in a large skillet, saute onions in 2 tsp. butter until tender. Add the garlic; cook 1 minute longer. Add the ham, tapenade and pepperoni; saute 2 minutes longer.
2. Cube remaining butter; stir butter and cream into skillet. Bring to a boil over medium heat. Reduce heat; simmer, uncovered, for 3 minutes.
3. Drain pasta; toss with ham mixture. Sprinkle with cheese.
1½ cups: 739 cal., 48g fat (21g sat. fat), 119mg chol., 1638mg sod., 48g carb. (2g sugars, 2g fiber), 27g pro.

SMOKED SAUSAGE & VEGGIE SHEET-PAN SUPPER

This recipe is tasty and quick, and it can easily be doubled for last-minute dinner guests. Cook it in the oven or on the grill, and add the veggies of your choice.
—Judy Batson, Tampa, FL

TAKES: 30 MIN. • **MAKES:** 4 SERVINGS

- 1 pkg. (13½ oz.) smoked sausage, cut into ½-in. slices
- 8 fresh Brussels sprouts, thinly sliced
- 1 large sweet onion, halved and sliced
- 1 medium yellow summer squash, halved and sliced
- 1 medium zucchini, halved and sliced
- 1 medium sweet yellow pepper, chopped
- 1 medium green pepper, chopped
- 1 medium tomato, chopped
- ¾ cup sliced fresh mushrooms
- ½ cup Greek vinaigrette

Preheat oven to 400°. Place first 9 ingredients into a greased 15x10x1-in. baking pan. Drizzle with vinaigrette; toss to coat. Bake, uncovered, 15 minutes. Remove pan from oven; preheat broiler. Broil sausage mixture 3-4 in. from heat until vegetables are lightly browned, 3-4 minutes.
2 cups: 491 cal., 37g fat (13g sat. fat), 64mg chol., 1430mg sod., 22g carb. (13g sugars, 5g fiber), 18g pro.

HEALTH TIP

Use smoked turkey sausage or fully cooked chicken sausage for a lighter version.

FISH & SEAFOOD FAVORITES

Whether you are a seafood lover or just want to mix up your beef-chicken routine, consider any of these fresh and flavorful options.

SEARED SALMON WITH STRAWBERRY BASIL RELISH

Take a sweet new approach to salmon fillets by topping them with a relish of strawberries, basil, honey and pepper.
—Stacy Mullens, Gresham, OR

TAKES: 20 MIN. • **MAKES:** 6 SERVINGS

- 6 salmon fillets (4 oz. each)
- 1 Tbsp. butter, melted
- ¼ tsp. salt
- ⅛ tsp. freshly ground pepper

RELISH
- 1¼ cups finely chopped fresh strawberries
- 1 Tbsp. minced fresh basil
- 1 Tbsp. honey
  Dash freshly ground pepper

1. Brush fillets with melted butter; sprinkle with salt and pepper. Heat a large skillet over medium-high heat. Add the fillets, skin side up, in batches if necessary; cook 2-3 minutes on each side or until fish just begins to flake easily with a fork.

2. In a small bowl, gently toss the strawberries with basil, honey and pepper. Serve salmon with relish.

1 salmon fillet with 3 Tbsp. relish: 215 cal., 12g fat (3g sat. fat), 62mg chol., 169mg sod., 6g carb. (5g sugars, 1g fiber), 19g pro. **Diabetic exchanges:** 3 lean meat, ½ starch, ½ fat.

COD WITH SWEET PEPPERS

This quick and delicious dish is a family favorite. I like to use three or four different colors of peppers.
—Judy Grebetz, Racine, WI

TAKES: 25 MIN. • **MAKES:** 4 SERVINGS

- 1 medium onion, halved and sliced
- 1 cup reduced-sodium chicken broth
- 1 Tbsp. lemon juice
- 3 garlic cloves, minced
- 1½ tsp. dried oregano
- ½ tsp. grated lemon zest
- ¼ tsp. salt
- 4 cod fillets (6 oz. each)
- ¾ cup julienned green pepper
- ¾ cup julienned sweet red pepper
- 2½ tsp. cornstarch
- 1 Tbsp. cold water
- 1 medium lemon, halved and sliced

1. In a large nonstick skillet, combine the first 7 ingredients. Bring to a boil. Reduce heat; cover and simmer until onion is tender, 6-8 minutes.

2. Arrange fish and peppers over onion mixture. Cover and simmer until the fish flakes easily with a fork and the peppers are tender, 6-9 minutes. Remove fish and vegetables; keep warm.

3. Combine cornstarch and water until smooth; gradually stir into pan juices. Bring to a boil; cook and stir until thickened, about 2 minutes. Spoon over fish and vegetables. Serve with lemon.

1 fillet with ⅓ cup pepper mixture: 168 cal., 1g fat (0 sat. fat), 65mg chol., 398mg sod., 10g carb. (4g sugars, 2g fiber), 29g pro. **Diabetic exchanges:** 4 lean meat, 1 vegetable.

SHRIMP PAD THAI

You can make this yummy Thai classic in no time. Find fish sauce and chili garlic sauce in the Asian foods aisle of your grocery store.
—Elise Ray, Shawnee, KS

TAKES: 30 MIN. • **MAKES:** 4 SERVINGS

- 4 oz. uncooked thick rice noodles
- ½ lb. uncooked shrimp (41-50 per lb.), peeled and deveined
- 2 tsp. canola oil
- 1 large onion, chopped
- 1 garlic clove, minced
- 1 large egg, lightly beaten
- 3 cups coleslaw mix
- 4 green onions, thinly sliced
- ⅓ cup rice vinegar
- ¼ cup sugar
- 3 Tbsp. reduced-sodium soy sauce
- 2 Tbsp. fish sauce or additional reduced-sodium soy sauce
- 2 to 3 tsp. chili garlic sauce
- 2 Tbsp. chopped salted peanuts
  Chopped fresh cilantro leaves

1. Cook noodles according to the package directions.
2. In a large nonstick skillet or wok, stir-fry shrimp in oil until shrimp turn pink; remove and set aside. Add onion and garlic to the pan. Make a well in the center of the onion mixture; add egg. Stir-fry for 2-3 minutes or until egg is completely set.
3. Add the coleslaw mix, green onions, vinegar, sugar, soy sauce, fish sauce, chili garlic sauce and peanuts; heat through. Return shrimp to the pan and heat through. Drain noodles; toss with shrimp mixture. Garnish with cilantro.

1¼ cups: 338 cal., 7g fat (1g sat. fat), 115mg chol., 1675mg sod., 52g carb. (23g sugars, 3g fiber), 17g pro.

GREEK FISH FILLETS

Olives, onion, dill and feta cheese combine in a tangy Greek-inspired topping to boost the flavor of tilapia or your favorite white fish. I usually serve this dish with a side of rice.
—Jennifer Maslowski, New York, NY

TAKES: 25 MIN. • **MAKES:** 4 SERVINGS

- 4 tilapia fillets (4 oz. each)
- ⅛ tsp. salt
- ⅛ tsp. pepper
- 2 Tbsp. plain yogurt
- 1 Tbsp. butter, softened
- 1½ tsp. lime juice
- ½ small red onion, finely chopped
- ¼ cup pitted Greek olives
- ½ tsp. dill weed
- ¼ tsp. paprika
- ⅛ tsp. garlic powder
- ¼ cup crumbled feta cheese

1. Sprinkle tilapia with salt and pepper. Place on a broiler pan coated with cooking spray.
2. Combine yogurt, butter and lime juice. Stir in onion, olives and seasonings. Spread down the middle of each fillet; sprinkle with feta cheese.
3. Broil 3-4 in. from the heat for 6-9 minutes or until fish flakes easily with a fork.

1 serving: 170 cal., 7g fat (3g sat. fat), 67mg chol., 344mg sod., 3g carb. (1g sugars, 1g fiber), 23g pro. **Diabetic exchanges:** 3 lean meat, 1½ fat.

ASPARAGUS & SHRIMP WITH ANGEL HAIR

We've all heard that the way to a man's heart is through his stomach, so when I plan a romantic dinner, this is one dish I like to serve. It's easy on the budget and turns out perfectly for two.
—Shari Neff, Takoma Park, MD

TAKES: 30 MIN. • **MAKES:** 2 SERVINGS

- 3 oz. uncooked angel hair pasta
- ½ lb. uncooked shrimp
  (16-20 per lb.),
  peeled and deveined
- ¼ tsp. salt
- ⅛ tsp. crushed
  red pepper flakes
- 2 Tbsp. olive oil, divided
- 8 fresh asparagus spears,
  trimmed and
  cut into 2-in. pieces
- ½ cup sliced fresh mushrooms
- ¼ cup chopped seeded tomato,
  peeled
- 4 garlic cloves, minced
- 2 tsp. chopped green onion
- ½ cup white wine or
  chicken broth
- 1½ tsp. minced fresh basil
- 1½ tsp. minced fresh oregano
- 1½ tsp. minced fresh parsley
- 1½ tsp. minced fresh thyme
- ¼ cup grated Parmesan cheese
  Lemon wedges

1. Cook pasta according to package directions. Meanwhile, sprinkle the shrimp with salt and pepper flakes. In a skillet or wok, heat 1 Tbsp. oil over medium-high heat. Add the shrimp; stir-fry until shrimp turn pink, 2-3 minutes. Remove shrimp; keep warm.

2. In same skillet, stir-fry the next 5 ingredients in remaining oil until vegetables are crisp-tender, about 5 minutes. Add the wine and the seasonings. Return shrimp to pan.

3. Drain pasta; add to shrimp mixture and toss gently. Cook and stir until heated through, 1-2 minutes. Sprinkle with Parmesan cheese. Serve with lemon wedges.

1¾ cups: 488 cal., 19g fat (4g sat. fat), 132mg chol., 584mg sod., 41g carb. (4g sugars, 3g fiber), 29g pro.

TEST KITCHEN TIP

Replace the fresh herbs in this recipe with dried if that's what you have on hand. Since dried herbs are more flavorful, use ½ teaspoon of each, then season to taste if needed.

BAKED TILAPIA

I've decided to cook healthier for my family, and that includes having more fish at home. This is an amazing recipe, and it's fast, too!
—Hope Stewart, Raleigh, NC

TAKES: 20 MIN. • **MAKES:** 4 SERVINGS

- 4   tilapia fillets (6 oz. each)
- 3   Tbsp. butter, melted
- 3   Tbsp. lemon juice
- 1½ tsp. garlic powder
- ⅛   tsp. salt
- 2   Tbsp. capers, drained
- ½   tsp. dried oregano
- ⅛   tsp. paprika

1. Place tilapia in an ungreased 13x9-in. baking dish. In a small bowl, combine the butter, lemon juice, garlic powder and salt; pour over fillets. Sprinkle with capers, oregano and paprika.
2. Bake, uncovered, at 425° until fish just begins to flake easily with a fork, 10-15 minutes.

1 fillet: 224 cal., 10g fat (6g sat. fat), 106mg chol., 304mg sod., 2g carb. (0 sugars, 0 fiber), 32g pro.

COD & ASPARAGUS BAKE

The lemon pulls this flavorful and healthy dish together. You can use grated Parmesan cheese instead of Romano if you'd like.
—Thomas Faglon, Somerset, NJ

TAKES: 30 MIN. • **MAKES:** 4 SERVINGS

- 4   cod fillets (4 oz. each)
- 1   lb. fresh thin asparagus, trimmed
- 1   pint cherry tomatoes, halved
- 2   Tbsp. lemon juice
- 1½ tsp. grated lemon zest
- ¼   cup grated Romano cheese

1. Preheat oven to 375°. Place cod and asparagus in a 15x10x1-in. baking pan brushed with oil. Add tomatoes, cut sides down. Brush the fish with lemon juice; sprinkle with lemon zest. Sprinkle fish and vegetables with Romano cheese. Bake until fish just begins to flake easily with a fork, about 12 minutes.
2. Remove pan from oven; preheat broiler. Broil cod mixture 3-4 in. from heat until vegetables are lightly browned, 2-3 minutes.

1 serving: 141 cal., 3g fat (2g sat. fat), 45mg chol., 184mg sod., 6g carb. (3g sugars, 2g fiber), 23g pro. **Diabetic exchanges:** 3 lean meat, 1 vegetable.

TEST KITCHEN TIP

If asparagus isn't in season, fresh green beans make a fine substitute and will cook in about the same amount of time. We tested cod fillets that were about ¾ in. thick. You'll need to adjust the bake time up or down a bit if your fillets are thicker or thinner.

1 lb. sole fillets,
   cut into 4 portions
¼ tsp. pepper
1 medium lemon, sliced
2 Tbsp. dry white wine or
   chicken broth
2 Tbsp. olive oil, divided
2 cups cherry tomatoes, halved
½ cup Greek olives, halved
1 Tbsp. capers, drained
1 Tbsp. lemon juice
2 garlic cloves, minced
2 Tbsp. minced fresh parsley

1. Preheat oven to 400°. Place each fillet on a piece of heavy-duty foil or parchment (about 12 in. square). Sprinkle fillets with pepper; top with lemon slices. Drizzle with wine and 1 Tbsp. oil.

2. In a small bowl, combine the tomatoes, olives, capers, lemon juice, garlic and remaining 1 Tbsp. oil; spoon over the fillets. Fold foil or parchment around fish, sealing tightly.

3. Place packets on a baking sheet. Bake until fish just begins to flake easily with a fork, 10-12 minutes. Open packets carefully to allow steam to escape. Sprinkle with minced parsley.

1 packet: 211 cal., 14g fat (2g sat. fat), 51mg chol., 669mg sod., 7g carb. (2g sugars, 2g fiber), 15g pro. **Diabetic exchanges:** 3 lean meat, 3 fat, 1 vegetable.

MEDITERRANEAN SOLE
Steaming in parchment is an easy and healthy way to cook fish and veggies. This is a simple recipe, but it's also elegant and incredibly flavorful. Any white fish will work in place of the sole.
—Andrea Potischman, Menlo Park, CA

TAKES: 25 MIN. • **MAKES:** 4 SERVINGS

HADDOCK WITH LIME-CILANTRO BUTTER

In Louisiana, the good times roll when we broil fish and serve it with lots of lime juice, cilantro and butter.
—Darlene Morris, Franklinton, LA

TAKES: 15 MIN. • **MAKES:** 4 SERVINGS

- 4 haddock fillets (6 oz. each)
- ½ tsp. salt
- ¼ tsp. pepper
- 3 Tbsp. butter, melted
- 2 Tbsp. minced fresh cilantro
- 1 Tbsp. lime juice
- 1 tsp. grated lime zest

1. Preheat broiler. Sprinkle fillets with salt and pepper. Place on a greased broiler pan. Broil 4-5 in. from heat until fish flakes easily with a fork, 5-6 minutes.
2. In a small bowl, mix remaining ingredients. Serve over fish.

1 fillet with 1 Tbsp. butter mixture: 227 cal., 10g fat (6g sat. fat), 121mg chol., 479mg sod., 1g carb. (0 sugars, 0 fiber), 32g pro. **Diabetic exchanges:** 4 lean meat, 2 fat.

FETA SHRIMP SKILLET

My husband and I tried a dish similar to this on our honeymoon in Greece. I re-created the flavors in this recipe when we got home. Whenever I make it now, it brings back so many wonderful memories.
—Sonali Ruder, New York, NY

TAKES: 30 MIN. • **MAKES:** 4 SERVINGS

- 1 Tbsp. olive oil
- 1 medium onion, finely chopped
- 3 garlic cloves, minced
- 1 tsp. dried oregano
- ½ tsp. pepper
- ¼ tsp. salt
- 2 cans (14½ oz. each) diced tomatoes, undrained
- ¼ cup white wine, optional
- 1 lb. uncooked shrimp (31-40 per lb.), peeled and deveined
- 2 Tbsp. minced fresh parsley
- ¾ cup crumbled feta cheese

1. In a large nonstick skillet, heat oil over medium-high heat. Add onion; cook and stir 4-6 minutes or until tender. Add garlic and seasonings; cook 1 minute longer. Stir in the tomatoes and, if desired, wine. Bring to a boil. Reduce heat; simmer, uncovered, 5-7 minutes or until sauce is slightly thickened.
2. Add shrimp and parsley; cook 5-6 minutes or until shrimp turn pink, stirring occasionally. Remove from heat; sprinkle with cheese. Let stand, covered, until cheese is softened.

1¼ cups: 240 cal., 8g fat (3g sat. fat), 149mg chol., 748mg sod., 16g carb. (9g sugars, 5g fiber), 25g pro. **Diabetic exchanges:** 3 lean meat, 1 starch, 1 fat.

HEALTH TIP

This saucy dish is terrific served over rice or pasta, but zucchini noodles and spaghetti squash also make delicious bases, and they're low-carb.

COCONUT CITRUS SAUCED COD

I love to make this fusion meal on weeknights when I am short on time but want something big in flavor.
—Roxanne Chan, Albany, CA

TAKES: 30 MIN. • **MAKES:** 4 SERVINGS

- 4 cod fillets (6 oz. each)
- 1 Tbsp. cornstarch
- 1 cup canned coconut milk
- ½ cup orange juice
- 2 Tbsp. sweet chili sauce
- 1 tsp. minced fresh gingerroot
- 1 tsp. soy sauce
- 1 can (11 oz.) mandarin oranges, drained
- 1 green onion, chopped
- 2 Tbsp. sliced almonds
- 1 Tbsp. sesame oil
  Minced fresh cilantro

1. In a large saucepan, place a steamer basket over 1 in. water. Place cod in basket. Bring water to a boil. Reduce heat to maintain a low boil; steam, covered, until fish just begins to flake easily with a fork, 8-10 minutes.
2. Meanwhile, in a small saucepan, whisk cornstarch, coconut milk and orange juice until smooth. Add chili sauce, ginger and soy sauce. Cook and stir over medium heat until thickened, 1-2 minutes. Stir in oranges, green onion, almonds and sesame oil; heat through. Serve with cod; sprinkle with fresh cilantro.

1 serving: 330 cal., 15g fat (10g sat. fat), 65mg chol., 316mg sod., 19g carb. (15g sugars, 1g fiber), 29g pro.

LEMONY SCALLOPS WITH ANGEL HAIR PASTA

This delicate dish tastes so bright with a touch of lemon and tender sauteed scallops. Serve with crusty whole grain bread, and you have an impressive dinner that comes together in a flash.
—Thomas Faglon, Somerset, NJ

TAKES: 25 MIN. • **MAKES:** 4 SERVINGS

- 8 oz. uncooked multigrain angel hair pasta
- 3 Tbsp. olive oil, divided
- 1 lb. sea scallops, patted dry
- 2 cups sliced radishes (about 1 bunch)
- 2 garlic cloves, sliced
- ½ tsp. crushed red pepper flakes
- 6 green onions, thinly sliced
- ½ tsp. kosher salt
- 1 Tbsp. grated lemon zest
- ¼ cup lemon juice

1. In a 6-qt. stockpot, cook pasta according to package directions; drain and return to pot.
2. Meanwhile, in a large skillet, heat 2 Tbsp. oil over medium-high heat; sear the scallops in batches until opaque and edges are golden brown, about 2 minutes per side. Remove from skillet; keep warm.
3. In the same skillet, saute the radishes, garlic and pepper flakes in remaining oil until radishes are tender, 2-3 minutes. Stir in green onions and salt; cook 1 minute. Add to pasta; toss to combine. Sprinkle with lemon zest and juice. Top with scallops to serve.

1½ cups: 404 cal., 13g fat (2g sat. fat), 27mg chol., 737mg sod., 48g carb. (4g sugars, 6g fiber), 25g pro.

TEST KITCHEN TIP

Not a fan of radishes? Simply leave them out, or replace them with green beans or chopped asparagus spears.

⑤ PARMESAN BAKED COD

This is a goof-proof way to keep oven-baked cod moist and flavorful. My mom shared this recipe with me years ago and I've been loving it ever since.
—Mary Jo Hoppe, Pewaukee, WI

TAKES: 25 MIN. • **MAKES:** 4 SERVINGS

- 4 cod fillets (4 oz. each)
- ⅔ cup mayonnaise
- 4 green onions, chopped
- ¼ cup grated Parmesan cheese
- 1 tsp. Worcestershire sauce

1. Preheat oven to 400°. Place the cod in an 8-in. square baking dish coated with cooking spray. Mix the remaining ingredients; spread over the fillets.
2. Bake, uncovered, until fish just begins to flake easily with a fork, 15-20 minutes.

1 fillet: 247 cal., 15g fat (2g sat. fat), 57mg chol., 500mg sod., 7g carb. (2g sugars, 0 fiber), 20g pro. **Diabetic exchanges:** 3 lean meat, 3 fat.

CAJUN SHRIMP

These zippy shrimp bring a lot of pizazz to the table. Use as much or as little of the cayenne pepper as you'd like, depending on your family's tastes. We love ours served alongside rice pilaf.
—Donna Thomason, El Paso, TX

TAKES: 10 MIN. • **MAKES:** 4 SERVINGS

- 2 tsp. paprika
- 1 tsp. dried thyme
- ½ tsp. salt
- ¼ tsp. ground nutmeg
- ¼ tsp. garlic powder
- ⅛ to ¼ tsp. cayenne pepper
- 1 Tbsp. olive oil
- 1 lb. uncooked shrimp (31-40 per lb.), peeled and deveined

In a large nonstick skillet, saute the paprika, thyme, salt, nutmeg, garlic powder and cayenne in oil for 30 seconds, stirring constantly. Add shrimp; saute for 2-3 minutes or until shrimp turn pink, stirring occasionally.

3 oz. cooked shrimp: 131 cal., 5g fat (1g sat. fat), 138mg chol., 430mg sod., 2g carb. (0 sugars, 1g fiber), 19g pro. **Diabetic exchanges:** 3 lean meat, ½ fat.

EASY GLAZED SALMON

It takes only four ingredients and a few moments to make this delightful main dish.
—Tara Ernspiker, Falling Waters, WV

TAKES: 25 MIN. • **MAKES:** 4 SERVINGS

- ⅓ cup packed brown sugar
- ¼ cup unsweetened pineapple juice
- 2 Tbsp. soy sauce
- 4 salmon fillets (6 oz. each)

1. Line a 15x10x1-in. baking pan with foil; grease the foil. Set aside. In a small bowl, combine brown sugar, pineapple juice and soy sauce. Place salmon skin side down on prepared pan. Spoon sauce mixture over fish.
2. Bake, uncovered, at 350° for 20-25 minutes or until fish flakes easily with a fork, basting frequently with pan juices.

1 fillet: 394 cal., 18g fat (4g sat. fat), 100mg chol., 568mg sod., 20g carb. (19g sugars, 0 fiber), 35g pro.

AIR-FRYER SCALLOPS

I never liked seafood until my husband urged me to try scallops, and now I love them. With the crunchy breading, these air-fryer scallops are the best you'll ever have.
—Martina Preston, Willow Grove, PA

TAKES: 25 MIN. • **MAKES:** 2 SERVINGS

- 1 **large egg**
- ⅓ **cup mashed potato flakes**
- ⅓ **cup seasoned bread crumbs**
- ⅛ **tsp. salt**
- ⅛ **tsp. pepper**
- 6 **sea scallops (about ¾ lb.), patted dry**
- 2 **Tbsp. all-purpose flour**
  Butter-flavored cooking spray

1. Preheat air fryer to 400°. In a shallow bowl, lightly beat egg. In another bowl, toss together potato flakes, bread crumbs, salt and pepper. In a third bowl, toss scallops with flour to coat lightly. Dip in egg, then in potato mixture, patting to adhere.
2. Arrange scallops in a single layer on greased tray in air-fryer basket; spritz with cooking spray. Cook until golden brown, 3-4 minutes. Turn; spritz with cooking spray. Cook until breading is golden brown and scallops are firm and opaque, 3-4 minutes longer.
3 scallops: 298 cal., 5g fat (1g sat. fat), 134mg chol., 1138mg sod., 33g carb. (2g sugars, 2g fiber), 28g pro.

TUNA & WHITE BEAN LETTUCE WRAPS

Here's a fabulous way to dress up ordinary tuna salad. This easy recipe makes a quick dinner or lunch at the office, and it's good for you.
—Heather Senger, Madison, WI

TAKES: 20 MIN. • **MAKES:** 4 SERVINGS

- 1 **can (12 oz.) light tuna in water, drained and flaked**
- 1 **can (15 oz.) cannellini beans, rinsed and drained**
- ¼ **cup chopped red onion**
- 2 **Tbsp. olive oil**
- 1 **Tbsp. minced fresh parsley**
- ⅛ **tsp. salt**
- ⅛ **tsp. pepper**
- 12 **Bibb or Boston lettuce leaves (about 1 medium head)**
- 1 **medium ripe avocado, peeled and sliced**

In a small bowl, combine the first 7 ingredients; toss lightly to combine. Serve in lettuce leaves; top with avocado.
3 wraps: 279 cal., 13g fat (2g sat. fat), 31mg chol., 421mg sod., 19g carb. (1g sugars, 7g fiber), 22g pro. **Diabetic exchanges:** 3 lean meat, 2 fat, 1 starch.

ROSEMARY SALMON & VEGGIES

My husband and I eat a lot of salmon. One night while in a rush to get dinner on the table, I created this meal. It's a keeper! You can also include sliced zucchini, small cauliflower florets or fresh green beans.
—Elizabeth Bramkamp, Gig Harbor, WA

TAKES: 30 MIN. • **MAKES:** 4 SERVINGS

- 1½ lbs. salmon fillets, cut into 4 portions
- 2 Tbsp. melted coconut oil or olive oil
- 2 Tbsp. balsamic vinegar
- 2 tsp. minced fresh rosemary or ¾ tsp. dried rosemary, crushed
- 1 garlic clove, minced
- ½ tsp. salt
- 1 lb. fresh asparagus, trimmed
- 1 medium sweet red pepper, cut into 1-in. pieces
- ¼ tsp. pepper
   Lemon wedges

1. Preheat oven to 400°. Place salmon in a greased 15x10x1-in. baking pan. Combine oil, vinegar, rosemary, garlic and salt. Pour half over salmon. Place asparagus and red pepper in a large bowl; drizzle with remaining oil mixture and toss to coat. Arrange around salmon in pan; sprinkle with pepper.
2. Bake until salmon flakes easily with a fork and vegetables are tender, 12-15 minutes. Serve with lemon wedges.
1 serving: 357 cal., 23g fat (9g sat. fat), 85mg chol., 388mg sod., 7g carb. (4g sugars, 2g fiber), 31g pro.
Diabetic exchanges: 4 lean meat, 1½ fat, 1 vegetable.

LEMON-BATTER FISH

Fishing is a popular recreational activity where we live, so folks are always looking for ways to prepare their catches. My husband ranks this as one of his favorite methods.
—Jackie Hannahs, Cedar Springs, MI

TAKES: 25 MIN. • **MAKES:** 6 SERVINGS

- 1½ cups all-purpose flour, divided
- 1 tsp. baking powder
- ¾ tsp. salt
- ½ tsp. sugar
- 1 large egg, lightly beaten
- ⅔ cup water
- ⅔ cup lemon juice, divided
- 2 lbs. perch or walleye fillets, cut into serving-sized pieces
   Oil for frying
   Lemon wedges, optional

1. Combine 1 cup flour, baking powder, salt and sugar. In another bowl, combine egg, water and ⅓ cup lemon juice; stir into dry ingredients until smooth.
2. Place the remaining lemon juice and remaining flour in separate shallow bowls. Dip the fillets in lemon juice, then flour, then coat with the egg mixture.
3. In a large skillet, heat 1 in. oil over medium-high heat. Fry fillets until golden brown and fish flakes easily with a fork, 2-3 minutes on each side. Drain on paper towels. If desired, serve with lemon wedges.
5 oz. cooked fish: 384 cal., 17g fat (2g sat. fat), 167mg chol., 481mg sod., 22g carb. (1g sugars, 1g fiber), 33g pro.
Lime-batter fish: Substitute lime juice for the lemon juice.

TEST KITCHEN TIP

If your cooking oil is not preheated enough, the battered fish will sit in the oil too long and absorb excess oil, causing your fish to become soggy. For best results, slowly heat oil until a deep-fry or candy thermometer reads 350° to 375° and fry as directed.

- 3 to 4 garlic cloves, minced
- ¼ cup butter, cubed
- ¼ cup olive oil
- 1 lb. uncooked shrimp (31-40 per lb.), peeled and deveined
- ¼ cup lemon juice
- ½ tsp. pepper
- ¼ tsp. dried oregano
- ½ cup grated Parmesan cheese
- ¼ cup dry bread crumbs
- ¼ cup minced fresh parsley
  Hot cooked angel hair pasta

1. In a 10-in. ovenproof skillet, saute garlic in butter and oil until fragrant. Add the shrimp, lemon juice, pepper and oregano; cook and stir until shrimp turn pink. Sprinkle with the cheese, bread crumbs and parsley.

2. Broil 6 in. from the heat for 2-3 minutes or until topping is golden brown. Serve with pasta.

1 cup: 395 cal., 30g fat (11g sat. fat), 177mg chol., 420mg sod., 9g carb. (1g sugars, 1g fiber), 24g pro.

Grilled shrimp scampi: Omit the butter, oregano, Parmesan, bread crumbs and pasta. Substitute jumbo shrimp for the medium shrimp. In a large bowl, whisk the garlic, oil, lemon juice and pepper. Add shrimp; toss to coat. Refrigerate, covered, 30 minutes. Thread shrimp onto 4 metal or soaked wooden skewers. Grill, covered, over medium heat or broil 4 in. from heat 6-8 minutes or until shrimp turn pink, turning once. Serve with hot cooked rice; sprinkle with parsley.

Garlic lemon shrimp: Omit the butter, pepper, oregano, Parmesan and bread crumbs. In a large skillet, saute the shrimp in 2 Tbsp. oil for 3 minutes. Add the garlic, 1 Tbsp. lemon juice, 1 tsp. cumin and ¼ tsp. salt; cook and stir until shrimp turn pink. Stir in 2 Tbsp. minced fresh parsley. Serve with pasta.

SHRIMP SCAMPI

This shrimp scampi recipe looks as if you fussed, but it's easy to prepare. Lemon and herbs enhance the shrimp, and bread crumbs add a pleasing crunch. Served over pasta, this main dish is pretty enough for company.
—Lori Packer, Omaha, NE

TAKES: 20 MIN. • **MAKES:** 4 SERVINGS

CORNMEAL CATFISH WITH AVOCADO SAUCE

When I was growing up in California, my mother often made catfish. Now I cook it with my own twist. When only frozen catfish fillets are available, I thaw them in the refrigerator overnight, and they work just as well as fresh.
—Mary Lou Cook, Welches, OR

TAKES: 25 MIN.
MAKES: 4 SERVINGS (¾ CUP SAUCE)

- 1 medium ripe avocado, peeled and cubed
- ⅓ cup reduced-fat mayonnaise
- ¼ cup fresh cilantro leaves
- 2 Tbsp. lime juice
- ½ tsp. garlic salt
- ¼ cup cornmeal
- 1 tsp. seafood seasoning
- 4 catfish fillets (6 oz. each)
- 3 Tbsp. canola oil
- 1 medium tomato, chopped

1. Place the first 5 ingredients in a food processor; process until blended.
2. In a shallow bowl, mix cornmeal and seafood seasoning. Dip catfish in cornmeal mixture to coat both sides; shake off excess.
3. In a large skillet, heat oil over medium heat. Add the catfish in batches; cook 4-5 minutes on each side or until fish flakes easily with a fork. Top with avocado sauce and chopped tomato.

1 fillet with 3 Tbsp. sauce: 505 cal., 37g fat (6g sat. fat), 87mg chol., 649mg sod., 15g carb. (2g sugars, 4g fiber), 29g pro.

SHRIMP ORZO WITH FETA

Tender, hearty and flavorful, this recipe is one of my favorites! Garlic and a splash of lemon add to the fresh taste and heart-healthy benefits of shrimp.
—Sarah Hummel, Moon Township, PA

TAKES: 25 MIN. • **MAKES:** 4 SERVINGS

- 1¼ cups uncooked whole wheat orzo pasta
- 2 Tbsp. olive oil
- 2 garlic cloves, minced
- 2 medium tomatoes, chopped
- 2 Tbsp. lemon juice
- 1¼ lbs. uncooked shrimp (26-30 per lb.), peeled and deveined
- 2 Tbsp. minced fresh cilantro
- ¼ tsp. pepper
- ½ cup crumbled feta cheese

1. Cook orzo according to package directions. Meanwhile, in a large skillet, heat oil over medium heat. Add garlic; cook and stir 1 minute. Add tomatoes and lemon juice. Bring to a boil. Stir in shrimp. Reduce heat; simmer, uncovered, until shrimp turn pink, 4-5 minutes.
2. Drain orzo. Add orzo, cilantro and pepper to shrimp mixture; heat through. Sprinkle with feta cheese.

1 cup: 406 cal., 12g fat (3g sat. fat), 180mg chol., 307mg sod., 40g carb. (2g sugars, 9g fiber), 33g pro.
Diabetic exchanges: 4 lean meat, 2 starch, 1 fat.

TANGY PARMESAN TILAPIA

If you want a gluten-free fish coating, this works beautifully! Some reduced-fat mayos may contain gluten, though, so check the label on yours to be sure.
—Deborah Purdue, Westland, MI

TAKES: 15 MIN. • **MAKES:** 4 SERVINGS

- ¼ cup grated Parmesan cheese
- 2 Tbsp. reduced-fat mayonnaise
- 1 Tbsp. butter, softened
- 1 Tbsp. lime juice
- ⅛ tsp. garlic powder
- ⅛ tsp. dried basil
- ⅛ tsp. pepper
  Dash onion powder
- 4 tilapia fillets (5 oz. each)
- ¼ tsp. salt

1. Preheat broiler. Mix the first 8 ingredients until blended.
2. Line a 15x10x1-in. baking pan with foil; coat foil with cooking spray. Place the tilapia in pan; sprinkle with salt.
3. Broil fish 3-4 in. from heat 2-3 minutes per side. Spread cheese mixture over fillets. Broil until topping is golden brown and fish just begins to flake easily with a fork, 1-2 minutes.

1 fillet: 191 cal., 8g fat (4g sat. fat), 84mg chol., 359mg sod., 2g carb. (0 sugars, 0 fiber), 28g pro. **Diabetic exchanges:** 4 lean meat, 1½ fat.

CRAB-TOPPED FISH FILLETS

These fillets are elegant enough for company but truly no trouble to make. Fish is abundant here in South Florida, and we like to get together with friends in the afternoon, so I often need to whip up a quick dinner when we get home. This dish is one of my husband's all-time favorites.
—Mary Tuthill, Fort Myers Beach, FL

TAKES: 30 MIN. • **MAKES:** 4 SERVINGS

- 4 **sole or cod fillets, or fish fillets of your choice (6 oz. each)**
- 1 **can (6 oz.) crabmeat, drained and flaked, or 1 cup imitation crabmeat, chopped**
- ½ **cup grated Parmesan cheese**
- ½ **cup mayonnaise**
- 1 **tsp. lemon juice**
- ⅓ **cup slivered almonds, toasted Paprika, optional**

1. Preheat oven to 350°. Place fillets in a greased 13x9-in. baking pan. Bake, uncovered, until fish flakes easily with a fork, 18-22 minutes. Meanwhile, in large bowl, combine the crab, cheese, mayonnaise and lemon juice.
2. Drain cooking juices from baking dish; spoon the crab mixture over fillets. Broil 4-5 in. from the heat until topping is lightly browned, about 5 minutes. Sprinkle with almonds and, if desired, paprika.
1 fillet: 429 cal., 31g fat (6g sat. fat), 128mg chol., 1063mg sod., 3g carb. (0 sugars, 1g fiber), 33g pro.

TUSCAN FISH PACKETS

My husband does a lot of fishing, so I'm always looking for different ways to serve his catches. A professional chef was kind enough to share this recipe with me, and I played around with some different veggie combinations until I found the one my family liked best.
—Kathy Morrow, Hubbard, OH

TAKES: 30 MIN. • **MAKES:** 4 SERVINGS

- 1 **can (15 oz.) great northern beans, rinsed and drained**
- 4 **plum tomatoes, chopped**
- 1 **small zucchini, chopped**
- 1 **medium onion, chopped**
- 1 **garlic clove, minced**
- ¼ **cup white wine**
- ¾ **tsp. salt, divided**
- ¼ **tsp. pepper, divided**
- 4 **tilapia fillets (6 oz. each)**
- 1 **medium lemon, cut into 8 thin slices**

1. Preheat oven to 400°. In a bowl, combine beans, tomatoes, zucchini, onion, garlic, wine, ½ tsp. salt and ⅛ tsp. pepper.
2. Rinse the fish and pat dry. Place each fillet on an 18x12-in. piece of heavy-duty foil; season with remaining salt and pepper. Spoon bean mixture over fish; top with lemon slices. Fold foil around fish and crimp edges to seal. Transfer packets to a baking sheet.
3. Bake until fish just begins to flake easily with a fork and vegetables are tender, 15-20 minutes. Be careful of escaping steam when opening packets.
1 serving: 270 cal., 2g fat (1g sat. fat), 83mg chol., 658mg sod., 23g carb. (4g sugars, 7g fiber), 38g pro.
Diabetic exchanges: 5 lean meat, 1 starch, 1 vegetable.

TEST KITCHEN TIP

If you hate to open a bottle of wine for just ¼ cup, look for wine in single-portion plastic bottles. These small bottles are convenient for use in recipes.

PRESSURE-COOKER SIMPLE POACHED SALMON

I love this recipe because it's healthy and almost effortless. The salmon always cooks to perfection and is ready in hardly any time!
—Erin Chilcoat, Central Islip, NY

TAKES: 15 MIN. • **MAKES:** 4 SERVINGS

- 2 cups water
- 1 cup white wine
- 1 medium onion, sliced
- 1 celery rib, sliced
- 1 medium carrot, sliced
- 2 Tbsp. lemon juice
- 3 fresh thyme sprigs
- 1 fresh rosemary sprig
- 1 bay leaf
- ½ tsp. salt
- ¼ tsp. pepper
- 4 salmon fillets
  (1¼ in. thick and 6 oz. each)
  Lemon wedges

1. Combine the first 11 ingredients in a 6-qt. electric pressure cooker; top with salmon. Lock lid; close pressure-release valve. Adjust to pressure-cook on high for 3 minutes. Quick-release pressure. A thermometer inserted in fish should read at least 145°.
2. Remove fish from pressure cooker. Serve warm or cold with lemon wedges.

1 salmon fillet: 270 cal., 16g fat (3g sat. fat), 85mg chol., 115mg sod., 0 carb. (0 sugars, 0 fiber), 29g pro. **Diabetic exchanges:** 4 lean meat.

PARMESAN-CRUSTED TILAPIA

I usually serve this crispy fish with tartar sauce and seasoned steamed veggies. It's like a Friday night fish fry without all the calories!
—Christi McElroy, Neenah, WI

TAKES: 25 MIN. • **MAKES:** 4 SERVINGS

- ½ cup all-purpose flour
- 1 large egg, beaten
- ½ cup crushed Ritz crackers
  (about 10 crackers)
- ¼ cup grated Parmesan cheese
- ½ tsp. salt
- 4 tilapia fillets (5 oz. each)
- 2 Tbsp. olive oil
  Lemon wedges

1. Place flour and egg in separate shallow bowls. In another shallow bowl, combine the crackers, cheese and salt. Dip the fillets in the flour, then egg, then cracker mixture; turn until coated.
2. In a large cast-iron or other heavy skillet, cook fillets in oil over medium heat until fish just begins to flake easily with a fork. Serve with lemon wedges.

1 fillet: 287 cal., 13g fat (3g sat. fat), 125mg chol., 440mg sod., 12g carb. (1g sugars, 0 fiber), 31g pro.

TUNA WITH CITRUS PONZU SAUCE

I like this Asian-inspired tuna because it's easy to prepare, delicious and healthy, too. It's a popular dish with my friends.
—Diane Halferty, Corpus Christi, TX

TAKES: 20 MIN. • **MAKES:** 4 SERVINGS

- ½ tsp. Chinese five-spice powder
- ¼ tsp. salt
- ¼ tsp. cayenne pepper
- 4 tuna steaks (6 oz. each)
- 1 Tbsp. canola oil
- ¼ cup orange juice
- 2 green onions, thinly sliced
- 1 Tbsp. lemon juice
- 1 Tbsp. reduced-sodium soy sauce
- 2 tsp. rice vinegar
- 1 tsp. brown sugar
- ¼ tsp. minced fresh gingerroot

1. Combine the five-spice powder, salt and cayenne; sprinkle over the tuna steaks. In a large skillet, cook the tuna in oil over medium heat for 2-3 minutes on each side for medium-rare or until slightly pink in the center; remove tuna and keep warm.
2. Combine orange juice, onions, lemon juice, soy sauce, vinegar, brown sugar and ginger; pour into skillet. Cook for 1-2 minutes or until slightly thickened. Serve with tuna.

1 tuna steak with 1 Tbsp. sauce: 234 cal., 5g fat (1g sat. fat), 77mg chol., 364mg sod., 5g carb. (3g sugars, 0 fiber), 40g pro. **Diabetic exchanges:** 5 lean meat, ½ fat.

FAJITA-STYLE SHRIMP & GRITS

I combined two of my all-time favorite dishes—shrimp with cheesy grits, and fajitas—into this spicy one-dish meal. For more heat, use pepper jack cheese instead of Mexican cheese blend.
—Arlene Erlbach, Morton Grove, IL

TAKES: 30 MIN. • **MAKES:** 4 SERVINGS

- 1 **lb. uncooked shrimp (16-20 per lb.), peeled and deveined**
- 2 **Tbsp. fajita seasoning mix**
- 1 **cup quick-cooking grits**
- 4 **cups boiling water**
- 1½ **cups shredded Mexican cheese blend**
- 3 **Tbsp. 2% milk**
- 2 **Tbsp. canola oil**
- 3 **medium sweet peppers, seeded and cut into 1-in. strips**
- 1 **medium sweet onion, cut into 1-in. strips**
- 1 **jar (15½ to 16 oz.) chunky medium salsa**
- ¼ **cup orange juice**
- ¼ **cup plus 1 Tbsp. fresh cilantro leaves, divided**

1. Sprinkle the shrimp with fajita seasoning; toss to coat. Set aside.
2. Slowly stir the grits into boiling water. Reduce heat to medium; cook, covered, stirring occasionally, until thickened, 5-7 minutes. Remove from heat. Stir in cheese until melted; stir in milk. Keep warm.
3. In a large skillet, heat oil over medium-high heat. Add peppers and onion; cook and stir until tender and pepper edges are slightly charred. Add the salsa, orange juice and shrimp. Cook, stirring constantly, until shrimp turn pink, 4-6 minutes. Stir in ¼ cup cilantro. Remove from heat.

4. Spoon grits into serving bowls; top with shrimp mixture. Sprinkle with remaining cilantro.
1 serving: 561 cal., 23g fat (8g sat. fat), 176mg chol., 1324mg sod., 55g carb. (12g sugars, 4g fiber), 33g pro.

TEST KITCHEN TIP

Watch the shrimp while they're cooking and remove them from the heat as soon as they're done. Overcooked shrimp are tough and rubbery.

MEATLESS MAINSTAYS

Whether vegetarian dishes are your way of life or you simply like to add meatless Mondays to your meal plan, don't miss these simply fantastic recipes.

SUN-DRIED TOMATO LINGUINE

At my house, this dish is known as Gus's Special Pasta. My oldest child claimed it as his own when he was 8, and I am always happy to oblige his request for this cheesy, garlicky, pungent meal.
—Courtney Gaylord, Columbus, IN

TAKES: 25 MIN. • **MAKES:** 6 SERVINGS

- 1 pkg. (16 oz.) linguine
- 1 jar (7 oz.) julienned oil-packed sun-dried tomatoes
- 6 garlic cloves, minced
- 1 Tbsp. lemon juice
- ½ cup minced fresh parsley
- 1½ cups crumbled feta cheese
- 1½ cups grated Parmesan cheese

1. In a 6-qt. stockpot, cook linguine according to package directions for al dente. Drain, reserving ½ cup pasta water; return linguine to pot.
2. Meanwhile, drain the tomatoes, reserving 2 Tbsp. oil. In a small microwave-safe bowl, combine garlic and reserved oil; microwave on high 45 seconds. Stir in drained tomatoes and lemon juice.
3. Add tomato mixture to linguine. Toss with parsley, cheeses and enough pasta water to moisten.

1⅓ cups: 542 cal., 21g fat (8g sat. fat), 32mg chol., 726mg sod., 68g carb. (3g sugars, 6g fiber), 23g pro.

CRISPY TOFU WITH BLACK PEPPER SAUCE

Sometimes tofu can be boring and tasteless, but not in this recipe! Here the crispy vegetarian bean curd is so loaded with flavor, you'll never shy away from tofu again.
—Nick Iverson, Denver, CO

TAKES: 30 MIN. • **MAKES:** 4 SERVINGS

- 2 Tbsp. reduced-sodium soy sauce
- 2 Tbsp. chili garlic sauce
- 1 Tbsp. packed brown sugar
- 1 Tbsp. rice vinegar
- 4 green onions
- 8 oz. extra-firm tofu, drained
- 3 Tbsp. cornstarch
- 6 Tbsp. canola oil, divided
- 8 oz. fresh sugar snap peas (about 2 cups), trimmed and thinly sliced
- 1 tsp. freshly ground pepper
- 3 garlic cloves, minced
- 2 tsp. grated fresh gingerroot

1. Mix first 4 ingredients. Mince white parts of green onions; thinly slice green parts.
2. Cut tofu into ½-in. cubes; pat dry with paper towels. Toss tofu with cornstarch. In a large skillet, heat 4 Tbsp. oil over medium-high heat. Add the tofu; cook until crisp and golden brown, 5-7 minutes, stirring occasionally. Remove from pan; drain on paper towels.
3. In same pan, heat 1 Tbsp. oil over medium-high heat. Add sugar snap peas; stir-fry until crisp-tender, 2-3 minutes. Remove from pan.
4. In same pan, heat remaining oil over medium-high heat. Add pepper; cook 30 seconds. Add garlic, ginger and minced green onions; stir-fry 30-45 seconds. Stir in soy sauce mixture; cook and stir until slightly thickened. Remove from heat; stir in tofu and peas. Sprinkle with sliced green onions.

1 cup: 316 cal., 24g fat (2g sat. fat), 0 chol., 583mg sod., 20g carb. (8g sugars, 2g fiber), 7g pro.

TEST KITCHEN TIP

To prevent the tofu from sticking, use a nonstick skillet or a cast-iron pan with a generous amount of oil. Make sure the oil is nice and hot before adding the tofu, and allow the tofu to sear in the pan for a few minutes before flipping it. We also recommend using firm or extra-firm tofu.

PENNE WITH VEGGIES & BLACK BEANS

Chock-full of zucchini, sweet pepper, tomato and carrot, this hearty pasta dish puts your garden harvest to good use.
—Vickie Spoerle, Carmel, IN

TAKES: 25 MIN. • **MAKES:** 2 SERVINGS

- ¾ cup uncooked penne pasta
- ⅓ cup sliced zucchini
- ⅓ cup sliced fresh carrot
- 4 medium fresh mushrooms, sliced
- ½ small green pepper, thinly sliced
- ½ small onion, thinly sliced
- 1 small garlic clove, minced
- ¼ tsp. each dried basil, oregano and thyme
- ¼ tsp. salt
- ⅛ tsp. pepper
- 2 tsp. olive oil, divided
- 1 cup canned black beans, rinsed and drained
- ¼ cup chopped seeded tomato
- 2 Tbsp. shredded Parmesan cheese
- 2 tsp. minced fresh parsley

1. Cook pasta according to package directions. Meanwhile, in a large nonstick skillet, saute the zucchini, carrot, mushrooms, green pepper, onion, garlic and seasonings in 1 tsp. oil until crisp-tender. Stir in the beans.
2. Drain pasta; add to vegetable mixture. Add tomato and remaining olive oil; toss gently. Sprinkle with Parmesan cheese and parsley.
1⅓ cups: 300 cal., 7g fat (2g sat. fat), 4mg chol., 643mg sod., 47g carb. (6g sugars, 8g fiber), 14g pro.

MUSHROOM & BROWN RICE HASH WITH POACHED EGGS

I made my mother's famous roast beef hash healthier by using cremini mushrooms instead of beef and brown rice instead of potatoes. It's ideal for a light main dish.
—Lily Julow, Lawrenceville, GA

TAKES: 30 MIN. • **MAKES:** 4 SERVINGS

- 2 Tbsp. olive oil
- 1 lb. sliced baby portobello mushrooms
- ½ cup chopped sweet onion
- 1 pkg. (8.8 oz.) ready-to-serve brown rice
- 1 large carrot, grated
- 2 green onions, thinly sliced
- ½ tsp. salt
- ¼ tsp. pepper
- ¼ tsp. caraway seeds
- 4 large eggs, cold

1. In a large skillet, heat the oil over medium-high heat; saute mushrooms until lightly browned, 5-7 minutes. Add sweet onion; cook 1 minute. Add rice and carrot; cook and stir until vegetables are tender, 4-5 minutes. Stir in green onions, salt, pepper and caraway seeds; heat through.
2. Meanwhile, place 2-3 in. water in a large saucepan or skillet with high sides. Bring to a boil; adjust heat to maintain a gentle simmer. Break cold eggs, 1 at a time, into a small bowl; holding bowl close to surface of water, slip each egg into water.
3. Cook, uncovered, until whites are completely set and yolks begin to thicken but are not hard, 3-5 minutes. Using a slotted spoon, lift eggs out of water. Serve over rice mixture.
1 serving: 282 cal., 13g fat (3g sat. fat), 186mg chol., 393mg sod., 26g carb. (4g sugars, 3g fiber), 13g pro.
Diabetic exchanges: 1½ starch, 1½ fat, 1 medium-fat meat.

BLACK BEAN & SWEET POTATO TOSTADAS

These spicy veggie-packed tostadas won over my meat-loving husband. To make them even faster, shop for baked tostada shells.
—Lauren Delaney-Wallace, Glen Carbon, IL

TAKES: 30 MIN. • **MAKES:** 4 SERVINGS

- 1 medium sweet potato, peeled and cut into ½-in. cubes
- ¼ cup fat-free mayonnaise
- 2 tsp. lime juice
- 1 to 3 tsp. minced chipotle pepper in adobo sauce
- 2 tsp. olive oil
- 1 small onion, chopped
- 2 garlic cloves, minced
- 1½ tsp. ground cumin
- ½ tsp. onion powder
- ½ tsp. pepper
- ¼ tsp. cayenne pepper
- ¼ tsp. salt
- 1 can (15 oz.) black beans, rinsed and drained
- 8 corn tortillas (6 in.) Cooking spray
- 1 cup shredded Monterey Jack cheese Shredded lettuce, optional

1. Preheat broiler. Place sweet potato in a microwave-safe bowl; microwave, covered, on high until tender, 2-3 minutes. For sauce, mix mayonnaise, lime juice and chipotle pepper.

2. In a large saucepan, heat the oil over medium heat; saute onion until tender, 3-4 minutes. Add garlic and seasonings; cook and stir 1 minute. Stir in beans; heat through. Stir in sweet potato; keep warm.

3. In 2 batches, spritz both sides of tortillas with cooking spray and place on a baking sheet; broil 4-5 in. from the heat until crisp and lightly browned, about 1 minute per side. Sprinkle immediately with cheese. To serve, top tortillas with sauce, bean mixture and, if desired, shredded lettuce.

2 tostadas: 407 cal., 15g fat (6g sat. fat), 27mg chol., 676mg sod., 54g carb. (8g sugars, 10g fiber), 16g pro.

DID YOU KNOW?

The best place to store sweet potatoes is in a cool, dark area, not in the fridge. Cold temperatures change a potato's cell structure and make a spud hard in the center.

ONE-POT BLACK BEAN ENCHILADA PASTA

This is an easy vegetarian one-dish recipe you can make for lunch or dinner. My kids love it, so I'm sure your family will be all over it, too! It's ready in less than 30 minutes and full of healthy ingredients—just what a busy weeknight meal calls for.
—Nora Ruöhev, Reitnau, AA

TAKES: 30 MIN. • **MAKES:** 6 SERVINGS

- 4 cups uncooked mini penne or other small pasta
- 4 cups vegetable broth or water
- 1 can (15 oz.) black beans, rinsed and drained
- 1 can (14½ oz.) diced tomatoes, undrained
- 1 medium sweet yellow pepper, chopped
- 1 medium sweet red pepper, chopped
- 1 cup fresh or frozen corn, thawed
- 1 can (10 oz.) enchilada sauce
- 2 Tbsp. taco seasoning
- ½ cup shredded cheddar cheese
  Optional: Fresh cilantro leaves, cherry tomatoes and lime wedges

In a Dutch oven or large skillet, combine the first 9 ingredients. Bring to a boil; reduce heat. Simmer, uncovered, until pasta is al dente and the sauce has thickened slightly, 12-15 minutes. Add cheese; stir until melted. Serve with desired toppings.
1¾ cups: 444 cal., 5g fat (2g sat. fat), 9mg chol., 1289mg sod., 84g carb. (8g sugars, 8g fiber), 18g pro.

5i
POLENTA LASAGNA

Using polenta instead of pasta gives you an amazing twist on lasagna. We love the easy assembly.
—Yevgeniya Farrer, Fremont, CA

TAKES: 25 MIN. • **MAKES:** 4 SERVINGS

- 1½ cups marinara sauce
- 1 tsp. garlic powder
- 1 tsp. herbes de Provence
- 1 tube (18 oz.) polenta, cut into 10 slices
- 1½ cups shredded part-skim mozzarella cheese

1. In a small bowl, mix marinara sauce, garlic powder and herbes de Provence. Arrange half the polenta slices in a greased 8-in. skillet. Top with half the sauce; sprinkle with ¾ cup cheese. Repeat the layers.

2. Cook, uncovered, over medium heat 12-14 minutes or until bubbly. Cover; cook 2-3 minutes longer or until cheese is melted.
Note: Look for herbes de Provence in the spice aisle.
1 piece: 280 cal., 10g fat (5g sat. fat), 25mg chol., 1120mg sod., 32g carb. (8g sugars, 3g fiber), 14g pro.

NUTTY CHEESE TORTELLINI

I like to plant Italian flat-leaf parsley in a long terra-cotta planter so I always have some on hand. It adds bright, fresh flavor to this pasta dish.
—Barbara Penatzer, Vestal, NY

TAKES: 20 MIN. • **MAKES:** 3 SERVINGS

- 1 pkg. (9 oz.) refrigerated cheese tortellini
- ½ cup butter, cubed
- ½ cup minced fresh parsley
- ⅓ cup chopped walnuts, toasted
- ¼ cup shredded Parmesan cheese
  Coarsely ground pepper to taste

Cook tortellini according to package directions; drain and keep warm. In same pan, melt butter. Stir in the tortellini, parsley and walnuts; toss to coat. Sprinkle with cheese and pepper.
1 cup: 650 cal., 48g fat (25g sat. fat), 123mg chol., 677mg sod., 42g carb. (3g sugars, 3g fiber), 17g pro.

2 cups thinly sliced Brussels sprouts
1 cup julienned carrots
1 medium sweet red pepper, julienned
½ tsp. sesame oil
½ tsp. salt
⅛ tsp. freshly ground pepper
1 Tbsp. water
4 large eggs
  Minced fresh chives
  Additional pepper

1. Cook rice according to package directions; cool slightly. Press a fourth of the rice into a ½-cup measuring cup that has been moistened lightly with water; invert onto a large sheet of plastic wrap. Fold plastic around rice; shape rice into a ½-in.-thick patty. Repeat 3 times.
2. In a large nonstick skillet, heat 1 Tbsp. canola oil over medium-high heat. Cook patties until crisp, 3-5 minutes per side; brush the tops with soy sauce after turning. Remove from pan; keep warm.
3. In the same pan, cook and stir vegetables over medium-high heat until lightly browned. Stir in sesame oil, salt and pepper. Add water; reduce heat to medium. Cook, covered, until vegetables are crisp-tender, 1-2 minutes. Remove from pan; keep warm.
4. In same pan, heat remaining canola oil over medium heat. Break the eggs, 1 at a time, into pan; immediately reduce heat to low. Cook, uncovered, until whites are completely set and yolks just begin to thicken, about 5 minutes. To serve, top the rice patties with vegetables and eggs. Sprinkle with chives and additional pepper.
1 serving: 320 cal., 11g fat (2g sat. fat), 186mg chol., 447mg sod., 43g carb. (4g sugars, 3g fiber), 11g pro. **Diabetic exchanges:** 3 starch, 1 medium-fat meat, 1 fat.

CRISPY RICE PATTIES WITH VEGETABLES & EGGS

Serve these patties at any time of day. The recipe features protein, grains and vegetables all in one dish. It's also an amazing way to use leftover rice.
—Megumi Garcia, Milwaukee, WI

TAKES: 30 MIN. • **MAKES:** 4 SERVINGS

2 pkg. (7.4 oz. each) ready-to-serve white sticky rice
1 Tbsp. plus 2 tsp. canola oil, divided
1 tsp. reduced-sodium soy sauce

PERSONAL MARGHERITA PIZZAS

This family-friendly supper is simplicity at its finest. A sprinkling of basil and delectable fresh mozzarella give these little pies Italian flair.

—Jerry Gulley, Pleasant Prairie, WI

TAKES: 25 MIN. • **MAKES:** 3 SERVINGS

- 1 pkg. (6½ oz.) pizza crust mix
- ½ tsp. dried oregano
- ¾ cup pizza sauce
- 6 oz. fresh mozzarella cheese, thinly sliced
- ¼ cup thinly sliced fresh basil leaves

1. Preheat oven to 425°. Prepare pizza dough according to package directions, adding oregano before mixing. Divide into 3 portions.
2. Pat each portion of dough into an 8-in. circle on a greased baking sheet. Bake until the edges are lightly browned, 8-10 minutes.
3. Spread each crust with ¼ cup pizza sauce to within ½ in. of edge. Top with cheese. Bake until the crust is golden and cheese is melted, 5-10 minutes longer. Sprinkle with basil.

1 pizza: 407 cal., 15g fat (8g sat. fat), 45mg chol., 675mg sod., 48g carb. (7g sugars, 3g fiber), 18g pro.

BEANS & RICE DINNER

On cold or rainy days, this comforting dish really fills the tummy. Sometimes I use pinto beans instead of kidney beans or white rice instead of brown. Add rolls and a green salad, and dinner is served!

—Lorraine Caland, Shuniah, ON

TAKES: 30 MIN. • **MAKES:** 4 SERVINGS

- 1 Tbsp. canola oil
- 2 celery ribs, chopped
- 1 medium green pepper, chopped
- 1 medium onion, chopped
- 1 can (28 oz.) diced tomatoes, undrained
- 1 can (16 oz.) kidney beans, rinsed and drained
- 2 cups cooked brown rice
- 2 tsp. Worcestershire sauce
- 1½ tsp. chili powder
- ¼ tsp. pepper
- ¼ cup shredded cheddar cheese
- ¼ cup reduced-fat sour cream
- 2 green onions, chopped

1. In a large nonstick skillet, heat oil over medium-high heat. Add celery, green pepper and onion; cook and stir until tender.
2. Stir in the tomatoes, beans, rice, Worcestershire sauce, chili powder and pepper; bring to a boil. Reduce the heat; simmer, covered, until heated through, 7-9 minutes. Top with the cheese, sour cream and green onions.

1½ cups: 354 cal., 8g fat (3g sat. fat), 13mg chol., 549mg sod., 58g carb. (13g sugars, 12g fiber), 15g pro.

BUDGET MACARONI & CHEESE

You can't beat this comforting recipe to please the family and go easy on the budget. It's a classic, satisfying meatless entree.

—Debbie Carlson, San Diego, CA

TAKES: 20 MIN. • **MAKES:** 4 SERVINGS

- 1 pkg. (7 oz.) elbow macaroni
- 3 Tbsp. butter
- 3 Tbsp. all-purpose flour
- ¼ tsp. salt
  Dash pepper
- 1 cup whole milk
- 1 cup shredded cheddar cheese

1. Cook the macaroni according to package directions. Meanwhile, in a large saucepan, melt butter over medium-low heat. Add the flour, salt and pepper; stir until smooth. Gradually add milk. Bring to a boil; cook and stir for 2 minutes or until thickened. Remove from the heat; stir in cheese until melted.
2. Drain the macaroni. Add to the cheese mixture; toss to coat.

1 serving: 412 cal., 20g fat (13g sat. fat), 61mg chol., 437mg sod., 44g carb. (5g sugars, 2g fiber), 15g pro.

⑤ⓘ FETA-STUFFED PORTOBELLO MUSHROOMS

My husband adores mushrooms, and portobello mushrooms have loads of room for stuffing with feta cheese and pesto. I usually plan on one mushroom per person.
—Amy Martell, Canton, PA

TAKES: 20 MIN. • **MAKES:** 4 SERVINGS

- 4 **large portobello mushrooms (4 to 4½ in. each)**
- 2 **Tbsp. olive oil**
- 1 **garlic clove, minced**
- ¼ **tsp. salt**
- 1 **cup (4 oz.) crumbled feta cheese**
- ½ **cup prepared pesto**

1. Remove and discard stems from mushrooms; with a spoon, scrape and remove gills. In a small bowl, combine oil and garlic; brush over mushrooms. Sprinkle with salt. In a small bowl, combine the cheese and pesto.
2. Place mushrooms on a piece of greased heavy-duty foil (about 12-in. square). Grill mushrooms, stem side up, covered, over medium heat or broil 4 in. from the heat 8-10 minutes, until mushrooms are tender. Spoon the cheese mixture into mushrooms; grill, covered, 2-3 minutes or until the filling is heated through.

1 stuffed mushroom: 273 cal., 22g fat (5g sat. fat), 15mg chol., 783mg sod., 9g carb. (3g sugars, 3g fiber), 9g pro.

CAULIFLOWER & TOFU CURRY

Cauliflower, garbanzo beans and tofu are each subtle on their own, but together they make an awesome base for curry. We have this recipe weekly because one of us is always craving it.
—Patrick McGilvray, Cincinnati, OH

TAKES: 30 MIN. • **MAKES:** 6 SERVINGS

- 1 **Tbsp. olive oil**
- 2 **medium carrots, sliced**
- 1 **medium onion, chopped**
- 3 **tsp. curry powder**
- ¼ **tsp. salt**
- ¼ **tsp. pepper**
- 1 **small head cauliflower, broken into florets (about 3 cups)**
- 1 **can (14½ oz.) fire-roasted crushed tomatoes**
- 1 **pkg. (14 oz.) extra-firm tofu, drained and cut into ½-in. cubes**
- 1 **cup vegetable broth**
- 1 **can (15 oz.) garbanzo beans or chickpeas, rinsed and drained**
- 1 **can (13.66 oz.) coconut milk**
- 1 **cup frozen peas**
  Hot cooked rice
  Chopped fresh cilantro

1. In a 6-qt. stockpot, heat oil over medium-high heat. Add carrots and onion; cook and stir until onion is tender, 4-5 minutes. Stir in the seasonings.
2. Add cauliflower, tomatoes, tofu and broth; bring to a boil. Reduce heat; simmer, covered, 10 minutes. Stir in garbanzo beans, coconut milk and peas; return to a boil. Reduce heat to medium; cook, uncovered, stirring occasionally, until slightly thickened and the cauliflower is tender, 5-7 minutes.
3. Serve with rice. Sprinkle with chopped cilantro.

1⅓ cups: 338 cal., 21g fat (13g sat. fat), 0 chol., 528mg sod., 29g carb. (9g sugars, 7g fiber), 13g pro.

HEALTH TIP

Just a half cup cooked cauliflower provides nearly half the daily value of vitamin C, not to mention compounds that may help protect against certain cancers.

GARDEN VEGETABLE GNOCCHI

When we go meatless, we toss gnocchi (my husband's favorite) with veggies and a dab of prepared pesto. I use zucchini in this 30-minute dish, too.
—Elisabeth Larsen, Pleasant Grove, UT

TAKES: 30 MIN. • **MAKES:** 4 SERVINGS

- 2 medium yellow summer squash, sliced
- 1 medium sweet red pepper, chopped
- 8 oz. sliced fresh mushrooms
- 1 Tbsp. olive oil
- ¼ tsp. salt
- ¼ tsp. pepper
- 1 pkg. (16 oz.) potato gnocchi
- ½ cup Alfredo sauce
- ¼ cup prepared pesto
  Chopped fresh basil, optional

1. Preheat oven to 450°. In a greased 15x10x1-in. baking pan, toss vegetables with oil, salt and pepper. Roast 18-22 minutes or until tender, stirring once.
2. Meanwhile, in a large saucepan, cook gnocchi according to package directions. Drain and return to pan.
3. Stir in the roasted vegetables, Alfredo sauce and pesto. If desired, sprinkle with basil.

1½ cups: 402 cal., 14g fat (4g sat. fat), 17mg chol., 955mg sod., 57g carb. (12g sugars, 5g fiber), 13g pro.

WHITE BEANS & BOW TIES

When we have fresh veggies, we toss them with pasta shapes like penne or bow ties. What a tasty way to enjoy a meatless meal!
—Angela Buchanan, Longmont, CO

TAKES: 25 MIN. • **MAKES:** 4 SERVINGS

- 2½ cups uncooked whole wheat bow tie pasta (about 6 oz.)
- 1 Tbsp. olive oil
- 1 medium zucchini, sliced
- 2 garlic cloves, minced
- 2 large tomatoes, chopped (about 2½ cups)
- 1 can (15 oz.) cannellini beans, rinsed and drained
- 1 can (2¼ oz.) sliced ripe olives, drained
- ¾ tsp. freshly ground pepper
- ½ cup crumbled feta cheese

1. Cook pasta according to package directions. Drain, reserving ½ cup pasta water.
2. Meanwhile, in a large skillet, heat oil over medium-high heat; saute zucchini until crisp-tender, 2-4 minutes. Add garlic; cook and stir 30 seconds. Stir in tomatoes, beans, olives and pepper; bring to a boil. Reduce heat; simmer, uncovered, until tomatoes are softened, 3-5 minutes, stirring occasionally.
3. Stir in pasta and enough pasta water to moisten as desired. Stir in cheese.

1½ cups: 348 cal., 9g fat (2g sat. fat), 8mg chol., 394mg sod., 52g carb. (4g sugars, 11g fiber), 15g pro.

HEALTH TIP

Boost protein in meatless pasta dishes by using whole wheat noodles, adding white beans or stirring in a little cheese—or all three.

CUMIN QUINOA PATTIES

This easy-to-make veggie burger packs an amazing taste, and the crunch from the addition of quinoa makes the texture to die for. This is a simple and delicious vegetarian burger option that you must try. Pan frying adds a perfect crisp that takes it to the next level. The mixture can be made ahead of time, and it freezes very well. Enjoy!
—Beth Klein, Arlington, VA

TAKES: 30 MIN. • **MAKES:** 4 SERVINGS

- 1   **cup water**
- ½   **cup quinoa, rinsed**
- 1   **medium carrot,**
       cut into 1-in. pieces
- 1   **cup canned cannellini beans,**
       rinsed and drained
- ¼   **cup panko bread crumbs**
- 3   **green onions, chopped**
- 1   **large egg, lightly beaten**
- 3   **tsp. ground cumin**
- ¼   **tsp. salt**
- ⅛   **tsp. pepper**
- 2   **Tbsp. olive oil**
       Optional: Sour cream, salsa
       and minced fresh cilantro

1. In a small saucepan, bring water to a boil. Add quinoa. Reduce heat; simmer, covered, until the liquid is absorbed, 12-15 minutes. Remove from heat; fluff with a fork.
2. Meanwhile, place carrot in a food processor; pulse until coarsely chopped. Add beans; process until chopped. Transfer mixture to a large bowl. Mix in cooked quinoa, bread crumbs, green onions, egg and seasonings. Shape mixture into 8 patties.

3. In a large skillet, heat oil over medium heat. Add patties; cook until a thermometer reads 160°, 3-4 minutes on each side, turning carefully. If desired, serve with optional ingredients.
2 patties: 235 cal., 10g fat (1g sat. fat), 47mg chol., 273mg sod., 28g carb. (2g sugars, 5g fiber), 8g pro.
Diabetic exchanges: 2 starch, 1½ fat, 1 lean meat.

51
CHEESY SUMMER SQUASH FLATBREADS

When you want a meatless meal with Mediterranean style, these flatbreads smothered with squash, hummus and mozzarella deliver the goods.
—Matthew Hass, Ellison Bay, WI

TAKES: 30 MIN. • **MAKES:** 4 SERVINGS

- 3 small yellow summer squash, sliced ¼ in. thick
- 1 Tbsp. olive oil
- ½ tsp. salt
- 2 cups fresh baby spinach, coarsely chopped
- 2 naan flatbreads
- ⅓ cup roasted red pepper hummus
- 1 carton (8 oz.) fresh mozzarella cheese pearls
    Pepper

1. Preheat oven to 425°. Toss squash with oil and salt; spread evenly in a 15x10x1-in. baking pan. Roast until tender, 8-10 minutes. Transfer to a bowl; stir in spinach.
2. Place naan on a baking sheet; spread with hummus. Top with squash mixture and cheese. Bake on a lower oven rack just until the cheese is melted, 4-6 minutes. Sprinkle with pepper.

½ topped flatbread: 332 cal., 20g fat (9g sat. fat), 47mg chol., 737mg sod., 24g carb. (7g sugars, 3g fiber), 15g pro.

BLACK BEAN & SWEET POTATO RICE BOWLS

With three hungry boys in my house, dinners need to be quick and filling—it helps to get in some veggies, too. This meal-in-a-bowl is a favorite because it's hearty and fun to tweak with different ingredients.
—Kim Van Dunk, Caldwell, NJ

TAKES: 30 MIN. • **MAKES:** 4 SERVINGS

- ¾ cup uncooked long grain rice
- ¼ tsp. garlic salt
- 1½ cups water
- 3 Tbsp. olive oil, divided
- 1 large sweet potato, peeled and diced
- 1 medium red onion, finely chopped
- 4 cups chopped fresh kale (tough stems removed)
- 1 can (15 oz.) black beans, rinsed and drained
- 2 Tbsp. sweet chili sauce
    Optional: Lime wedges and additional sweet chili sauce

1. Place rice, garlic salt and water in a large saucepan; bring to a boil. Reduce the heat; simmer, covered, until water is absorbed and rice is tender, 15-20 minutes. Remove from heat; let stand 5 minutes.
2. Meanwhile, in a large skillet, heat 2 Tbsp. oil over medium-high heat; saute sweet potato 8 minutes. Add the onion; cook and stir until the potato is tender, 4-6 minutes. Add the kale; cook and stir until tender, 3-5 minutes. Stir in beans; heat through.
3. Gently stir 2 Tbsp. chili sauce and remaining oil into rice; add to potato mixture. If desired, serve with lime wedges and additional chili sauce.

2 cups: 435 cal., 11g fat (2g sat. fat), 0 chol., 405mg sod., 74g carb. (15g sugars, 8g fiber), 10g pro.

HEALTH TIP

When you add together the fiber per serving of the sweet potato, kale and black beans, the sum equals nearly a third of the daily value.

2 cups cavatappi or spiral pasta
3 Tbsp. butter, divided
⅓ cup panko bread crumbs
2 Tbsp. all-purpose flour
1½ cups 2% milk
¾ lb. Velveeta, cubed
¼ cup shredded cheddar cheese

1. Cook pasta according to package directions. Meanwhile, in a large nonstick skillet, melt 1 Tbsp. butter over medium-high heat. Add bread crumbs; cook and stir until golden brown. Remove to a small bowl and set aside.

2. In same skillet, melt remaining butter. Stir in flour until smooth. Gradually add the milk; bring to a boil. Cook and stir until thickened, about 2 minutes. Reduce heat. Stir in Velveeta until melted.

3. Drain pasta; add to the cheese mixture. Cook and stir until heated through, 3-4 minutes. Sprinkle with cheddar cheese and bread crumbs.

1¼ cups: 661 cal., 36g fat (21g sat. fat), 121mg chol., 1267mg sod., 58g carb. (11g sugars, 2g fiber), 27g pro.

TEST KITCHEN TIP

Turn up the fun on pasta night by serving this family favorite as the main attraction in a mac-and-cheese bar. Make it hearty with meaty toppings like crumbled bacon, shredded rotisserie chicken or leftover taco meat, and pile on the freshness with chopped tomatoes, bell peppers, green onions, jalapenos and more.

SAUCY MAC & CHEESE

I love the curly noodles in this creamy recipe. Cavatappi, also sold under the name cellentani, is a corkscrew pasta, but any type of spiral pasta will work. This dish is fun to make and looks so pretty topped with extra cheese and crunchy, golden crumbs. I like to add ground pepper to my serving.
—Sara Martin, Brookfield, WI

TAKES: 25 MIN. • **MAKES:** 4 SERVINGS

SAGE-PECAN BUTTERNUT SQUASH RAVIOLI

I am in love with this ravioli recipe! The sauce is delicious with any pasta, but I like the wow factor of squash ravioli. The flavor is sweet, salty, nutty, buttery and savory all at the same time.
—Barbara Miller, Oakdale, MN

TAKES: 25 MIN. • **MAKES:** 4 SERVINGS

- 1 pkg. (18 oz.) frozen butternut squash ravioli or 2 pkg. (9 oz. each) refrigerated cheese ravioli
- ¾ cup chopped pecans or walnuts
- 3 Tbsp. butter
- ¼ cup packed brown sugar
- ½ tsp. salt
- ¼ tsp. ground nutmeg
- Dash cayenne pepper
- ¼ cup heavy whipping cream
- 2 Tbsp. minced fresh sage or 2 tsp. rubbed sage
  Shaved or shredded Parmesan cheese

1. Cook the ravioli according to package directions.
2. Meanwhile, in a large dry skillet, toast pecans over medium-low heat 1-2 minutes or until lightly browned, stirring occasionally. Stir in butter until melted. Stir in brown sugar, salt, nutmeg and cayenne. Remove from heat; stir in cream and sage.
3. Drain ravioli; add to skillet and toss to coat. Top with cheese.

1 cup: 568 cal., 32g fat (11g sat. fat), 44mg chol., 637mg sod., 63g carb. (19g sugars, 5g fiber), 11g pro.

CHEDDAR BEAN BURRITOS

My family goes meatless several nights a week, and this recipe is one of our favorites. I usually puree a can or two of chipotle peppers in adobo and freeze them in ice cube trays so I can use a small amount when I need it.
—Amy Bravo, Ames, IA

TAKES: 25 MIN. • **MAKES:** 6 SERVINGS

- 2 tsp. canola oil
- 1 Tbsp. minced chipotle pepper in adobo sauce
- 2 garlic cloves, minced
- 2 tsp. chili powder
- 1 tsp. ground cumin
- ⅛ tsp. salt
- 2 cans (15 oz. each) black beans, rinsed and drained
- 2 Tbsp. water
- ½ cup pico de gallo
- 6 flour tortillas (8 in.), warmed
- 1 cup shredded cheddar or Monterey Jack cheese
- ½ cup sour cream
  Optional: Additional pico de gallo and sour cream

1. In a large skillet, heat oil over medium heat; saute the chipotle pepper, garlic and seasonings 2 minutes. Stir in beans and water; bring to a boil. Reduce the heat; simmer, uncovered, until flavors are blended, 5-7 minutes, stirring occasionally.
2. Coarsely mash bean mixture; stir in pico de gallo. Spoon onto tortillas; top with cheese and sour cream. Roll up. If desired, serve with additional pico de gallo and sour cream.

Freeze option: Cool filling before making burritos. Individually wrap burritos in paper towels and foil; freeze in an airtight container. To use, remove foil; place a paper towel-wrapped burrito on a microwave-safe plate. Microwave on high until heated through, 4-6 minutes, turning once. Let stand 2 minutes.

1 burrito: 410 cal., 16g fat (7g sat. fat), 23mg chol., 726mg sod., 50g carb. (2g sugars, 8g fiber), 16g pro.

QUINOA & BLACK BEAN STUFFED PEPPERS

If you're thinking about a meat-free meal, give these no-fuss peppers a try. They come together with just a few ingredients and put a tasty spin on a low-fat dinner!
—Cindy Reams, Philipsburg, PA

TAKES: 30 MIN. • **MAKES:** 4 SERVINGS

- 1½ cups water
- 1 cup quinoa, rinsed
- 4 large green peppers
- 1 jar (16 oz.) chunky salsa, divided
- 1 can (15 oz.) black beans, rinsed and drained
- ½ cup reduced-fat ricotta cheese
- ½ cup shredded Monterey Jack cheese, divided

1. Preheat oven to 400°. In a small saucepan, bring water to a boil. Add quinoa. Reduce the heat; simmer, covered, until water is absorbed, 10-12 minutes.
2. Meanwhile, cut and discard tops from peppers; remove seeds. Place in a greased 8-in. square baking dish, cut sides down. Microwave, uncovered, on high until crisp-tender, 3-4 minutes. Turn the peppers cut side up.
3. Reserve ⅓ cup salsa; add the remaining salsa to quinoa. Stir in beans, ricotta cheese and ¼ cup Monterey Jack cheese. Spoon the mixture into peppers; sprinkle with remaining cheese. Bake, uncovered, 10-15 minutes, until filling is heated through. Top with reserved salsa.

1 stuffed pepper: 393 cal., 8g fat (4g sat. fat), 20mg chol., 774mg sod., 59g carb. (10g sugars, 10g fiber), 18g pro.

VEGETARIAN PAD THAI

Here's my version of pad thai loaded with crisp, colorful vegetables and zesty flavor. Give fresh and simple a try.
—Colleen Doucette, Truro, NS

TAKES: 30 MIN. • **MAKES:** 4 SERVINGS

- 6 oz. uncooked thick rice noodles
- 2 Tbsp. brown sugar
- 3 Tbsp. reduced-sodium soy sauce
- 4 tsp. rice vinegar
- 2 tsp. lime juice
- 2 tsp. olive oil
- 3 medium carrots, shredded
- 1 medium sweet red pepper, cut into thin strips
- 4 green onions, chopped
- 3 garlic cloves, minced
- 4 large eggs, lightly beaten
- 2 cups bean sprouts
- ⅓ cup chopped fresh cilantro
     Chopped peanuts, optional
     Lime wedges

1. Prepare noodles according to package directions. Drain; rinse well and drain again. In a small bowl, mix together brown sugar, soy sauce, vinegar and lime juice.
2. In a large nonstick skillet, heat the oil over medium-high heat; stir-fry carrots and pepper until crisp-tender, 3-4 minutes. Add green onions and garlic; cook and stir 2 minutes. Remove from pan.
3. Reduce heat to medium. Pour eggs into same pan; cook and stir until no liquid egg remains. Stir in carrot mixture, noodles and sauce mixture; heat through. Add bean sprouts; toss to combine. Top with cilantro and, if desired, peanuts. Serve with lime wedges.

1¼ cups: 339 cal., 8g fat (2g sat. fat), 186mg chol., 701mg sod., 55g carb. (15g sugars, 4g fiber), 12g pro.

TORTELLINI WITH TOMATO-CREAM SAUCE

This tortellini with tomato cream sauce is mouthwatering. Put frozen spinach, canned tomatoes and other staples to use in this warm and satisfying dish.
—Barbra Stanger, West Jordan, UT

TAKES: 25 MIN. • **MAKES:** 6 SERVINGS

- 1 pkg. (16 oz.) frozen cheese tortellini
- 1 small onion, chopped
- 2 Tbsp. olive oil
- 3 garlic cloves, minced
- 1 can (14½ oz.) diced tomatoes, undrained
- 1 pkg. (10 oz.) frozen chopped spinach, thawed and squeezed dry
- 1½ tsp. dried basil
- 1 tsp. salt
- ½ tsp. pepper
- 1½ cups heavy whipping cream
- ½ cup grated Parmesan cheese
  Additional grated Parmesan cheese, optional

1. Cook tortellini according to the package directions. Meanwhile, in large skillet, saute onion in oil until tender. Add garlic; cook 1 minute longer. Add the tomatoes, spinach, basil, salt and pepper. Cook and stir over medium heat until liquid is absorbed, about 3 minutes.
2. Stir in cream and cheese. Bring to a boil. Reduce heat; simmer, uncovered, until thickened, 8-10 minutes.
3. Drain tortellini; toss with sauce. Sprinkle with additional cheese if desired.

1 cup: 459 cal., 33g fat (18g sat. fat), 99mg chol., 835mg sod., 29g carb. (4g sugars, 4g fiber), 13g pro.

SPICY VEGGIE PASTA BAKE

My dad cooked with cast-iron skillets, so when I do, I remember his amazing culinary skills. I keep the tradition going with this veggie pasta.
—Sonya Goergen, Moorhead, MN

TAKES: 30 MIN. • **MAKES:** 6 SERVINGS

- 3 cups uncooked spiral pasta
- 1 medium yellow summer squash
- 1 small zucchini
- 1 medium sweet red pepper
- 1 medium green pepper
- 1 Tbsp. olive oil
- 1 small red onion, halved and sliced
- 1 cup sliced fresh mushrooms
- ½ tsp. salt
- ¼ tsp. pepper
- ¼ tsp. crushed red pepper flakes
- 1 jar (24 oz.) spicy marinara sauce
- 8 oz. fresh mozzarella cheese pearls
  Optional: Grated Parmesan cheese and julienned fresh basil

1. Preheat oven to 375°. Cook pasta according to package directions for al dente; drain.
2. Cut squashes and peppers into ¼-in. julienne strips. In a 12-in. cast-iron or other ovenproof skillet, heat oil over medium-high heat. Add the onion, mushrooms and julienned vegetables; cook and stir until crisp-tender, 5-7 minutes. Stir in seasonings. Add marinara sauce and pasta; toss to combine. Top with cheese pearls.
3. Transfer skillet to oven; bake, uncovered, until cheese is melted, 10-15 minutes. If desired, sprinkle with Parmesan cheese and basil before serving.

1⅓ cups: 420 cal., 13g fat (6g sat. fat), 32mg chol., 734mg sod., 57g carb. (12g sugars, 5g fiber), 17g pro.

VEGETARIAN SKILLET ENCHILADAS

Whether served for meatless Monday or your family's everyday vegetarian meal, these unconventional enchiladas will satisfy everyone. Garnish with the optional toppings listed or other favorites like tortilla chips and extra shredded cheese.
—Susan Court, Pewaukee, WI

TAKES: 25 MIN. • **MAKES:** 4 SERVINGS

- 1 Tbsp. canola oil
- 1 medium onion, chopped
- 1 medium sweet red pepper, chopped
- 2 garlic cloves, minced
- 1 can (15 oz.) black beans, rinsed and drained
- 1 can (10 oz.) enchilada sauce
- 1 cup frozen corn
- 2 tsp. chili powder
- ½ tsp. ground cumin
- ⅛ tsp. pepper
- 8 corn tortillas (6 in.), cut into ½-in. strips
- 1 cup shredded Mexican cheese blend
  Optional: Chopped fresh cilantro, sliced avocado, sliced radishes, sour cream and lime wedges

1. Preheat oven to 400°. Heat oil in a 10-in. cast-iron or other ovenproof skillet over medium-high heat. Add onion and pepper; cook and stir until tender, 2-3 minutes. Add the garlic; cook 1 minute longer. Stir in beans, enchilada sauce, corn, chili powder, cumin and pepper. Stir in the tortillas.

2. Bring to a boil. Reduce heat; simmer, uncovered, until tortillas are softened, 3-5 minutes. Sprinkle with cheese. Bake, uncovered, until the sauce is bubbly and cheese is melted, 3-5 minutes. If desired, garnish with optional ingredients.
1½ cups: 307 cal., 14g fat (5g sat. fat), 25mg chol., 839mg sod., 33g carb. (5g sugars, 7g fiber), 14g pro.

TEST KITCHEN TIP

These vegetarian skillet enchiladas last for about 2-3 days in the fridge. If you'd like to enjoy this vegetarian dinner for longer, you can freeze it in an airtight container for up to 3 months.

GRILLED GREATS

What's better than a flame-broiled dinner? One that's ready in a pinch! Fire up the grill and savor the family-pleasing, no-fuss specialties found here.

PLUM-GLAZED PORK KABOBS

Get out there and heat up the grill for pork kabobs, a tasty alternative to chicken and beef. These sweet and gingery beauties always make dinnertime happy.
—Tonya Burkhard, Palm Coast, FL

TAKES: 30 MIN. • **MAKES:** 6 SERVINGS

- ⅓ cup plum jam
- 2 Tbsp. reduced-sodium soy sauce
- 1 garlic clove, minced
- ½ tsp. ground ginger
- 1 medium sweet red pepper
- 1 medium green pepper
- 1 small red onion
- 2 pork tenderloins (¾ lb. each)

1. For glaze, in a small bowl, mix jam, soy sauce, garlic and ginger. Cut the vegetables and pork into 1-in. pieces. On 6 metal or soaked wooden skewers, alternately thread pork and vegetables.

2. On a lightly greased grill rack, grill kabobs, covered, over medium heat 12-15 minutes or until pork is tender, turning occasionally and brushing with ¼ cup glaze during the last 5 minutes. Brush with remaining glaze before serving.

1 kabob: 196 cal., 4g fat (1g sat. fat), 64mg chol., 239mg sod., 15g carb. (12g sugars, 1g fiber), 24g pro. **Diabetic exchanges:** 3 lean meat, 1 starch.

CHICKEN WITH PEACH-CUCUMBER SALSA

To keep our kitchen cool, we grill chicken outdoors and serve it with a minty peach salsa that can easily be made ahead.
—Janie Colle, Hutchinson, KS

TAKES: 25 MIN. • **MAKES:** 4 SERVINGS

- 1½ cups chopped peeled fresh peaches (about 2 medium)
- ¾ cup chopped cucumber
- 4 Tbsp. peach preserves, divided
- 3 Tbsp. finely chopped red onion
- 1 tsp. minced fresh mint
- ¾ tsp. salt, divided
- 4 boneless skinless chicken breast halves (6 oz. each)
- ¼ tsp. pepper

1. For salsa, in a small bowl, combine the peaches, cucumber, 2 Tbsp. preserves, onion, mint and ¼ tsp. salt.

2. Sprinkle chicken with pepper and remaining salt. On a lightly oiled grill rack, grill chicken, covered, over medium heat 5 minutes. Turn; grill 7-9 minutes longer or until a thermometer reads 165°, brushing tops occasionally with remaining preserves. Serve with salsa.

1 chicken breast half with ½ cup salsa: 261 cal., 4g fat (1g sat. fat), 94mg chol., 525mg sod., 20g carb. (17g sugars, 1g fiber), 35g pro. **Diabetic exchanges:** 5 lean meat, ½ starch, ½ fruit.

SUBLIME LIME BEEF

It's fun to watch the happy reactions of others when they try these lime beef kabobs for the first time. They're so good it's hard not to smile.
—Diep Nguyen, Hanford, CA

TAKES: 25 MIN. • **MAKES:** 4 SERVINGS

- ⅓ cup lime juice
- 2 tsp. sugar
- 2 garlic cloves, minced
- 1 beef top sirloin steak (1 in. thick and 1 lb.)
- 1½ tsp. pepper
- ¾ tsp. salt
- 2 Tbsp. unsalted dry roasted peanuts, chopped
- 3 cups hot cooked brown rice

1. In a small bowl, mix lime juice, sugar and garlic until blended; set aside. Cut steak into 2x1x¾-in. pieces; toss with pepper and salt. Thread beef onto 4 metal or soaked wooden skewers.

2. Grill the kabobs, covered, over medium heat or broil 4 in. from heat 2-4 minutes on each side or until beef reaches desired doneness. Add peanuts to sauce; serve with kabobs and rice.

1 kabob with ¾ cup rice and 1 Tbsp. sauce: 352 cal., 8g fat (2g sat. fat), 46mg chol., 502mg sod., 39g carb. (3g sugars, 3g fiber), 29g pro. **Diabetic exchanges:** 3 lean meat, 2½ starch.

GRILLED SALMON WRAPS

We eat fish on Fridays, so I like to experiment with different types. I pulled salmon, spinach and avocado from the fridge for these wraps. My kids loved them, and I did, too! They're delicious, and they contain all five food groups right in one hand-held meal.
—Jennifer Krey, Clarence, NY

TAKES: 25 MIN. • **MAKES:** 4 SERVINGS

- 1 lb. salmon fillet (about 1 in. thick)
- ½ tsp. salt
- ¼ tsp. pepper
- ½ cup salsa verde
- 4 whole wheat tortillas (8 in.), warmed
- 1 cup chopped fresh spinach
- 1 medium tomato, seeded and chopped
- ½ cup shredded Monterey Jack cheese
- ½ medium ripe avocado, peeled and thinly sliced

1. Sprinkle salmon with salt and pepper; place on an oiled grill rack over medium heat, skin side down. Grill, covered, until the fish just begins to flake easily with a fork, 8-10 minutes.
2. Remove from grill. Break salmon into bite-sized pieces, removing skin if desired. Toss gently with salsa; serve in tortillas. Top with remaining ingredients.
1 wrap: 380 cal., 18g fat (5g sat. fat), 69mg chol., 745mg sod., 27g carb. (2g sugars, 5g fiber), 27g pro.
Diabetic exchanges: 3 lean meat, 2 starch, 2 fat.

HASH BROWN-TOPPED STEAK

My husband and I enjoy cooking together. One night we were craving grilled steak and cheese-stuffed baked potatoes but were feeling a little impatient. Here's the quicker meal-in-one idea we invented.
—Judy Armstrong, Prairieville, LA

TAKES: 30 MIN. • **MAKES:** 4 SERVINGS

- 2 Tbsp. butter
- 1 small onion, chopped
- 3 garlic cloves, minced
- 2 cups frozen shredded hash brown potatoes, thawed
- ¾ tsp. salt, divided
- 1 cup shredded Jarlsberg cheese
- 1 beef top sirloin steak (1 in. thick and 1½ lbs.), cut into four portions
- ½ tsp. pepper
- 2 Tbsp. minced fresh chives

1. In a large skillet, heat butter over medium-high heat. Add onion; cook and stir 2-3 minutes or until tender. Add garlic; cook 2 minutes longer.
2. Stir in hash browns and ¼ tsp. salt; spread in even layer. Reduce heat to medium; cook 5 minutes. Turn hash browns over; cook, covered, 5-6 minutes longer or until heated through and bottom is lightly browned. Sprinkle with cheese; cover and remove from heat. Keep warm.
3. Sprinkle beef with pepper and remaining salt. Grill, covered, over medium heat 5-7 minutes on each side or until meat reaches desired doneness (for medium-rare, a thermometer should read 135°; medium, 140°; medium-well, 145°).
4. Remove steaks from heat; top each with a fourth of the potato mixture. Sprinkle with chives.
1 serving: 403 cal., 20g fat (10g sat. fat), 102mg chol., 703mg sod., 10g carb. (1g sugars, 1g fiber), 45g pro.

DAD'S COLA BURGERS

Before you hand out the drinks, save a little soda to make these delectable burgers. Cola—used in the meat mixture and brushed on during cooking—sparks the flavor and takes this favorite to a whole new level.
—Emily Nelson, Green Bay, WI

TAKES: 25 MIN. • **MAKES:** 6 SERVINGS

- ½ cup crushed saltines (about 15 crackers)
- ½ cup (nondiet) cola, divided
- 6 Tbsp. French salad dressing, divided
- 1 large egg
- 2 Tbsp. grated Parmesan cheese
- ½ tsp. salt, divided
- 1½ lbs. lean ground beef (90% lean)
- 6 hamburger buns, split
  Optional toppings:
  Lettuce leaves and tomato and red onion slices

1. Combine saltine crumbs, ¼ cup cola, 3 Tbsp. salad dressing, egg, Parmesan cheese and ¼ tsp. salt. Add beef; mix well. Shape into six ¾-in.-thick patties (the mixture will be moist); sprinkle with remaining salt. Combine remaining ¼ cup cola and 3 Tbsp. salad dressing.
2. Grill patties, covered, over medium heat 3 minutes per side. Brush with cola mixture. Grill, brushing and turning occasionally, until a thermometer reads 160°, 3-4 minutes longer. Serve on buns; if desired, top with lettuce, tomato and onion.
1 burger: 419 cal., 20g fat (6g sat. fat), 103mg chol., 698mg sod., 30g carb. (7g sugars, 1g fiber), 28g pro.

TEST KITCHEN TIP

For a moist burger, don't overhandle the meat before grilling it. If you add seasonings to the ground beef, gently mix them in with 2 forks until just combined.

GRILLED GARDEN VEGGIE PIZZA

Pile on the veggies—the crisp, grilled crust can take it! This colorful, healthy pizza looks as fresh as it tastes.
—Diane Halferty, Corpus Christi, TX

TAKES: 30 MIN. • **MAKES:** 6 SERVINGS

- 1   medium red onion, cut crosswise into ½-in. slices
- 1   large sweet red pepper, halved, stemmed and seeded
- 1   small zucchini, cut lengthwise into ½-in. slices
- 1   yellow summer squash, cut lengthwise into ½-in. slices
- 2   Tbsp. olive oil
- ½   tsp. salt
- ¼   tsp. pepper
- 1   prebaked 12-in. thin whole wheat pizza crust
- 3   Tbsp. jarred roasted minced garlic
- 2   cups shredded part-skim mozzarella cheese, divided
- ⅓   cup torn fresh basil

1. Brush the vegetables with oil; sprinkle with salt and pepper. Grill, covered, over medium heat until tender, 4-5 minutes per side for onion and pepper, 3-4 minutes per side for zucchini and squash.
2. Separate onion into rings; cut pepper into strips. Spread pizza crust with garlic; sprinkle with 1 cup cheese. Top with grilled vegetables, then remaining cheese.
3. Grill pizza, covered, over medium heat until bottom is golden brown and cheese is melted, 5-7 minutes. Top with basil.

1 slice: 324 cal., 15g fat (6g sat. fat), 24mg chol., 704mg sod., 30g carb. (5g sugars, 5g fiber), 16g pro.
Diabetic exchanges: 2 starch, 2 medium-fat meat, 1 fat.

GRILLED PORK CHOPS WITH SMOKIN' SAUCE

While growing up, my husband always had pork chops that were pan-fried or baked, but he knew they could be better. So he combined his love of grilling with the desire to create his own signature sauce, and the result was this recipe.
—Vicky Drnek, Rome, GA

TAKES: 25 MIN. • **MAKES:** 4 SERVINGS

- ¼   cup water
- ¼   cup ketchup
- 1   Tbsp. Dijon mustard
- 1   Tbsp. molasses
- 1½ tsp. brown sugar
- 1   tsp. Worcestershire sauce
- ¼   tsp. kosher salt
- ¼   tsp. chipotle hot pepper sauce
- ⅛   tsp. pepper

PORK CHOPS
- 1¼ tsp. mustard seed
- 1¼ tsp. smoked paprika
- 1¼ tsp. whole peppercorns
- 1   tsp. onion powder
- 1   tsp. garlic powder
- ½   tsp. kosher salt
- ¼   tsp. cayenne pepper
- 1½ tsp. brown sugar
- 4   bone-in pork loin chops (7 oz. each)

1. In a small saucepan, mix first 9 ingredients; bring to a boil over medium heat. Reduce heat; simmer, uncovered, until slightly thickened, 10 minutes, stirring occasionally. Reserve ¼ cup sauce for serving.
2. Using a mortar and pestle or spice grinder, crush seasonings with brown sugar. Rub mixture over chops.

3. Place chops on an oiled grill over medium heat. Grill, covered, until a thermometer reads 145°, 5-6 minutes per side, brushing top with remaining sauce after turning. Let stand 5 minutes before serving. Serve with reserved sauce.

1 pork chop with 1 Tbsp. sauce: 263 cal., 9g fat (3g sat. fat), 86mg chol., 721mg sod., 13g carb. (11g sugars, 1g fiber), 31g pro. **Diabetic exchanges:** 4 lean meat, 1 starch.

1 lb. lean ground beef (90% lean)
½ tsp. salt
¼ tsp. pepper
8 Bibb lettuce leaves
⅓ cup crumbled feta cheese
2 Tbsp. Miracle Whip Light
½ medium ripe avocado, peeled and cut into 8 slices
¼ cup chopped red onion
  Chopped cherry tomatoes, optional

1. In a large bowl, combine beef, salt and pepper, mixing lightly but thoroughly. Shape into eight ½-in.-thick patties.
2. Grill burgers, covered, over medium heat or broil 3-4 in. from heat until a thermometer reads 160°, 3-4 minutes on each side. Place burgers in lettuce leaves. Combine feta and Miracle Whip; spread over burgers. Top with avocado, red onion and, if desired, tomatoes.

2 wraps: 252 cal., 15g fat (5g sat. fat), 78mg chol., 518mg sod., 5g carb. (2g sugars, 2g fiber), 24g pro. **Diabetic exchanges:** 3 lean meat, 2 fat.

TEST KITCHEN TIP

You can always use mayonnaise and a pinch of sugar if you don't have Miracle Whip on hand.

CALIFORNIA BURGER WRAPS

I love the way these fresh flavors blend. It's a snap to throw these wraps together for a quick, healthy lunch. The burgers can also be served on buns if you like.
—Rachelle McCalla, Atlantic, IA

TAKES: 30 MIN. • **MAKES:** 4 SERVINGS

BRUSCHETTA STEAK

My husband and I love bruschetta, especially in the summertime with tomatoes and herbs from our garden.
—Kristy Still, Broken Arrow, OK

TAKES: 25 MIN. • **MAKES:** 4 SERVINGS

- 3 medium tomatoes, chopped
- 3 Tbsp. minced fresh basil
- 3 Tbsp. chopped fresh parsley
- 2 Tbsp. olive oil
- 1 tsp. minced fresh oregano or ½ tsp. dried oregano
- 1 garlic clove, minced
- ¾ tsp. salt, divided
- 1 beef flat iron or top sirloin steak (1 lb.), cut into four portions
- ¼ tsp. pepper
   Grated Parmesan cheese, optional

1. Combine first 6 ingredients; stir in ¼ tsp. salt.

2. Sprinkle beef with pepper and remaining salt. Grill, covered, over medium heat or broil 4 in. from heat until meat reaches desired doneness (for medium-rare, a thermometer should read 135°; medium, 140°), 4-6 minutes per side. Top with tomato mixture. If desired, sprinkle with cheese.

1 steak with ½ cup tomato mixture: 280 cal., 19g fat (6g sat. fat), 73mg chol., 519mg sod., 4g carb. (2g sugars, 1g fiber), 23g pro. **Diabetic exchanges:** 3 lean meat, 1½ fat, 1 vegetable.

🟢**5i**

GRILLED CHICKEN SAUSAGES WITH HARVEST RICE

Try something new on the grill tonight. My husband loves chicken sausage, so I'm always creating new recipes to include it. We prefer the apple-flavored sausages, but any flavor would work well. Experiment to find your own personal favorite.
—Pamela Shank, Parkersburg, WV

TAKES: 25 MIN. • **MAKES:** 4 SERVINGS

- 1¾ cups chicken broth
- 2 cups instant brown rice
- 1 pkg. (12 oz.) frozen cooked winter squash, thawed and drained well
- ⅓ cup dried cranberries
- 1 pkg. (12 oz.) fully cooked apple chicken sausage links or flavor of your choice

1. Bring broth to a boil in a large saucepan. Stir in the rice. Reduce the heat; cover and simmer for 3 minutes. Add squash and simmer, uncovered, for 4-6 minutes or until liquid is absorbed. Remove from the heat. Stir in cranberries; cover and let stand for 5 minutes.

2. Grill sausages, uncovered, over medium heat or broil 4 in. from heat for 8-10 minutes or until heated through, turning often. Slice the sausages and serve with the rice mixture.

1 serving: 421 cal., 9g fat (2g sat. fat), 62mg chol., 911mg sod., 69g carb. (19g sugars, 5g fiber), 20g pro.

GRILLED BRATS WITH SRIRACHA MAYO

I am a Sriracha fanatic, so that's what inspired this dish. Boil the brats in your favorite beer to reduce the fat and give them flavor before grilling, or simply spread garlic butter on lightly toasted buns.
—Quincie Ball, Olympia, WA

TAKES: 20 MIN. • **MAKES:** 4 SERVINGS

- ½ cup mayonnaise
- ⅓ cup minced roasted sweet red peppers
- 3 Tbsp. Sriracha chili sauce
- 1 tsp. hot pepper sauce
- 4 fully cooked bratwurst links
- 4 brat buns or hot dog buns, split
- ½ cup dill pickle relish
- ½ cup finely chopped red onion
  Ketchup, optional

Mix first 4 ingredients. Grill the bratwursts, covered, over medium-low heat until browned and heated through, 7-10 minutes, turning occasionally. Serve in buns with mayonnaise mixture, relish, onion and, if desired, ketchup.

1 serving: 742 cal., 49g fat (13g sat. fat), 65mg chol., 2020mg sod., 54g carb. (10g sugars, 2g fiber), 20g pro.

SIMPLE GRILLED STEAK FAJITAS

After moving to a new state with two toddlers in tow, I came up with effortless fajitas. They make an easy weeknight meal on the grill or in a cast-iron skillet.
—Shannen Mahoney, Yelm, WA

TAKES: 30 MIN. • **MAKES:** 4 SERVINGS

- 1 beef top sirloin steak (¾ in. thick and 1 lb.)
- 2 Tbsp. fajita seasoning mix
- 1 large sweet onion, cut crosswise into ½-in. slices
- 1 medium sweet red pepper, halved
- 1 medium green pepper, halved
- 1 Tbsp. olive oil
- 4 whole wheat tortillas (8 in.), warmed
  Optional: Sliced avocado, minced fresh cilantro and lime wedges

1. Rub steak with seasoning mix. Brush onion and peppers with oil.
2. Grill steak and vegetables, covered, on a greased rack over medium direct heat 4-6 minutes on each side or until meat reaches desired doneness (for medium-rare, a thermometer should read 135°; medium, 140°; and medium-well, 145°) and vegetables are tender. Remove from grill. Let steak stand, covered, 5 minutes before slicing.
3. Cut vegetables and steak into strips; serve in tortillas. If desired, top with avocado and cilantro, and serve with lime wedges.

1 serving: 363 cal., 13g fat (4g sat. fat), 54mg chol., 686mg sod., 34g carb. (6g sugars, 5g fiber), 27g pro.
Diabetic exchanges: 3 lean meat, 2 starch, 1 vegetable, ½ fat.

SPICE-RUBBED CHICKEN THIGHS

Our go-to meal has always been baked chicken thighs. This easy grilled version takes the cooking outside with a zesty rub of turmeric, paprika and chili powder. Yum!
—Bill Staley, Monroeville, PA

TAKES: 20 MIN. • **MAKES:** 6 SERVINGS

- 1 tsp. salt
- 1 tsp. garlic powder
- 1 tsp. onion powder
- 1 tsp. dried oregano
- ½ tsp. ground turmeric
- ½ tsp. paprika
- ¼ tsp. chili powder
- ¼ tsp. pepper
- 6 boneless skinless chicken thighs (about 1½ lbs.)

1. In a small bowl, mix the first 8 ingredients. Sprinkle over both sides of chicken.

2. On a lightly greased grill rack, grill chicken, covered, over medium heat or broil 4 in. from the heat until a thermometer reads 170°, 6-8 minutes on each side.

1 chicken thigh: 169 cal., 8g fat (2g sat. fat), 76mg chol., 460mg sod., 1g carb. (0 sugars, 0 fiber), 21g pro. **Diabetic exchanges:** 3 lean meat.

TUNA WITH TUSCAN WHITE BEAN SALAD

This recipe is for tuna that is still pink in the middle (medium-rare). Increase the cooking time for tuna that is a bit more cooked through. Once the tuna steaks hit the grill, do not move them around or they may tear.
—Vance Werner Jr., Franklin, WI

TAKES: 30 MIN. • **MAKES:** 4 SERVINGS

- 1 can (15 oz.) cannellini beans, rinsed and drained
- 3 celery ribs, finely chopped
- 1 medium sweet red pepper, finely chopped
- 1 plum tomato, seeded and finely chopped
- ½ cup fresh basil leaves, thinly sliced
- ¼ cup finely chopped red onion
- 3 Tbsp. olive oil
- 2 Tbsp. red wine vinegar
- 1 Tbsp. lemon juice
- ¼ tsp. salt
- ¼ tsp. pepper

TUNA
- 4 tuna steaks (6 oz. each)
- 1 Tbsp. olive oil
- ¼ tsp. salt
- ¼ tsp. pepper

1. In a large bowl, combine first 6 ingredients. In a small bowl, whisk the oil, vinegar, lemon juice, salt and pepper. Pour over bean mixture; toss to coat. Refrigerate until serving.

2. Brush tuna with oil. Sprinkle with salt and pepper; place on greased grill rack. Cook, covered, over high heat or broil 3-4 in. from the heat until slightly pink in the center for medium-rare, 3-4 minutes on each side. Serve with salad.

1 tuna steak with 1 cup salad: 409 cal., 16g fat (2g sat. fat), 77mg chol., 517mg sod., 20g carb. (3g sugars, 6g fiber), 45g pro. **Diabetic exchanges:** 5 lean meat, 3 fat, 1 starch, 1 vegetable.

GRILLED CHICKEN CHOPPED SALAD

Layered desserts always grab my family's attention, but basic salads? Not so much. I wondered if I could get everyone on board by presenting a healthy salad in an eye-catching way. I'm happy to say that it worked.
—Christine Hadden, Whitman, MA

TAKES: 30 MIN. • **MAKES:** 4 SERVINGS

1 lb. chicken tenderloins
6 Tbsp. zesty Italian
   salad dressing, divided
2 medium zucchini,
   quartered lengthwise
1 medium red onion, quartered
2 medium ears sweet corn,
   husked
1 bunch romaine, chopped
1 medium cucumber, chopped
   Additional salad dressing,
   optional

1. In a bowl, toss the chicken with 4 Tbsp. dressing. Brush zucchini and onion with the remaining 2 Tbsp. dressing.
2. Place corn, zucchini and onion on a grill rack over medium heat; close lid. Grill zucchini and onion 2-3 minutes on each side or until tender. Grill corn 10-12 minutes or until tender, turning occasionally.
3. Drain the chicken, discarding marinade. Grill chicken, covered, over medium heat 3-4 minutes on each side or until no longer pink.
4. Cut corn from cobs; cut zucchini, onion and chicken into bite-sized pieces. In a 3-qt. trifle bowl or other glass bowl, layer romaine, cucumber, grilled vegetables and chicken. If desired, serve with additional dressing.
3 cups: 239 cal., 5g fat (0 sat. fat), 56mg chol., 276mg sod., 21g carb. (9g sugars, 5g fiber), 32g pro.
Diabetic exchanges: 3 lean meat, 2 vegetable, ½ starch, ½ fat.

HEALTH TIP

Amp up the nutrition factor on this salad by substituting fresh spinach, kale or a combo of both for the romaine.

CILANTRO LIME SHRIMP

A quick garlicky lime marinade works magic on these juicy shrimp. They come off the grill with huge flavors perfect for your next cookout.
—Melissa Rodriguez, Van Nuys, CA

TAKES: 30 MIN. • **MAKES:** 4 SERVINGS

- ⅓ cup chopped fresh cilantro
- 1½ tsp. grated lime zest
- ⅓ cup lime juice
- 1 jalapeno pepper, seeded and minced
- 2 Tbsp. olive oil
- 3 garlic cloves, minced
- ¼ tsp. salt
- ¼ tsp. ground cumin
- ¼ tsp. pepper
- 1 lb. uncooked shrimp (16-20 per lb.), peeled and deveined
  Lime slices

1. Mix first 9 ingredients; toss with shrimp. Let stand 15 minutes.
2. Thread shrimp and lime slices onto 4 metal or soaked wooden skewers. Grill, covered, over medium heat until shrimp turn pink, 2-4 minutes per side.
1 kabob: 167 cal., 8g fat (1g sat. fat), 138mg chol., 284mg sod., 4g carb. (1g sugars, 0 fiber), 19g pro. **Diabetic exchanges:** 3 lean meat, 1½ fat.

GRILLED WHISKEY CHOPS

This is a family favorite for summer. The molasses butter nicely contrasts with the whiskey and peppercorn taste of the chops.
—Kelly Hodson, Anderson, IN

TAKES: 25 MIN. • **MAKES:** 4 SERVINGS

- ¼ cup butter, softened
- 1 Tbsp. molasses
- ½ tsp. ground cinnamon
- ½ tsp. lemon juice
- 3 Tbsp. coarsely ground pepper
- ⅓ cup whiskey
- ½ tsp. salt
- 4 bone-in pork loin chops (¾ in. thick)

1. In a small bowl, mix butter, molasses, cinnamon and lemon juice; refrigerate until serving.
2. Place pepper in a shallow bowl. In a separate shallow bowl, mix whiskey and salt. Dip chops in whiskey mixture, then in pepper.
3. Grill chops, covered, on a lightly greased rack over medium heat or broil 4 in. from heat 4-5 minutes on each side, until a thermometer reads 145°. Let stand 5 minutes. Serve with molasses butter.
1 pork chop with 1 Tbsp. butter mixture: 459 cal., 30g fat (14g sat. fat), 141mg chol., 286mg sod., 7g carb. (3g sugars, 1g fiber), 37g pro.

⑤ⓘ
ROSEMARY-THYME LAMB CHOPS

My father loves lamb, so I make this dish whenever he visits. It's a wonderful main course for holidays or special get-togethers.
—Kristina Mitchell, Clearwater, FL

TAKES: 30 MIN. • **MAKES:** 4 SERVINGS

- 8 lamb loin chops (3 oz. each)
- ½ tsp. pepper
- ¼ tsp. salt
- 3 Tbsp. Dijon mustard
- 1 Tbsp. minced fresh rosemary
- 1 Tbsp. minced fresh thyme
- 3 garlic cloves, minced

1. Sprinkle the lamb chops with pepper and salt. In a small bowl, mix the mustard, rosemary, thyme and garlic.
2. Grill chops, covered, on an oiled rack over medium heat 6 minutes. Turn; spread herb mixture over chops. Grill 6-8 minutes longer or until meat reaches desired doneness (for medium-rare, a thermometer should read 135°; medium, 140°; medium-well, 145°).
2 lamb chops: 231 cal., 9g fat (4g sat. fat), 97mg chol., 493mg sod., 3g carb. (0 sugars, 0 fiber), 32g pro.

4 medium ears sweet corn, husked
1 small red onion, cut crosswise into ½-in. slices
2 Tbsp. olive oil, divided
8 corn tortillas (6 in.)
1 container (8 oz.) hummus
¼ tsp. ground chipotle pepper
1 cup cherry tomatoes, halved
½ tsp. salt
1 medium ripe avocado, peeled and sliced
½ cup crumbled feta cheese
1 jalapeno pepper, thinly sliced
   Optional: Lime wedges, fresh cilantro leaves and Mexican hot pepper sauce

1. Brush corn and onion with 1 Tbsp. oil. Grill corn and onion, covered, over medium-high heat until tender and lightly charred, 5-7 minutes, turning occasionally. Cool slightly.

2. Meanwhile, brush tortillas with remaining oil. Grill, covered, until crisp and lightly browned, 2-3 minutes per side.

3. Cut corn from cobs. Process the hummus, chipotle pepper and 2 cups cut corn in a food processor until almost smooth. Coarsely chop grilled onion; toss with tomatoes, salt and any remaining corn.

4. Spread hummus mixture over tortillas; top with onion mixture, avocado, cheese and jalapeno. If desired, serve with limes, cilantro and pepper sauce.

Note: Wear disposable gloves when cutting hot peppers; the oils can burn skin. Avoid touching your face.

2 tostadas: 453 cal., 23g fat (5g sat. fat), 8mg chol., 692mg sod., 55g carb. (9g sugars, 12g fiber), 14g pro.

GRILLED CORN HUMMUS TOSTADAS

This recipe is a combination of Mediterranean and Mexican cuisines, giving it a unique taste. Avocado and hummus may sound like a weird mix, but they really go together well.
—Lauren McAnelly, Des Moines, IA

TAKES: 30 MIN. • **MAKES:** 4 SERVINGS

GRILLED ZUCCHINI & PESTO PIZZA

Fellow campers who don't think it is possible to have pizza in the backwoods are surprised by this recipe.
—Jesse Arriaga, Reno, NV

TAKES: 20 MIN. • **MAKES:** 6 SERVINGS

- 4   naan flatbreads
- ½   cup prepared pesto
- 2   cups shredded part-skim mozzarella cheese
- 1   medium zucchini, thinly sliced
- 1   small red onion, thinly sliced
- ¼   lb. thinly sliced hard salami, chopped
- ½   cup fresh basil leaves, thinly sliced
- ¼   cup grated Romano cheese

1. Over each naan, spread 2 Tbsp. pesto; top with ½ cup mozzarella and a fourth each of the zucchini, onion and salami.
2. Grill, covered, over medium-low heat until mozzarella has melted and vegetables are tender, 4-6 minutes. Rotate naan halfway through grilling for an evenly browned crust.
3. Remove from heat. Top each naan with basil and Romano; cut into thirds.
2 pieces: 391 cal., 24g fat (9g sat. fat), 51mg chol., 1276mg sod., 25g carb. (4g sugars, 1g fiber), 20g pro.

SPICY SHRIMP & WATERMELON KABOBS

My three sons can polish off a whole watermelon in one sitting. Before they dig in, I set aside a few slices to make these zesty shrimp kabobs.
—Jennifer Fisher, Austin, TX

TAKES: 30 MIN. • **MAKES:** 4 SERVINGS

- 1   Tbsp. reduced-sodium soy sauce
- 1   Tbsp. Sriracha chili sauce
- 1   Tbsp. honey
- 1   garlic clove, minced
- 4   cups cubed seedless watermelon (1 in.), divided
- 1   lb. uncooked shrimp (16-20 per lb.), peeled and deveined
- 1   medium red onion, cut into 1-in. pieces
- ½   tsp. sea salt
- ¼   tsp. coarsely ground pepper
      Minced fresh cilantro, optional

1. For glaze, place soy sauce, chili sauce, honey, garlic and 2 cups watermelon in a blender; cover and process until pureed. Transfer to a small saucepan; bring to a boil. Cook, uncovered, over medium-high heat until mixture is reduced by half, about 10 minutes. Reserve ¼ cup glaze for serving.
2. On 4 metal or soaked wooden skewers, alternately thread shrimp, onion and remaining watermelon. Sprinkle with salt and pepper.
3. Place kabobs on an oiled grill rack over medium heat. Grill, covered, 3-4 minutes on each side or until shrimp turn pink, brushing with remaining glaze during the last 2 minutes. If desired, sprinkle with cilantro. Serve with reserved glaze.
1 kabob with 1 Tbsp. glaze: 172 cal., 2g fat (0 sat. fat), 138mg chol., 644mg sod., 23g carb. (19g sugars, 2g fiber), 20g pro. **Diabetic exchanges:** 3 lean meat, 1 fruit, ½ starch.

HEALTH TIP

A serving of fruit with dinner? Check! You'll event get 20% of your daily value of vitamin C.

SESAME BEEF SKEWERS

A bottle of sesame ginger dressing makes this amazing dish doable on any weeknight. And the pineapple-y salad easily caps off dinner. You can broil the beef, too, but we live in the South where people grill pretty much all year long.
—Janice Elder, Charlotte, NC

TAKES: 30 MIN. • **MAKES:** 4 SERVINGS

- 1   lb. beef top sirloin steak, cut into 1-in. cubes
- 6   Tbsp. sesame ginger salad dressing, divided
- 1   Tbsp. reduced-sodium soy sauce
- 2   cups chopped fresh pineapple
- 2   medium apples, chopped
- 1   Tbsp. sweet chili sauce
- 1   Tbsp. lime juice
- ¼   tsp. pepper
- 1   Tbsp. sesame seeds, toasted

1. In a bowl, toss beef with 3 Tbsp. dressing and soy sauce; let stand 10 minutes. Meanwhile, in a large bowl, combine pineapple, apples, chili sauce, lime juice and pepper; toss to combine.

2. Thread beef onto 4 metal or soaked wooden skewers; discard remaining marinade. Grill kabobs, covered, over medium heat or broil 4 in. from heat until desired doneness, 7-9 minutes, turning occasionally; brush generously with remaining dressing during the last 3 minutes. Sprinkle with sesame seeds. Serve with the pineapple mixture.

1 kabob with 1 cup salad: 311 cal., 11g fat (3g sat. fat), 46mg chol., 357mg sod., 28g carb. (21g sugars, 3g fiber), 25g pro. **Diabetic exchanges:** 3 lean meat, 1 starch, 1 fruit, ½ fat.

LEMON-DILL SALMON PACKETS

Grilling in foil is an easy technique I use with foods that cook quickly, like fish, shrimp, bite-sized meats and fresh veggies. The options are endless and the cleanup is easy.
—A.J. Weinhold, McArthur, CA

TAKES: 25 MIN. • **MAKES:** 4 SERVINGS

- 1   Tbsp. butter, softened
- 4   salmon fillets (6 oz. each)
- ½   tsp. salt
- ¼   tsp. pepper
- ½   medium onion, sliced
- 4   garlic cloves, sliced
- 4   fresh dill sprigs
- 1   Tbsp. minced fresh basil
- 1   medium lemon, sliced

1. Prepare campfire or grill for medium heat. Ready 4 pieces of a double thickness of foil (about 12 in. square). Spread butter in the center of each. Place 1 salmon fillet in the center of each; sprinkle with salt and pepper. Top with onion, garlic, dill, basil and lemon. Fold foil around fillets; seal.

2. Place packets on a grill grate over a campfire or grill. Cook until fish just begins to flake easily with a fork, 8-10 minutes. Open carefully to allow steam to escape.

1 fillet: 305 cal., 19g fat (5g sat. fat), 93mg chol., 405mg sod., 4g carb. (1g sugars, 1g fiber), 29g pro. **Diabetic exchanges:** 5 lean meat, 1 fat.

TEST KITCHEN TIP

No grill? No problem! Just place these packets evenly spaced on a baking sheet and pop them into a 350° oven instead.

TOMATO-HERB GRILLED TILAPIA

This super tilapia with ginger and lemon takes dinner over the top with minimal prep. Grilling the fish in foil is about as easy as it gets.
—Trisha Kruse, Eagle, ID

TAKES: 30 MIN. • **MAKES:** 4 SERVINGS

- 1 cup fresh cilantro leaves
- 1 cup fresh parsley leaves
- 2 Tbsp. olive oil
- 2 tsp. grated lemon zest
- 2 Tbsp. lemon juice
- 1 Tbsp. coarsely chopped fresh gingerroot
- ¾ tsp. sea salt or kosher salt, divided
- 2 cups grape tomatoes, halved lengthwise
- 1½ cups fresh or frozen corn (about 8 oz.), thawed
- 4 tilapia fillets (6 oz. each)

1. Place first 6 ingredients in a food processor; add ½ tsp. salt. Pulse until mixture is finely chopped.
2. In a bowl, combine tomatoes and corn; stir in 1 Tbsp. herb mixture and remaining salt.
3. Place each fillet on a piece of heavy-duty foil (about 12 in. square). Top with herb mixture; spoon tomato mixture alongside fish. Fold foil around fish and vegetables, sealing tightly.
4. Grill, covered, over medium-high heat until fish just begins to flake easily with a fork, 6-8 minutes. Open foil carefully to allow steam to escape.
1 serving: 270 cal., 9g fat (2g sat. fat), 83mg chol., 443mg sod., 15g carb. (6g sugars, 3g fiber), 35g pro.
Diabetic exchanges: 5 lean meat, 1½ fat, 1 vegetable, ½ starch.

GRILLED STEAK & ONION TACOS

Fire up the grill for soft tacos stuffed with zesty beef, sweet and tender red onions, and health-boosting avocado. Oh, yeah!
—*Taste of Home* Test Kitchen

TAKES: 30 MIN. • **MAKES:** 4 SERVINGS

- 1 beef top sirloin steak (1 to 2 lbs.)
- 2 Tbsp. taco seasoning
- 2 medium red onions, cut into ½-in. slices
- 2 tsp. olive oil
- 8 flour tortillas (6 in.)
- 2 medium ripe avocados, peeled and sliced
  Sour cream, fresh cilantro leaves and lime wedges

1. Sprinkle steak with the taco seasoning. Grill steak, covered, on lightly greased rack over medium heat or broil 4 in. from the heat for 6-8 minutes on each side, until meat reaches desired doneness (for medium-rare, a thermometer should read 135°; medium, 140°; medium-well, 145°). Let stand for 5 minutes.
2. Meanwhile, brush onions with oil. Grill, uncovered, over medium heat for 3-4 minutes on each side or until tender.
3. Grill tortillas on each side until warm. Thinly slice the steak. Top tortillas with steak, avocado and onions. Serve with sour cream, cilantro and lime wedges.
2 tacos: 536 cal., 24g fat (6g sat. fat), 46mg chol., 871mg sod., 48g carb. (4g sugars, 9g fiber), 31g pro.

VEGETABLE, STEAK & EGGS

Low-carb doesn't mean skimpy. Here's a lighter take on steak and eggs. I love cooking with squash, but feel free to toss in any vegetable combination you like.
—Robert Deskin, Plantation, FL

TAKES: 30 MIN. • **MAKES:** 4 SERVINGS

- 1 beef skirt steak or flank steak (1 lb.)
- 1 tsp. Montreal steak seasoning
- 2 Tbsp. butter or coconut oil, divided
- 1 medium zucchini, halved lengthwise and cut into ¼-in. slices
- 1 medium yellow summer squash, halved lengthwise and cut into ¼-in. slices
- 1 medium sweet red pepper, chopped
- 5 oz. fresh baby spinach (about 6 cups)
- ½ tsp. salt
- ¼ tsp. pepper
- 4 large eggs
- ¼ cup shredded Parmesan cheese

1. Rub steak with seasoning. Grill steak, covered, over medium-high heat or broil 3-4 in. from the heat 3-5 minutes on each side, until meat reaches desired doneness (for medium-rare, a thermometer should read 135°; medium, 140°; medium-well, 145°). Let stand 5 minutes.

2. Meanwhile, in a large nonstick skillet, heat 1 Tbsp. butter over medium-high heat. Saute zucchini, squash and red pepper until crisp-tender, 5-7 minutes. Add spinach, salt and pepper; cook and stir until wilted, 2 minutes. Divide among 4 plates; keep warm.

3. In the same skillet, heat remaining butter. Break eggs, 1 at a time, into pan; reduce heat to low. Cook to desired doneness. Thinly slice steak across the grain; serve over vegetables. Top with egg and cheese.

1 serving: 344 cal., 21g fat (10g sat. fat), 259mg chol., 770mg sod., 7g carb. (4g sugars, 2g fiber), 33g pro.

TEST KITCHEN TIP

This is a veggie-packed version of steak and eggs. Sirloin steak could be used, too, if you're partial to that cut.

MEXICAN HOT DOGS

My stepmom was born in Mexico and introduced us to hot dogs with avocado and bacon. We were instantly hooked. Now our whole family makes them.
—Amanda Brandenburg, Hamilton, OH

TAKES: 20 MIN. • **MAKES:** 6 SERVINGS

½   medium ripe avocado, peeled
1   Tbsp. lime juice
¼   tsp. salt
⅛   tsp. pepper
6   hot dogs
6   hot dog buns, split
1   small tomato, chopped
3   Tbsp. finely chopped red onion
3   bacon strips,
     cooked and crumbled

1. In a small bowl, mash avocado with a fork, stirring in lime juice, salt and pepper. Grill hot dogs, covered, over medium heat until heated through, 7-9 minutes, turning occasionally.
2. Serve in buns. Top with avocado mixture, tomato, onion and bacon.
1 serving: 310 cal., 19g fat (7g sat. fat), 29mg chol., 844mg sod., 25g carb. (4g sugars, 2g fiber), 11g pro.

5i
GARLIC-RUBBED T-BONES WITH BURGUNDY MUSHROOMS

T-bone steak is a fairly tender cut, so there's no need to marinate. Punch up the flavor using loads of garlic.
—Kevin Black, Cedar Rapids, IA

TAKES: 25 MIN. • **MAKES:** 4 SERVINGS

12   garlic cloves, minced or sliced
1   Tbsp. olive oil
1   tsp. salt
4   beef T-bone or
     porterhouse steaks
     (¾ in. thick and 12 oz. each)
½   cup butter, cubed
1   lb. baby portobello
     mushrooms, thickly sliced
½   cup Burgundy wine or
     reduced-sodium beef broth

1. In a small bowl, combine garlic, oil and salt; rub over both sides of steaks. Grill steaks, covered, over medium heat or broil 4 in. from heat for 4-7 minutes on each side, until meat reaches desired doneness (for medium-rare, a thermometer should read 135°; medium, 140°; medium-well, 145°).
2. Meanwhile, in a large skillet, melt butter over medium-high heat. Add mushrooms; cook and stir for 3-5 minutes or until almost tender. Stir in the wine; bring to a boil. Cook until the liquid is reduced by half, stirring occasionally. Serve over the steaks.
1 steak with ½ cup mushrooms: 621 cal., 42g fat (20g sat. fat), 159mg chol., 886mg sod., 8g carb. (2g sugars, 2g fiber), 51g pro.

TEST KITCHEN TIP

With their large size and meaty texture, portobello mushrooms are well suited for grilling or broiling. They are popularly used as vegetarian burgers and in other vegetarian recipes.

4 tsp. lemon juice
4 halibut fillets (4 to 6 oz. each)
1 tsp. minced fresh gingerroot
¼ to ¾ tsp. salt, divided
¼ tsp. pepper
½ cup water
10 oz. (about 2½ cups) fresh
Brussels sprouts, halved
Crushed red pepper flakes
1 Tbsp. canola oil
5 garlic cloves,
sliced lengthwise
2 Tbsp. sesame oil
2 Tbsp. soy sauce
Lemon slices, optional

1. Brush lemon juice over halibut
fillets. Sprinkle with minced ginger,
¼ tsp. salt and pepper.
2. Place fish on an oiled grill rack,
skin side down. Grill, covered, over
medium heat (or broil 6 in. from
heat) until fish just begins to flake
easily with a fork, 6-8 minutes.
3. In a large skillet, bring water
to a boil over medium-high heat.
Add Brussels sprouts, pepper
flakes and, if desired, remaining
salt. Cook, covered, until tender,
5-7 minutes. Meanwhile, in a small
skillet, heat oil over medium heat.
Add garlic cloves; cook until golden
brown. Drain on paper towels.
4. Drizzle sesame oil and soy sauce
over halibut. Serve with Brussels
sprouts; sprinkle with fried garlic.
If desired, serve with lemon slices.
1 fillet with Brussels sprouts:
234 cal., 12g fat (2g sat. fat), 56mg
chol., 701mg sod., 7g carb. (2g
sugars, 3g fiber), 24g pro. **Diabetic
exchanges:** 3 lean meat, 2 fat,
1 vegetable.

GINGER HALIBUT WITH BRUSSELS SPROUTS

*I moved to the United States from
Russia and love cooking Russian food
for family and friends. Halibut with soy
sauce, ginger and pepper is a favorite.*
—Margarita Parker, New Bern, NC

TAKES: 25 MIN. • **MAKES:** 4 SERVINGS

GRILLED RIBEYES WITH GREEK RELISH

The classic Grecian flavors of olives, feta cheese and tomatoes are a surefire hit. Combine them to complement a perfectly grilled steak, and it's magic.
—Mary Lou Cook, Welches, OR

TAKES: 30 MIN. • **MAKES:** 4 SERVINGS

- 4 plum tomatoes, seeded and chopped
- 1 cup chopped red onion
- ⅔ cup pitted Greek olives
- ¼ cup minced fresh cilantro
- ¼ cup lemon juice, divided
- 2 Tbsp. olive oil
- 2 garlic cloves, minced
- 2 beef ribeye steaks (¾ lb. each)
- 1 cup crumbled feta cheese

1. For relish, combine tomatoes, onion, olives, cilantro, 2 Tbsp. lemon juice, oil and garlic.
2. Drizzle remaining lemon juice over steaks. Grill steaks, covered, over medium heat or broil 4 in. from heat 5-7 minutes on each side, until meat reaches desired doneness (for medium-rare, a thermometer should read 135°; medium, 140°; medium-well, 145°). Let stand 5 minutes before cutting steaks in half. Serve with the relish and cheese.

4 oz. cooked beef with ⅔ cup relish and ¼ cup cheese: 597 cal., 44g fat (16g sat. fat), 115mg chol., 723mg sod., 11g carb. (4g sugars, 3g fiber), 37g pro.

GRILLED SHRIMP & TOMATOES WITH LINGUINE

This pasta came about one night when I started making up dinner as I went along, using what I had on hand. We knew it turned out amazing with the very first bite.
—Lisa Bynum, Brandon, MS

TAKES: 30 MIN. • **MAKES:** 4 SERVINGS

- 8 oz. uncooked linguine
- 16 cherry tomatoes
- 2 Tbsp. olive oil
- 1 lb. uncooked shrimp (26-30 per lb.), peeled and deveined
- ½ tsp. pepper
- ¼ tsp. salt
- ¼ tsp. garlic powder
- ¼ tsp. Italian seasoning
- 2 Tbsp. butter
- ¼ cup grated Parmesan cheese
- 2 Tbsp. torn fresh basil

1. In a large saucepan, cook linguine according to package directions. Meanwhile, thread tomatoes onto metal or soaked wooden skewers; brush with 1 Tbsp. oil. Thread shrimp onto skewers; brush with remaining oil. Mix seasonings; sprinkle over shrimp.
2. Grill shrimp, covered, over medium heat 3-4 minutes on each side or until shrimp turn pink. Grill tomatoes, covered, over medium heat 2-3 minutes or until slightly softened, turning occasionally.
3. Drain linguine, reserving ¼ cup pasta water. In same saucepan, melt butter over medium heat. Add linguine, cheese and reserved pasta water, tossing to combine. Remove shrimp and tomatoes from skewers; serve with pasta. Sprinkle with basil.

1 serving: 445 cal., 17g fat (6g sat. fat), 158mg chol., 416mg sod., 45g carb. (4g sugars, 3g fiber), 29g pro. **Diabetic exchanges:** 3 starch, 3 lean meat, 3 fat.

SPEEDY
SIDE DISHES

Whether seasoned fresh veggies or old-fashioned biscuits, any of these fast fixes will make a fantastic addition to your very next meal.

EASY CHEESY BISCUITS

I'm a big fan of homemade biscuits, but not the rolling and cutting that goes into making them. The drop biscuit method solves everything!
—Christina Addison, Blanchester, OH

TAKES: 30 MIN. • **MAKES:** 1 DOZEN

- 3 cups all-purpose flour
- 3 tsp. baking powder
- 1 Tbsp. sugar
- 1 tsp. salt
- ¾ tsp. cream of tartar
- ½ cup cold butter
- 1 cup shredded sharp cheddar cheese
- 1 garlic clove, minced
- ¼ to ½ tsp. crushed red pepper flakes
- 1¼ cups 2% milk

1. Preheat oven to 450°. In a large bowl, whisk flour, baking powder, sugar, salt and cream of tartar. Cut in butter until mixture resembles coarse crumbs. Stir in the cheese, garlic and pepper flakes. Add milk; stir just until moistened.
2. Drop dough by heaping ¼ cupfuls 2 in. apart onto a greased baking sheet. Bake 18-20 minutes or until golden brown. Serve warm.
1 biscuit: 237 cal., 12g fat (7g sat. fat), 32mg chol., 429mg sod., 26g carb. (2g sugars, 1g fiber), 7g pro.

TABBOULEH

Tabbouleh is a classic Middle Eastern salad. The fresh veggies and mint leaves make it light and refreshing on a hot day.
—Michael & Mathil Chebat, Lake Ridge, VA

TAKES: 30 MIN. • **MAKES:** 8 SERVINGS

- ¼ cup bulgur
- 3 bunches fresh parsley, minced (about 2 cups)
- 3 large tomatoes, finely chopped
- 1 small onion, finely chopped
- ¼ cup lemon juice
- ¼ cup olive oil
- 5 fresh mint leaves, minced
- ½ tsp. salt
- ½ tsp. pepper
- ¼ tsp. cayenne pepper

Prepare bulgur according to the package directions; cool. Transfer to a large bowl. Stir in remaining ingredients. If desired, chill mixture before serving.
⅔ cup: 100 cal., 7g fat (1g sat. fat), 0 chol., 164mg sod., 9g carb. (3g sugars, 2g fiber), 2g pro. **Diabetic exchanges:** 1½ fat, ½ starch.

PARMESAN ROASTED BROCCOLI

Sure, it's simple and healthy but, oh, this roasted broccoli is also delicious. Cutting the stalks into tall trees turns the ordinary veggie into a standout side dish.
—Holly Sander, Lake Mary, FL

TAKES: 30 MIN. • **MAKES:** 4 SERVINGS

- 2 small broccoli crowns (about 8 oz. each)
- 3 Tbsp. olive oil
- ½ tsp. salt
- ½ tsp. pepper
- ¼ tsp. crushed red pepper flakes
- 4 garlic cloves, thinly sliced
- 2 Tbsp. grated Parmesan cheese
- 1 tsp. grated lemon zest

1. Preheat oven to 425°. Cut broccoli crowns into quarters from top to bottom. Drizzle with oil; sprinkle with salt, pepper and pepper flakes. Place in a parchment-lined 15x10x1-in. pan.
2. Roast until crisp-tender, 10-12 minutes. Sprinkle with garlic; roast 5 minutes longer. Sprinkle with cheese; roast until cheese is melted and stalks of broccoli are tender, 2-4 minutes longer. Sprinkle with lemon zest.
2 broccoli pieces: 144 cal., 11g fat (2g sat. fat), 2mg chol., 378mg sod., 9g carb. (2g sugars, 3g fiber), 4g pro. **Diabetic exchanges:** 2 fat, 1 vegetable.

GARDEN SALAD WITH CHICKPEAS

Toss crisp veggies in a light vinaigrette for a chickpea salad that tastes as if it's straight from your garden.
—*Taste of Home* Test Kitchen

TAKES: 25 MIN. • **MAKES:** 6 SERVINGS

⅓ cup olive oil
¼ cup lemon juice
2 Tbsp. red wine vinegar
½ tsp. salt
¼ tsp. pepper
¼ tsp. garlic powder
SALAD
1 can (15 oz.) chickpeas or garbanzo beans, rinsed and drained
2 medium carrots, julienned
1 medium zucchini, julienned
½ cup chopped tomato
4 green onions, thinly sliced
4 radishes, thinly sliced
½ cup chopped pecans, toasted
½ cup coarsely chopped fresh parsley
½ cup crumbled goat cheese
6 cups spring mix salad greens

1. In a small bowl, whisk oil, lemon juice, vinegar, salt, pepper and garlic powder.
2. In a large bowl, combine the chickpeas, carrots, zucchini, tomato, green onions, radishes, pecans, parsley and cheese. Stir in ½ cup dressing. Arrange the greens in a serving bowl; top with chickpea mixture. Drizzle with the remaining dressing.
1 serving: 294 cal., 23g fat (4g sat. fat), 12mg chol., 394mg sod., 21g carb. (5g sugars, 7g fiber), 7g pro.

MISO-BUTTERED SUCCOTASH

The miso paste used in this super simple recipe gives depth and a hint of savoriness to canned or fresh vegetables. To brighten the flavor profile even more, you could add a splash of your favorite white wine.
—William Milton III, Clemson, SC

TAKES: 20 MIN. • **MAKES:** 6 SERVINGS

2 tsp. canola oil
1 small red onion, chopped
2 cans (15¼ oz. each) whole kernel corn, drained
1½ cups frozen shelled edamame, thawed
½ medium sweet red pepper, chopped (about ½ cup)
2 Tbsp. unsalted butter, softened
1 tsp. white miso paste
3 green onions, thinly sliced
Coarsely ground pepper

1. In a large skillet, heat oil over medium-high heat. Add red onion; cook and stir until crisp-tender, 2-3 minutes. Add the corn, edamame and red pepper. Cook until vegetables reach desired tenderness, 4-6 minutes longer.
2. In a small bowl, mix butter and miso paste until combined; stir into pan until melted. Sprinkle with green onions and pepper before serving.
¾ cup: 193 cal., 9g fat (3g sat. fat), 10mg chol., 464mg sod., 20g carb. (11g sugars, 6g fiber), 8g pro.

TEST KITCHEN TIP

White miso paste has a subtle, salty flavor. You can increase the amount of miso in this recipe for more flavor. Leftover miso paste is especially delicious in soups. Or try mixing a bit of leftover miso paste into cold spreads—mix it with mayonnaise, cream cheese or sour cream, for example. It can give salad dressings and marinades a lift, too.

RIB SHACK LOADED MASHED POTATOES

Idaho is well known for being the potato state—even our license plates say "Famous Potatoes"! This is my version of the scrumptious smashers that are served at a local barbecue joint. Everyone who tries them there begs for the recipe, which the place won't give out, so I made my own copycat version. These can be made ahead and kept warm in the slow cooker.
—Trisha Kruse, Eagle, ID

TAKES: 30 MIN. • **MAKES:** 12 SERVINGS

- 2½ lbs. potatoes, peeled and cubed
- 1 cup 2% milk, warmed
- ½ cup spreadable garlic and herb cream cheese
- 3 Tbsp. butter, softened
- 1 lb. bacon strips, cooked and crumbled
- 1 cup shredded cheddar cheese
- ½ cup shredded Parmesan cheese
- 3 green onions, chopped
- 2 Tbsp. minced fresh parsley or 2 tsp. dried parsley flakes
- ¼ tsp. salt
- ¼ tsp. pepper

Place the potatoes in a Dutch oven; add water to cover. Bring to a boil. Reduce heat; cook, uncovered, until tender, 15-20 minutes. Drain and return to pan; gently mash potatoes while gradually adding milk, cream cheese spread and butter to reach desired consistency. Stir in the remaining ingredients.

⅔ cup: 238 cal., 15g fat (8g sat. fat), 41mg chol., 477mg sod., 15g carb. (2g sugars, 1g fiber), 10g pro.

5i

GREAT GARLIC BREAD

This tasty garlic bread topped with cheese adds wow to any pasta dish.
—*Taste of Home* Test Kitchen

TAKES: 15 MIN. • **MAKES:** 8 SERVINGS

- ½ cup butter, melted
- ¼ cup grated Romano cheese
- 4 garlic cloves, minced
- 1 loaf (1 lb.) French bread, halved lengthwise
- 2 Tbsp. minced fresh parsley

1. Preheat oven to 350°. In a small bowl, mix butter, cheese and garlic; brush over cut sides of bread. Place on a baking sheet, cut sides up. Sprinkle with parsley.
2. Bake 7-9 minutes or until light golden brown. Cut bread into slices; serve warm.

1 slice: 283 cal., 14g fat (8g sat. fat), 34mg chol., 457mg sod., 33g carb. (1g sugars, 1g fiber), 8g pro.

5i

CILANTRO GINGER CARROTS

Peppery-sweet ginger and cooling cilantro have starring roles in this colorful side of crisp-tender carrots. The veggie goes from pan to plate in a twinkling.
—*Taste of Home* Test Kitchen

TAKES: 15 MIN. • **MAKES:** 4 SERVINGS

- 1 Tbsp. butter
- 1 lb. fresh carrots, sliced diagonally
- 1½ tsp. minced fresh gingerroot
- 2 Tbsp. chopped fresh cilantro
- ½ tsp. salt
- ¼ tsp. pepper

In a large cast-iron or other heavy skillet, heat butter over medium-high heat. Add carrots; cook and stir until crisp-tender, 4-6 minutes. Add ginger; cook 1 minute longer. Stir in cilantro, salt and pepper.

½ cup: 73 cal., 3g fat (2g sat. fat), 8mg chol., 396mg sod., 11g carb. (5g sugars, 3g fiber), 1g pro. **Diabetic exchanges:** 1 vegetable, ½ fat.

BALSAMIC BRUSSELS SPROUTS

These balsamic Brussels sprouts couldn't be easier to make—and you need only a few ingredients!
—Kallee Krong-Mccreery, Escondido, CA

TAKES: 15 MIN. • **MAKES:** 4 SERVINGS

- 3 to 4 Tbsp. extra virgin olive oil
- 1 pkg. (16 oz.) frozen Brussels sprouts, thawed
- 2 Tbsp. balsamic vinegar
- 2 Tbsp. torn fresh basil leaves
- ½ to 1 tsp. flaky sea salt
- ½ tsp. coarsely ground pepper

In a large skillet, heat oil over medium-high heat. Add Brussels sprouts to skillet and cook until heated through, 5-7 minutes. Transfer to a serving bowl. Drizzle with vinegar; sprinkle with basil, salt and pepper.

⅔ cup: 145 cal., 11g fat (2g sat. fat), 0 chol., 252mg sod., 11g carb. (2g sugars, 4g fiber), 4g pro. **Diabetic exchanges:** 2 fat, 1 vegetable.

AIR-FRYER SWEET POTATO FRIES

I can never get enough of these sweet potato fries! Even though my grocery store sells them in the frozen foods section, I still love to pull sweet potatoes out of my garden and chop them up fresh for this popular side.
—Amber Massey, Argyle, TX

TAKES: 20 MIN. • **MAKES:** 4 SERVINGS

- 2 large sweet potatoes, cut into thin strips
- 2 Tbsp. canola oil
- 1 tsp. garlic powder
- 1 tsp. paprika
- 1 tsp. kosher salt
- ¼ tsp. cayenne pepper

Preheal air fryer to 400°. Combine all ingredients; toss to coat. Place potato strips on greased tray in air-fryer basket. Cook until lightly browned, 10-12 minutes, stirring once. Serve immediately.

1 serving: 243 cal., 7g fat (1g sat. fat), 0 chol., 498mg sod., 43g carb. (17g sugars, 5g fiber), 3g pro.

TEST KITCHEN TIP

If you don't have an air fryer, you can make this recipe in an oven.

EASY CITRUS SEAFOOD SALAD

This super simple, deceptively delicious recipe was inspired by a seafood salad I had in the Bahamas that featured conch. I substituted crab and shrimp for the conch and like it even more!
—Cindy Heyd, Edmond, OK

TAKES: 15 MIN. • **MAKES:** 4 SERVINGS

- 1 medium orange
- 1 medium lemon
- 1 medium lime
- ½ lb. peeled and deveined cooked shrimp (31-40 per lb.), coarsely chopped
- ½ lb. refrigerated fresh or imitation crabmeat, coarsely chopped
- 2 Tbsp. finely chopped sweet onion
- 2 Tbsp. finely chopped sweet red pepper
  Shredded lettuce
  Assorted crackers

Finely grate zest from orange. Cut orange crosswise in half; squeeze juice from orange. Transfer zest and juice to a large bowl. Repeat with lemon and lime. Add shrimp, crab, onion and pepper; toss to coat. Serve on lettuce with crackers.

¾ cup: 128 cal., 2g fat (0 sat. fat), 141mg chol., 309mg sod., 6g carb. (3g sugars, 1g fiber), 22g pro.
Diabetic exchanges: 3 lean meat.

GREEK BROWN & WILD RICE BOWLS

This fresh rice dish tastes like the Mediterranean in a bowl! It is short on ingredients but packs in so much flavor. For a hand-held entree, leave out the rice and tuck the rest of the ingredients in a pita pocket.
—Darla Andrews, Boerne, TX

TAKES: 15 MIN. • **MAKES:** 2 SERVINGS

- 1 pkg. (8½ oz.) ready-to-serve whole grain brown and wild rice medley
- ¼ cup Greek vinaigrette, divided
- ½ medium ripe avocado, peeled and sliced
- ¾ cup cherry tomatoes, halved
- ¼ cup crumbled feta cheese
- ¼ cup pitted Greek olives, sliced
  Minced fresh parsley, optional

In a microwave-safe bowl, combine the rice mix and 2 Tbsp. vinaigrette. Cover and cook on high until heated through, about 2 minutes. Divide between 2 bowls. Top with avocado, tomatoes, cheese, olives, remaining dressing and, if desired, parsley.

1 serving: 433 cal., 25g fat (4g sat. fat), 8mg chol., 1355mg sod., 44g carb. (3g sugars, 6g fiber), 8g pro.

HEALTH TIP

These otherwise healthy bowls are a bit high in sodium because of the prepared rice, dressing, feta cheese and Greek olives. Save on sodium by cooking rice from scratch and using a simple oil and vinegar dressing.

5i BALSAMIC ZUCCHINI SAUTE

This super fast vegetarian dish is flavorful and uses only a few ingredients, so it's easy to whip up as your entree is cooking.
—Elizabeth Bramkamp, Gig Harbor, WA

TAKES: 20 MIN. • **MAKES:** 4 SERVINGS

- 1 Tbsp. olive oil
- 3 medium zucchini, cut into thin slices
- ½ cup chopped sweet onion
- ½ tsp. salt
- ½ tsp. dried rosemary, crushed
- ¼ tsp. pepper
- 2 Tbsp. balsamic vinegar
- ⅓ cup crumbled feta cheese

In a large skillet, heat oil over medium-high heat; saute zucchini and onion until crisp-tender, 6-8 minutes. Stir in seasonings. Add the vinegar; cook and stir 2 minutes. Top with cheese.
½ cup: 94 cal., 5g fat (2g sat. fat), 5mg chol., 398mg sod., 9g carb. (6g sugars, 2g fiber), 4g pro. **Diabetic exchanges:** 1 vegetable, 1 fat.

EDAMAME SALAD WITH SESAME GINGER DRESSING

This bright baby kale salad is packed with a little bit of everything: hearty greens, a nutty crunch, a zip of citrusy goodness and a big protein punch. It's pure bliss in a bowl.
—Darla Andrews, Boerne, TX

TAKES: 15 MIN. • **MAKES:** 6 SERVINGS

- 6 cups baby kale salad blend (about 5 oz.)
- 1 can (15 oz.) garbanzo beans or chickpeas, rinsed and drained
- 2 cups frozen shelled edamame (about 10 oz.), thawed
- 3 clementines, peeled and segmented
- 1 cup fresh bean sprouts
- ½ cup salted peanuts
- 2 green onions, diagonally sliced
- ½ cup sesame ginger salad dressing

Divide salad blend among 6 bowls. Top with all remaining ingredients except salad dressing. Serve with the dressing.
1 serving: 317 cal., 17g fat (2g sat. fat), 0 chol., 355mg sod., 32g carb. (14g sugars, 8g fiber), 13g pro.

DID YOU KNOW?

Edamame is the Japanese name for immature or green soybeans, which are then steamed or boiled. In the frozen vegetable section, they are available shelled or still in their pods.

3 Tbsp. coconut oil
10 oz. medium fresh mushrooms, quartered (about 4 cups)
1 lb. fresh asparagus, trimmed and cut into 1½-in. pieces
2 garlic cloves, thinly sliced
½ tsp. dried oregano
¼ tsp. salt
¼ tsp. pepper
2 cups chopped fresh kale
2 tsp. fish sauce or soy sauce
1 tsp. balsamic vinegar
  Toasted sesame seeds, optional

In a large cast-iron or other heavy skillet, heat oil over medium-high heat. Add the mushrooms; cook, stirring occasionally, until lightly browned, 4-6 minutes. Add the asparagus, garlic, oregano, salt and pepper; cook and stir until crisp-tender, 2-4 minutes. Stir in the kale; cook and stir until wilted, 2-4 minutes. Remove from heat; stir in fish sauce and vinegar. If desired, top with sesame seeds.

¾ cup: 129 cal., 11g fat (9g sat. fat), 0 chol., 383mg sod., 7g carb. (1g sugars, 1g fiber), 4g pro.

TEST KITCHEN TIP

The key ingredient in this side dish—besides the tasty mix of herbs and spices—is fish sauce. It is a smart way to supply a burst of rich flavor even when you're short on time.

FRESH THAI ASPARAGUS, KALE & GARLICKY MUSHROOMS

Hit the local farmers market and stock up! This quick, simple side is a perfect complement to any meal. The fish sauce gives it a wonderful depth of flavor without much effort.
—Julie Peterson, Crofton, MD

TAKES: 30 MIN. • **MAKES:** 4 SERVINGS

KALE CAESAR SALAD

I love Caesar salads, so I created this blend of kale and romaine lettuces with a creamy Caesar salad dressing. It's perfect paired with chicken or steak for a light weeknight meal.
—Rashanda Cobbins, Milwaukee, WI

TAKES: 15 MIN. • **MAKES:** 8 SERVINGS

- 4 cups chopped fresh kale
- 4 cups torn romaine
- 1 cup Caesar salad croutons
- ½ cup shredded Parmesan cheese
- ½ cup mayonnaise
- 2 Tbsp. lemon juice
- 1 Tbsp. Worcestershire sauce
- 2 tsp. Dijon mustard
- 2 tsp. anchovy paste
- 1 garlic clove, minced
- ¼ tsp. salt
- ¼ tsp. pepper

In a large salad bowl, toss kale, romaine, croutons and cheese. For dressing, combine remaining ingredients in a small bowl; pour over the salad and toss to coat. Serve immediately.

1 cup: 148 cal., 13g fat (3g sat. fat), 10mg chol., 417mg sod., 6g carb. (1g sugars, 1g fiber), 3g pro. **Diabetic exchanges:** 2½ fat, 1 vegetable.

5i
OLD BAY CAULIFLOWER

Ready in 10 minutes, this bowl of veggies has three ingredients and a whole lot of flavor. It's the ideal cauliflower side dish.
—Elizabeth Bramkamp, Gig Harbor, WA

TAKES: 10 MIN. • **MAKES:** 4 SERVINGS

- 1 pkg. (16 oz.) frozen cauliflower
- 1 to 2 Tbsp. butter, melted
- 1 to 2 tsp. seafood seasoning

Prepare cauliflower according to package directions; drain. Drizzle with butter; sprinkle with the seafood seasoning.

1 cup: 53 cal., 3g fat (2g sat. fat), 8mg chol., 216mg sod., 5g carb. (3g sugars, 3g fiber), 2g pro. **Diabetic exchanges:** 1 vegetable, ½ fat.

PRESSURE-COOKER CRANBERRY APPLE RED CABBAGE

When I was looking for something new, I started playing with flavors and came up with this very tasty dish. My German grandmother would be impressed, I think! The colorful side is just right with pork.
—Ann Sheehy, Lawrence, MA

TAKES: 20 MIN. • **MAKES:** 8 SERVINGS

- 1 medium head red cabbage, coarsely chopped
- 1 can (14 oz.) whole-berry cranberry sauce
- 2 medium Granny Smith apples, peeled and coarsely chopped
- 1 medium onion, chopped
- ½ cup cider vinegar
- ¼ cup sweet vermouth, white wine or unsweetened apple juice, optional
- 1 tsp. kosher salt
- ¾ tsp. caraway seeds
- ½ tsp. coarsely ground pepper

Combine all ingredients; transfer to a 6-qt. electric pressure cooker. Lock lid; close pressure-release valve. Adjust to pressure-cook on high for 3 minutes. Allow pressure to naturally release for 5 minutes. Quick-release any remaining pressure. Serve cabbage with a slotted spoon.

¾ cup: 144 cal., 0 fat (0 sat. fat), 0 chol., 296mg sod., 34g carb. (21g sugars, 4g fiber), 2g pro.

⑤ⁱ

GRANDMA'S BISCUITS

Homemade biscuits add a warm and comforting touch to any meal. My grandmother makes these tender biscuits to go with her seafood chowder. They're a family favorite.
—Melissa Obernesser, Oriskany, NY

TAKES: 25 MIN. • **MAKES:** 10 BISCUITS

- 2 cups all-purpose flour
- 3 tsp. baking powder
- 1 tsp. salt
- ⅓ cup shortening
- ⅔ cup 2% milk
- 1 large egg, lightly beaten

1. Preheat oven to 450°. In a large bowl, whisk flour, baking powder and salt. Cut in shortening until mixture resembles coarse crumbs. Add milk; stir just until moistened.
2. Turn dough onto a lightly floured surface; knead gently 8-10 times. Pat dough into a 10x4-in. rectangle. Cut rectangle lengthwise in half; cut crosswise to make 10 squares.
3. Place 1 in. apart on an ungreased baking sheet; brush tops with the egg. Bake until golden brown, 8-10 minutes. Serve warm.
1 biscuit: 165 cal., 7g fat (2g sat. fat), 20mg chol., 371mg sod., 20g carb. (1g sugars, 1g fiber), 4g pro.

CARIBBEAN ISLAND COLESLAW

After trying a similar version of this coleslaw while visiting the island of St. Kitts, I returned home and wanted to make it myself. I've taken it to so many events, and it's always a hit.
—Noreen McCormick Danek, Cromwell, CT

TAKES: 15 MIN. • **MAKES:** 10 SERVINGS

- 2 pkg. (14 oz. each) coleslaw mix
- 1 cup unsweetened pineapple tidbits
- ½ cup sweetened shredded coconut
- ½ cup golden raisins
- ½ cup finely chopped sweet red pepper
- 1½ cups mayonnaise
- ½ cup unsweetened pineapple juice
- ¾ tsp. salt
- ¼ tsp. celery seed
- ¼ tsp. pepper

Place the first 5 ingredients in a serving bowl. In a small bowl, combine remaining ingredients. Pour over slaw mix; toss to coat. Refrigerate until serving.
¾ cup: 305 cal., 26g fat (5g sat. fat), 2mg chol., 378mg sod., 19g carb. (14g sugars, 3g fiber), 2g pro.

TEST KITCHEN TIP

Remember this change-of-pace salad the next time you need a potluck or picnic contribution.

5i
SYRIAN GREEN BEANS WITH FRESH HERBS

This is how my mom always made green beans. She got the recipe from a neighbor when we lived in Turkey. I often make a double batch, as the beans make an excellent healthy snack straight from the fridge. Add a thinly sliced onion and red bell pepper if you like. Another idea is to make them ahead to add to a salad.
—Trisha Kruse, Eagle, ID

TAKES: 25 MIN. • **MAKES:** 6 SERVINGS

- 2 Tbsp. olive oil
- 2 garlic cloves, minced
- 1 lb. fresh green beans, cut into 2-in. pieces
- ½ tsp. salt
- ¼ tsp. pepper
- 2 Tbsp. each minced fresh cilantro, parsley and mint

In a large skillet, heat the oil over medium heat. Add garlic; cook for 1 minute. Add green beans, salt and pepper. Cook, covered, until crisp-tender, 8-10 minutes, stirring occasionally. Add herbs; cook and stir just until beans are tender, 1-2 minutes.
¾ cup: 66 cal., 5g fat (1g sat. fat), 0 chol., 203mg sod., 6g carb. (2g sugars, 3g fiber), 2g pro. **Diabetic exchanges:** 1 vegetable, 1 fat.

CAPRESE MACARONI SALAD

When tomatoes and basil are abundant in the summer, I like to do everything I can with these wonderful ingredients, including preparing this salad.
—Debbie Glasscock, Conway, AR

TAKES: 20 MIN. • **MAKES:** 7 SERVINGS

- 2 cups uncooked elbow macaroni
- 1 cup mayonnaise
- 1 Tbsp. Italian salad dressing mix
- 2 tsp. sugar
- ¾ tsp. ground mustard
- ¼ tsp. salt
- ⅛ tsp. pepper
- 1 pint cherry tomatoes, halved
- 1 cup fresh mozzarella cheese pearls
- ¼ cup fresh basil leaves, slivered
- 2 Tbsp. grated Parmesan cheese

1. Cook macaroni according to the package directions; drain and rinse with cold water. Cool completely.
2. For the dressing, in a small bowl, combine mayonnaise, dressing mix, sugar, mustard, salt and pepper. In a large bowl, combine tomatoes, mozzarella and macaroni. Add the dressing; gently toss to coat. Refrigerate until serving. Top with basil and Parmesan before serving.
¾ cup: 397 cal., 31g fat (8g sat. fat), 29mg chol., 458mg sod., 20g carb. (4g sugars, 1g fiber), 10g pro.

DID YOU KNOW?
Caprese salad is said to be named after the island of Capri, where it's believed the salad was first created.

⑤ⓘ SHAVED FENNEL SALAD

This salad tastes even more impressive than it looks. It's got an incredible crunch thanks to the cucumbers, radishes and apples, and the finish of fennel fronds adds just the faintest hint of licorice flavor.
—William Milton III, Clemson, SC

TAKES: 15 MIN. • **MAKES:** 8 SERVINGS

- 1 large fennel bulb, fronds reserved
- 1 English cucumber
- 1 medium Honeycrisp apple
- 2 Tbsp. extra virgin olive oil
- ½ tsp. kosher salt
- ¼ tsp. coarsely ground pepper
- 2 radishes, thinly sliced

With a mandoline or vegetable peeler, cut the fennel, cucumber and apple into very thin slices. Transfer to a large bowl; toss with olive oil, salt and pepper. Top with radishes and reserved fennel fronds to serve.

¾ cup: 55 cal., 4g fat (1g sat. fat), 0 chol., 138mg sod., 6g carb. (4g sugars, 2g fiber), 1g pro. **Diabetic exchanges:** 1 vegetable, 1 fat.

PARMESAN SCONES

The addition of onions gives these scones a nice bite. You can even stir in some basil or oregano if you like.
—Jolie Stinson, Marion, IN

TAKES: 25 MIN. • **MAKES:** 1 DOZEN

- 2 cups finely chopped onions
- 2 Tbsp. olive oil
- 6 garlic cloves, minced
- 4 cups all-purpose flour
- 2 cups grated Parmesan cheese
- 4 tsp. baking powder
- 1 tsp. salt
- 2 cups heavy whipping cream
  Additional grated Parmesan cheese, optional

1. In a large skillet, saute onions in oil until tender. Add garlic; saute 1 minute longer.
2. In a large bowl, combine flour, cheese, baking powder and salt. Stir in cream just until moistened. Stir in onion mixture.
3. Turn onto a floured surface; knead 10 times. Divide dough in half. Pat each portion into a 6-in. circle. Cut each circle into 6 wedges. Separate wedges and place on a greased baking sheet.
4. Bake at 400° for 12-15 minutes or until light golden brown. If desired, sprinkle with additional cheese in last 5 minutes of baking. Serve scones warm.

1 scone: 378 cal., 21g fat (12g sat. fat), 66mg chol., 551mg sod., 36g carb. (2g sugars, 2g fiber), 11g pro.

TEST KITCHEN TIP

For a tasty grab-and-go breakfast, set the English muffins or flour tortillas aside and turn these savory scones into egg and cheese sandwiches.

5i GRILLED GARLIC NAAN

Indian food is my all-time favorite and no meal is complete without some naan. I like to brush grilled or baked naan with lots of butter, garlic and a little chopped cilantro.
—Jerry Gulley, Pleasant Prairie, WI

TAKES: 10 MIN. • **MAKES:** 4 SERVINGS

- 2 Tbsp. butter, melted
- 3 garlic cloves, minced
- 2 naan flatbreads

Stir together the butter and garlic. Place naan on grill rack; grill over medium-high heat until bottom is golden brown, about 2 minutes. Flip and brush top with the garlic butter. Grill until golden brown on bottom. Remove; cut each naan in half.

1 slice: 134 cal., 8g fat (4g sat. fat), 18mg chol., 286mg sod., 15g carb. (2g sugars, 1g fiber), 2g pro.

SUMMER ZUCCHINI PASTA

This simple and healthy pasta is a wonderful side or meatless entree, but you can add shredded chicken or grilled salmon for a heartier dish.
—Beth Berlin, Oak Creek, WI

TAKES: 25 MIN. • **MAKES:** 10 SERVINGS

- 1 pkg. (16 oz.) pappardelle or tagliatelle pasta
- ¼ cup olive oil
- 2 small zucchini, cut into thin ribbons
- 2 small yellow summer squash, cut into thin ribbons
- 4 garlic cloves, thinly sliced
- 2 cans (14½ oz. each) diced tomatoes with roasted garlic, undrained
- ⅓ cup loosely packed basil leaves, torn
- 1 Tbsp. coarsely chopped fresh rosemary
- ½ tsp. salt
- ¼ tsp. crushed red pepper flakes

Cook pasta according to package directions. Meanwhile, in a Dutch oven, heat oil over medium-high heat. Add zucchini and yellow squash; cook and stir until crisp-tender, 3-4 minutes. Add garlic; cook 1 minute longer. Add the tomatoes, basil, rosemary, salt and pepper flakes; heat through. Drain pasta; serve with zucchini mixture. If desired, top with additional basil.

1 cup: 254 cal., 7g fat (1g sat. fat), 0 chol., 505mg sod., 42g carb. (8g sugars, 3g fiber), 7g pro.

SPICY FRIED OKRA

This fried veggie is a southern delicacy that's sure to add excitement to any summer meal.
—Rashanda Cobbins, Milwaukee, WI

TAKES: 30 MIN. • **MAKES:** 4 SERVINGS

- 3 cups sliced fresh or frozen okra, thawed
- 6 Tbsp. buttermilk
- 2 tsp. Louisiana-style hot sauce
- ¼ cup all-purpose flour
- ¼ cup cornmeal
- ½ tsp. seasoned salt
- ¼ tsp. cayenne pepper
  Oil for deep-fat frying
  Optional: Additional salt and pepper

1. Pat okra dry with paper towels. Place buttermilk and hot sauce in a shallow bowl. In another shallow bowl, combine the flour, cornmeal, salt and pepper. Dip the okra in buttermilk mixture, then roll in cornmeal mixture.
2. In a cast-iron or other heavy skillet, heat 1 in. oil to 375°. Fry okra, a few pieces at a time, until golden brown, 1½-2½ minutes on each side. Drain on paper towels. If desired, season with additional salt and pepper.

¾ cup: 237 cal., 16g fat (1g sat. fat), 1mg chol., 326mg sod., 20g carb. (4g sugars, 3g fiber), 5g pro.

CHERRY TOMATO PASTA WITH AVOCADO SAUCE

Heart-healthy avocado makes this pasta dish feel indulgent without being overly rich. The flavorful sauce is so luscious, you'll think there is cream hiding in there. It's guilt-free and dairy-free, but with a texture and consistency that's similar to traditional cream-based sauces.
—Julie Peterson, Crofton, MD

TAKES: 30 MIN. • **MAKES:** 10 SERVINGS

- 1 pkg. (14½ oz.) protein-enriched rotini (about 3½ cups uncooked)
- 2 medium ripe avocados, peeled and pitted
- 1 cup fresh spinach
- ¼ cup loosely packed basil leaves
- 2 garlic cloves, halved
- 2 Tbsp. lime juice
- ½ tsp. kosher salt
- ¼ tsp. coarsely ground pepper
- ⅓ cup olive oil
- 1 cup assorted cherry tomatoes, halved
- ½ cup pine nuts
  Optional: Shredded Parmesan cheese, shredded mozzarella cheese and grated lime zest

1. Cook rotini according to package directions for al dente. Meanwhile, place avocados, spinach, basil, garlic, lime juice, salt and pepper in a food processor; pulse until chopped. Continue processing while gradually adding oil in a steady stream.
2. Drain the rotini; transfer to a large bowl. Add avocado mixture and tomatoes; toss to coat. Sprinkle with pine nuts, and add toppings as desired.

¾ cup: 314 cal., 18g fat (2g sat. fat), 0 chol., 125mg sod., 32g carb. (2g sugars, 5g fiber), 9g pro.

TEST KITCHEN TIP

This pasta will last about 3 days in the fridge if you keep it covered tightly, but the avocado sauce will start to brown slightly, which is natural and normal. The lime juice in the sauce does help slow the browning process.

🟠 ORANGE & OLIVES SALAD

My grandmother made sure this salad was on our holiday table every year. We always celebrated the rustic Italian way, and she made lots of delicious food. This is simple to make and so light—it didn't fill us up before one of her marvelous meals. It even looks pretty on the table.
—Angela David, Lakeland, FL

TAKES: 10 MIN. • **MAKES:** 16 SERVINGS

- 4 **large navel oranges, peeled and sliced**
- 2 **cans (6 oz. each) pitted ripe olives, drained**
- 1 **Tbsp. canola oil**
- ⅛ **tsp. pepper**

Arrange orange slices along outer edge of a serving dish, leaving center open. Place olives in center of dish. Drizzle with oil; sprinkle with pepper.

1 serving: 54 cal., 3g fat (0 sat. fat), 0 chol., 185mg sod., 7g carb. (4g sugars, 2g fiber), 1g pro. **Diabetic exchanges:** ½ fruit, ½ fat.

🟠 QUICK CHEESY BROCCOLI

Topped with crumbs, this cheesy broccoli is a decadent side dish for any occasion. Plus, it can be on the table in just 10 minutes!
—Joan Hallford, North Richland Hills, TX

TAKES: 10 MIN. • **MAKES:** 4 SERVINGS

- 1 **pkg. (16 oz.) frozen broccoli florets**
- ⅓ **cup panko bread crumbs, toasted**
- ⅓ **cup extra-sharp shredded cheddar cheese**
- ½ **tsp. salt**
- ¼ **tsp. pepper**
- ¼ **tsp. garlic powder**

Prepare broccoli according to the package directions; drain. Combine bread crumbs, cheese, salt, pepper and garlic powder; sprinkle over the broccoli.

1 cup: 101 cal., 4g fat (2g sat. fat), 9mg chol., 109mg sod., 9g carb. (3g sugars, 3g fiber), 5g pro. **Diabetic exchanges:** 1 vegetable, ½ fat.

HONEY-LEMON ASPARAGUS

Everyone who tastes my glazed asparagus takes a second helping, so I usually double the recipe. For another option, try using a root vegetable like turnip or parsnip.
—Lorraine Caland, Shuniah, ON

TAKES: 15 MIN. • **MAKES:** 8 SERVINGS

- 2 **lbs. fresh asparagus, trimmed**
- ¼ **cup honey**
- 2 **Tbsp. butter**
- 2 **Tbsp. lemon juice**
- 1 **tsp. sea salt**
- 1 **tsp. balsamic vinegar**
- 1 **tsp. Worcestershire sauce**
  Additional sea salt, optional

1. In a large saucepan, bring 8 cups water to a boil. Add the asparagus in batches; cook, uncovered, 1-2 minutes or just until crisp-tender. Drain and pat dry.
2. Meanwhile, in a small saucepan, combine next 6 ingredients. Bring to a boil. Reduce the heat; simmer, uncovered, 2 minutes or until slightly thickened.
3. Transfer asparagus to a large bowl; drizzle with glaze and toss gently to coat. If desired, sprinkle with additional sea salt.

1 serving: 73 cal., 3g fat (2g sat. fat), 8mg chol., 276mg sod., 12g carb. (10g sugars, 1g fiber), 2g pro. **Diabetic exchanges:** 1 vegetable, ½ starch, ½ fat.

NO-BAKE DESSERTS

Life is too short to pass up dessert, even on your busiest nights! Surrender to temptation with these fast-to-fix sweets that don't require you to heat up the oven.

NUTTY RICE KRISPIE COOKIES

My mom and I used to prepare these treats for Christmas every year. Making them with just the microwave means they're super easy and fun to mix with the kids.
—Savanna Chapdelaine, Orlando, FL

TAKES: 15 MIN.
MAKES: ABOUT 2 DOZEN

- 1 pkg. (10 to 12 oz.) white baking chips
- ¼ cup creamy peanut butter
- 1 cup miniature marshmallows
- 1 cup Rice Krispies
- 1 cup salted peanuts

In a large microwave-safe bowl, melt baking chips; stir until smooth. Stir in peanut butter until blended. Add marshmallows, Rice Krispies and peanuts. Drop by heaping tablespoonfuls onto waxed paper-lined baking sheets. Cool completely. Store in an airtight container.
1 cookie: 127 cal., 8g fat (3g sat. fat), 2mg chol., 49mg sod., 11g carb. (9g sugars, 1g fiber), 3g pro.

SIMPLE TURTLE CHEESECAKE

For an almost instant dessert, I spread homemade ganache and caramel sauce over premade cheesecake. It always makes busy holidays feel slightly less hectic.
—Laura McDowell, Lake Villa, IL

TAKES: 25 MIN. • **MAKES:** 8 SERVINGS

- 1 frozen New York-style cheesecake (30 oz.), thawed
- ½ cup semisweet chocolate chips
- ½ cup heavy whipping cream, divided
- 3 Tbsp. chopped pecans, toasted
- ¼ cup butter, cubed
- ½ cup plus 2 Tbsp. packed brown sugar
- 1 Tbsp. light corn syrup

1. Place cheesecake on a serving plate. Place chocolate chips in a small bowl. In a small saucepan, bring ¼ cup cream just to a boil. Pour over chocolate; stir with a whisk until smooth. Cool slightly, stirring occasionally. Pour over cheesecake; sprinkle with pecans. Refrigerate until set.
2. In a small saucepan, melt butter; stir in brown sugar and corn syrup. Bring to a boil. Reduce heat; cook and stir until sugar is dissolved. Stir in remaining cream and return to a boil. Remove from heat. Serve warm with the cheesecake or, if desired, cool completely and drizzle over cheesecake.
1 piece: 585 cal., 40g fat (20g sat. fat), 94mg chol., 276mg sod., 53g carb. (23g sugars, 1g fiber), 7g pro.

TEST KITCHEN TIP

Ganache is a French term referring to a smooth mixture of chocolate and cream that's used for glazes and cake fillings as well as in candymaking. Traditionally, ganache is made by pouring hot cream over chopped chocolate and stirring until the mixture is velvety smooth. The proportions of cream to chocolate vary depending on the use. Flavorings, as well as corn syrup, can be added to the chocolate mixture. Corn syrup gives a shiny finish to a poured ganache.

APRICOT-PECAN SUGARPLUMS

We deliver these fast and easy sweets to an assisted living home during the holidays and the residents love them! We also layer the ingredients in a canning jar, attach an instruction card around the lid and give the festive jars as gifts. These no-bake treats look beautiful in individual cookie tins, too!
—Mandy Nall, Montgomery, AL

TAKES: 20 MIN. • **MAKES:** 2 DOZEN

- ½ cup packed dried apricots
- ½ cup chopped pecans
- ¼ cup sweetened shredded coconut
- ¼ cup golden raisins
- ¼ cup packed dried figs
- 3 Tbsp. orange juice
- ¼ tsp. almond extract
- ¼ cup coarse sugar

Place the first 7 ingredients in a food processor; pulse until the mixture just comes together. Shape mixture into 1-in. balls; roll in sugar. Store between layers of waxed paper in an airtight container in the refrigerator.

1 sugarplum: 42 cal., 2g fat (0 sat. fat), 0 chol., 3mg sod., 6g carb. (5g sugars, 1g fiber), 0 pro.

PUMPKIN TOFFEE TRIFLE

I wanted to use pumpkin for a quick party dessert. This twist on a cream cheese pie tastes divine and keeps well, so it can be made ahead.
—Jodie Jensen, Draper, UT

TAKES: 25 MIN. • **MAKES:** 14 SERVINGS

- 2 pkg. (8 oz. each) cream cheese, softened
- ¾ cup sugar
- 1 can (15 oz.) pumpkin
- 2 Tbsp. ground cinnamon
- 2 tsp. ground nutmeg
- ½ tsp. ground cloves
- 2 tsp. vanilla extract
- 1 carton (16 oz.) frozen whipped topping, thawed
- 1 pkg. (11.3 oz.) toffee shortbread cookies, broken into pieces
- 1 pkg. (5¼ oz.) thin ginger cookies, coarsely crushed
- ½ cup plus 2 Tbsp. hot caramel ice cream topping, divided
- 1 cup milk chocolate English toffee bits, divided

1. Beat cream cheese and sugar until blended. Beat in pumpkin and spices; set aside. In another bowl, stir vanilla extract into whipped topping.

2. In a 4-qt. glass bowl, layer half each of the shortbread cookie pieces, pumpkin mixture and crushed ginger cookies. Drizzle with ¼ cup caramel topping; top with half the whipped topping and ¾ cup toffee bits. Repeat layers, using remaining toffee bits. Drizzle with remaining caramel topping. Refrigerate until serving.

1 cup: 553 cal., 32g fat (17g sat. fat), 49mg chol., 353mg sod., 63g carb. (35g sugars, 2g fiber), 4g pro.

NO-BAKE CORNFLAKE COOKIES

I grew up on a farm where we hand-milked cows and had plenty of milk and cream to use for cooking, so sometimes we'd substitute light cream for the evaporated milk in this recipe. We'd rarely let these cookies cool before sampling them, and a batch never lasted a day!
—Denise Marnell, Hereford, TX

TAKES: 25 MIN.
MAKES: ABOUT 4 DOZEN

- 4 **cups cornflakes**
- 1½ **cups sweetened shredded coconut**
- ¾ **cup chopped pecans**
- 1½ **cups sugar**
- ½ **cup light corn syrup**
- ½ **cup evaporated milk**
- ¼ **cup butter**
  Dash salt

Combine the cornflakes, coconut and pecans; set aside. In a small heavy saucepan, combine the remaining ingredients. Cook, stirring constantly, over medium heat until a candy thermometer reads 240° (soft-ball stage). Add syrup mixture to dry ingredients; stir well. Drop by tablespoonfuls onto waxed paper. Let cookies stand until set.
1 cookie: 81 cal., 3g fat (2g sat. fat), 3mg chol., 68mg sod., 13g carb. (11g sugars, 0 fiber), 1g pro.

MOCHA PECAN BALLS

Dusted in either confectioners' sugar or cocoa, this six-ingredient dough rolls into truffle-like treats. Best of all, there's no baking required.
—Lorraine Darocha, Mountain City, TN

TAKES: 25 MIN. • **MAKES:** 4 DOZEN

- 2½ **cups crushed vanilla wafers (about 65 wafers)**
- 2 **cups plus ¼ cup confectioners' sugar, divided**
- ⅔ **cup finely chopped pecans, toasted**
- 2 **Tbsp. baking cocoa**
- ¼ **cup reduced-fat evaporated milk**
- ¼ **cup cold strong brewed coffee**
  Additional baking cocoa, optional

1. In a large bowl, combine the wafer crumbs, 2 cups confectioners' sugar, pecans and cocoa. Stir in milk and coffee (mixture will be sticky).
2. With hands dusted in confectioners' sugar, shape dough into ¾-in. balls; roll in remaining confectioners' sugar or additional baking cocoa if desired. Store in an airtight container.
1 cookie: 61 cal., 2g fat (0 sat. fat), 1mg chol., 20mg sod., 10g carb. (8g sugars, 0 fiber), 0 pro.
Diabetic exchanges: 1 starch.

TEST KITCHEN TIP

When making truffle-like treats, it's key to stick to the liquid-to-solid ratio called for in the recipe. Not doing so could make it difficult to shape the mixture into balls.

NO-BAKE CHERRY DESSERT

I adapted this fast and easy recipe from one given to me by my first best friend in 1966. I often made it for my children, and now when they visit, they still love it.
—Judy Harris, McRae, GA

TAKES: 15 MIN. • **MAKES:** 4 SERVINGS

- ⅔ cup graham cracker crumbs
- 2 Tbsp. brown sugar
- 2 Tbsp. butter, melted
- 4 oz. cream cheese, softened
- 1 Tbsp. confectioners' sugar
- 1 cup whipped topping
- 1¼ cups cherry pie filling

1. In a small bowl, combine the cracker crumbs, brown sugar and butter; press into an ungreased 9x5-in. loaf pan.
2. In a large bowl, beat cream cheese and confectioners' sugar until smooth; fold in whipped topping. Spread over crust. Top with pie filling. Chill until serving.

1 piece: 332 cal., 13g fat (9g sat. fat), 28mg chol., 270mg sod., 48g carb. (36g sugars, 1g fiber), 4g pro.

EASY BERRY CHEESECAKE PARFAITS

These sweet little parfaits take everything that's wonderful about cheesecake and make it way easier. You get the rich creaminess, graham cracker crunch and bright berry flavor all in fun individual portions.
—*Taste of Home* Test Kitchen

TAKES: 15 MIN. • **MAKES:** 2 SERVINGS

- 2 oz. cream cheese, softened
- ⅔ cup marshmallow creme
- ½ cup frozen whipped topping
- 4 Tbsp. graham cracker crumbs
- 1 cup fresh raspberries
- 1 cup fresh blueberries

1. Beat the cream cheese and marshmallow creme until blended; fold in whipped topping.
2. Sprinkle 2 Tbsp. cracker crumbs into each of 2 glasses or dessert dishes. Layer each with ½ cup cream cheese mixture, ¼ cup raspberries and ¼ cup blueberries; repeat the layers. Refrigerate, covered, until serving.

1 parfait: 396 cal., 15g fat (9g sat. fat), 29mg chol., 174mg sod., 54g carb. (39g sugars, 6g fiber), 4g pro.

RUM BALLS

I use this recipe for special occasions with my treasured family and friends. The sweet cookies are so easy to make and pack a festive rum punch.
—Diane Duschanek, Council Bluffs, IA

TAKES: 30 MIN.
MAKES: ABOUT 2½ DOZEN

- 2 cups confectioners' sugar
- ¼ cup baking cocoa
- 1 pkg. (12 oz.) vanilla wafers, finely crushed
- 1 cup finely chopped walnuts
- ½ cup light corn syrup
- ¼ cup rum
  Additional confectioners' sugar

1. In a large bowl, mix the confectioners' sugar and cocoa until blended. Add crushed wafers and walnuts; toss to combine. In another bowl, mix corn syrup and rum; stir into wafer mixture.
2. Shape into 1-in. balls. Roll in additional confectioners' sugar. Store in an airtight container.
1 ball: 125 cal., 4g fat (1g sat. fat), 2mg chol., 43mg sod., 21g carb. (16g sugars, 0 fiber), 1g pro.

CHOCOLATE CHEESECAKE PIE

Guests always go for this rich but simple pie. I like topping it with fresh raspberries or cherry pie filling.
—Sandy Schwartz, Brooklyn, NY

TAKES: 30 MIN. • **MAKES:** 8 SERVINGS

- 1 pkg. (8 oz.) cream cheese, softened
- ¼ cup butter, softened
- ⅓ cup sugar
- 1½ tsp. vanilla extract
- 1½ cups milk chocolate chips, melted and cooled
- 1 carton (8 oz.) frozen whipped topping, thawed
- 1 graham cracker crust (9 in.)
  Chocolate curls, optional

In a large bowl, beat the cream cheese, butter, sugar and vanilla until smooth. Beat in the cooled chocolate. Fold in whipped topping. Spoon into crust. Refrigerate until serving. Decorate with chocolate curls as desired.
1 piece: 535 cal., 35g fat (20g sat. fat), 53mg chol., 270mg sod., 48g carb. (38g sugars, 1g fiber), 6g pro.

TEST KITCHEN TIP

Substitute a chocolate- or Oreo-crumb crust for the graham cracker crust. You can also top the pie with strawberries, a dollop of whipped topping or a drizzle of chocolate sauce.

RASPBERRY BREEZE PIE

One way to my loved one's heart is through marvelous-tasting food. Luckily, I've learned to take a few shortcuts. This no-bake pie uses canned pie filling and a prepared crust to get me out of the kitchen quickly.
—Pamela Baldwin, Columbia, TN

TAKES: 20 MIN. • **MAKES:** 8 SERVINGS

- 1 pkg. (8 oz.) cream cheese, softened
- 1 cup confectioners' sugar
- 1 tsp. vanilla extract
- 1 cup whipped topping
- 1 graham cracker crust (9 in.)
- 1¾ cups raspberry, cherry or strawberry pie filling
- ¼ tsp. almond extract
  Sliced almonds

In a large bowl, beat the cream cheese, sugar and vanilla until smooth. Fold in whipped topping. Spoon into crust. Combine the pie filling and extract; spread over the cream cheese layer. Garnish with sliced almonds. Chill until set.
1 piece: 351 cal., 16g fat (9g sat. fat), 31mg chol., 202mg sod., 47g carb. (30g sugars, 2g fiber), 4g pro.

EASY CHEESECAKE PIE

This is so quick, you'll have it ready in less than 10 minutes. And it's so good!
—Cathy Shortall, Easton, MD

TAKES: 5 MIN. • **MAKES:** 8 SERVINGS

- 1 carton (24.3 oz.) Philadelphia ready-to-serve cheesecake filling
- 1½ cups coarsely crushed Oreos (about 12 cookies), divided
- 1 chocolate crumb crust (9 in.)

In a large bowl, combine the cheesecake filling and 1¼ cups crushed cookies. Spoon into crust; sprinkle with remaining cookies. Chill until serving.
1 piece: 443 cal., 28g fat (14g sat. fat), 80mg chol., 492mg sod., 43g carb. (29g sugars, 1g fiber), 6g pro.

PEANUT BUTTER CUP TRIFLE

The billowing layers of this trifle are a nice contrast to the peanut butter cups. You can add a little extra decoration with chocolate jimmies, too.
—Chris Nelson, Decatur, AR

TAKES: 20 MIN. • **MAKES:** 12 SERVINGS

- 4 cups cold 2% milk
- 2 pkg. (3.9 oz. each) instant chocolate pudding mix
- 1 prepared angel food cake (8 to 10 oz.), cut into 1-in. cubes
- 1 carton (12 oz.) frozen whipped topping, thawed
- 2 pkg. (8 oz. each) Reese's mini peanut butter cups

In a large bowl, whisk milk and pudding mixes 2 minutes. Let stand 2 minutes or until soft-set. In a 3-qt. trifle bowl or glass bowl, layer half each of the cake cubes, pudding, whipped topping and peanut butter cups. Repeat layers. Refrigerate trifle until serving.
¾ cup: 429 cal., 19g fat (12g sat. fat), 11mg chol., 365mg sod., 60g carb. (38g sugars, 2g fiber), 7g pro.

In a small bowl, combine peanut butter, honey and vanilla. Stir in milk powder, oats and graham cracker crumbs. Shape into 1-in. balls. Cover and refrigerate until serving.

1 serving: 70 cal., 3g fat (1g sat. fat), 1mg chol., 46mg sod., 9g carb. (6g sugars, 1g fiber), 3g pro. **Diabetic exchanges:** ½ starch, ½ fat.

TINY BANANA CREAM PIES

These petite pies take very little time to prepare and make a splendid, delicious dessert.
—Jennifer Loewen, Altona, BC

TAKES: 15 MIN. • **MAKES:** 4 SERVINGS

- 1   cup cold milk
- ⅓   cup instant vanilla pudding mix
- 1   small banana, sliced
- 4   individual graham cracker tart shells
- ½   cup whipped topping
- 2   Tbsp. sweetened shredded coconut, toasted
     Additional banana slices, optional

1. In a small bowl, whisk the milk and pudding mix for 2 minutes. Arrange banana slices over tart shell bottoms; top with pudding.
2. Cover with whipped topping; sprinkle with coconut. Cover and refrigerate until serving. Garnish with additional banana slices if desired.

1 pie: 258 cal., 10g fat (5g sat. fat), 6mg chol., 345mg sod., 38g carb. (23g sugars, 1g fiber), 3g pro.

TEST KITCHEN TIP

This recipe is so fast and simple, you can double it without much additional time. Trust us—the bite-sized treats will vanish in no time!

NO-BAKE PEANUT BUTTER TREATS

This quick and tasty snack is perfect for a road trip. The treats won't stick to your hands, travel well and promise to satisfy everyone. I like to keep them in the fridge at home for a no-fuss bite.
—Sonia Rohda, Waverly, NE

TAKES: 10 MIN. • **MAKES:** 15 TREATS

- ⅓   cup chunky peanut butter
- ¼   cup honey
- ½   tsp. vanilla extract
- ⅓   cup nonfat dry milk powder
- ⅓   cup quick-cooking oats
- 2   Tbsp. graham cracker crumbs

5i ALMOND-VANILLA YOGURT PARFAITS

I'm a night-shift nurse. When I get home, I make a crunchy parfait with yogurt for a protein boost before heading off to a good day's sleep.
—Meredith Brazinski, Neptune, NJ

TAKES: 15 MIN. • **MAKES:** 4 SERVINGS

- 4 cups reduced-fat plain Greek yogurt
- 1 pkg. (3.4 oz.) instant vanilla or cheesecake pudding mix
- ½ cup almond butter
- 1 cup granola with fruit and nuts
  Toasted chopped almonds, optional

In a large bowl, mix yogurt and pudding mix until well blended; gently stir in almond butter to swirl. Layer ½ cup yogurt mixture and 2 Tbsp. granola in each of 4 parfait glasses. Repeat layers. If desired, sprinkle with almonds. Serve immediately.

1 parfait: 560 cal., 26g fat (5g sat. fat), 13mg chol., 508mg sod., 56g carb. (34g sugars, 5g fiber), 32g pro.

5i NO-BAKE CHOCOLATE TORTE

Here's a delightful dessert that only looks as if you fussed all day. With its attractive appearance and wonderful taste, no one will know that you saved time by spreading an easy-to-prepare frosting on a store-bought pound cake.
—Taste of Home Test Kitchen

TAKES: 20 MIN. • **MAKES:** 6 SERVINGS

- 1 frozen pound cake (10¾ oz.), thawed
- 2 cups heavy whipping cream
- 6 Tbsp. confectioners' sugar
- 6 Tbsp. baking cocoa
- ½ tsp. almond extract
- ½ cup sliced almonds, toasted, optional

1. Slice pound cake into 3 layers and set aside. In a large bowl, beat cream until soft peaks form. Gradually add sugar and cocoa; beat until stiff peaks form. Stir in extract.
2. Place 1 layer of cake on a serving platter; top with 1 cup frosting. Repeat layers. Frost top and sides with remaining frosting. Garnish with the almonds if desired. Chill at least 15 minutes. Refrigerate any leftovers.

1 piece: 511 cal., 38g fat (23g sat. fat), 181mg chol., 215mg sod., 38g carb. (23g sugars, 2g fiber), 6g pro.

FRESH FRUIT PARFAITS

I fix this simple recipe when I want to prepare something impressive yet low-calorie for company.
—Karin Christian, Plano, TX

TAKES: 30 MIN. • **MAKES:** 4 SERVINGS

- ½ cup mixed berry yogurt
- ¾ cup reduced-fat whipped topping
- 1 cup sliced ripe banana
- 1 cup sliced fresh strawberries
- 1 cup cubed fresh pineapple
- 1 cup fresh blueberries
- 4 whole strawberries

1. In a small bowl, combine yogurt and whipped topping; set aside 4 tsp. for topping. Spoon half the remaining yogurt mixture into 4 parfait glasses; layer with half each of the banana, sliced strawberries, pineapple and blueberries. Repeat the layers.
2. Top each parfait with 1 tsp. reserved yogurt mixture and a whole strawberry. Chill parfaits until serving.

1 parfait: 149 cal., 2g fat (2g sat. fat), 2mg chol., 22mg sod., 31g carb. (24g sugars, 4g fiber), 2g pro. **Diabetic exchanges:** 1½ fruit, ½ starch, ½ fat.

PEPPERMINT CANDY SANDWICH COOKIES

I love to include a little homemade treat in teacher and hostess gifts, and these delicious lovelies (that come together in minutes) never fail to charm. They store very well in an airtight container at room temperature.
—Jennifer Beckman, Falls Church, VA

TAKES: 20 MIN.
MAKES: 20 SANDWICH COOKIES

- ¼ cup butter, softened
- ¼ cup shortening
- 1 tsp. vanilla extract
- ½ tsp. peppermint extract
- 2 cups confectioners' sugar
- ½ cup finely crushed peppermint candies
- 1 pkg. (9 oz.) chocolate wafers

1. In a large bowl, beat butter, shortening and extracts until blended. Gradually beat in confectioners' sugar until thick and creamy. Stir in candies.
2. Spread about 1 Tbsp. mixture on bottoms of half the cookies. Cover with remaining cookies.
1 sandwich cookie: 154 cal., 7g fat (3g sat. fat), 6mg chol., 93mg sod., 24g carb. (18g sugars, 0 fiber), 1g pro.

5i

CRUNCHY APRICOT-COCONUT BALLS

My mom gave me this no-bake cookie recipe years ago when she had them on her Christmas buffet. I can't believe how simple they are to make.
—Jane Whittaker, Pensacola, FL

TAKES: 30 MIN. • **MAKES:** 2 DOZEN

- 1¼ cups sweetened shredded coconut
- 1 cup dried apricots, finely chopped
- ⅔ cup chopped pecans
- ½ cup fat-free sweetened condensed milk
- ½ cup confectioners' sugar

1. In a small bowl, combine the coconut, apricots and pecans. Add condensed milk; mix well (mixture will be sticky).

2. Shape into 1¼-in. balls and roll in confectioners' sugar. Store in an airtight container in the refrigerator.
1 ball: 87 cal., 4g fat (2g sat. fat), 1mg chol., 19mg sod., 12g carb. (10g sugars, 1g fiber), 1g pro.

BERRY-MARSHMALLOW TRIFLE

My guests say that this is almost too pretty to eat! I like the way it can be made a day ahead for convenience, and neither the taste nor appearance is compromised.
—Shannon Aldridge, Suwanee, GA

TAKES: 25 MIN. • **MAKES:** 10 SERVINGS

- 1¾ cups cold fat-free milk
- 1 pkg. (1 oz.) sugar-free instant vanilla pudding mix
- 1 carton (8 oz.) frozen fat-free whipped topping, thawed, divided
- 1 loaf (10¾ oz.) frozen reduced-fat pound cake, thawed and cut into 1-in. cubes
- 3 cups fresh strawberries, halved
- 2 cups miniature marshmallows
- 3 Tbsp. sliced almonds

1. In a small bowl, whisk the milk and pudding mix for 2 minutes. Let stand for 2 minutes or until soft-set. Fold in 2½ cups whipped topping; set aside.
2. Place half the cake cubes in a 3-qt. trifle bowl; spoon half the pudding mixture over the top. Top with half each of the strawberries and marshmallows. Repeat layers. Top with the remaining whipped topping; sprinkle with almonds. Chill until serving.
1 cup: 230 cal., 6g fat (1g sat. fat), 18mg chol., 298mg sod., 40g carb. (23g sugars, 2g fiber), 4g pro.

BERRY, LEMON & DOUGHNUT HOLE TRIFLE

After my son called and said he was bringing home his college roommates, I was able to whip up this quick yet scrumptious dessert in only a few minutes. It's been a family favorite ever since.
—Ellen Riley, Murfreesboro, TN

TAKES: 25 MIN. • **MAKES:** 10 SERVINGS

- 2 cups cold 2% milk
- 1 pkg. (3.4 oz.) instant lemon pudding mix
- 1 carton (8 oz.) frozen whipped topping, thawed and divided
- 16 to 32 plain doughnut holes
- 3 cups fresh strawberries, halved
- 2 cups fresh blueberries

1. Whisk milk and pudding mix for 2 minutes. Let stand for 2 minutes or until soft-set. Fold in 2½ cups whipped topping; set aside.
2. Place half the doughnut holes in a 3-qt. trifle bowl; spread half the pudding mixture over the top. Top pudding with half the strawberries and blueberries. Repeat layers. Top with remaining whipped topping. Chill until serving.
1 cup: 250 cal., 11g fat (7g sat. fat), 6mg chol., 250mg sod., 33g carb. (24g sugars, 2g fiber), 3g pro.

BUTTERSCOTCH-RUM RAISIN TREATS

I love making rum raisin rice pudding around the holidays—and those classic flavors inspired this quick confection. Crispy rice cereal adds crunch, but nuts, toasted coconut or candied pineapple could do the job, too.
—Crystal Schlueter, Northglenn, CO

TAKES: 20 MIN.
MAKES: ABOUT 4½ DOZEN

- 1 pkg. (10 to 11 oz.) butterscotch chips
- 1 pkg. (10 to 12 oz.) white baking chips
- ½ tsp. rum extract
- 3 cups Rice Krispies
- 1 cup raisins

1. Line 56 mini-muffin cups with paper liners. In a large bowl, combine butterscotch and white chips. Microwave, uncovered, on high for 30 seconds; stir. Microwave in additional 30-second intervals, stirring until smooth.
2. Stir in extract, Rice Krispies and raisins. Drop by rounded tablespoonfuls into prepared mini-muffin cups. Chill until set.
1 treat: 76 cal., 4g fat (3g sat. fat), 1mg chol., 21mg sod., 11g carb. (9g sugars, 0 fiber), 0 pro.

TEST KITCHEN TIP

You can easily freeze these fast little treats for future snacking. Simply set them in a freezer container, separating the layers with waxed paper. Thaw before serving.

RECIPE INDEX

//